The European Tour
Yearbook 1998

O F F I C I A L  P U B L I C A T I O N

Lennard
Queen Anne Press

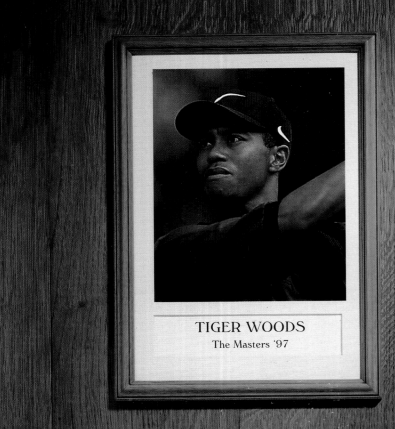

TIGER WOODS
The Masters '97

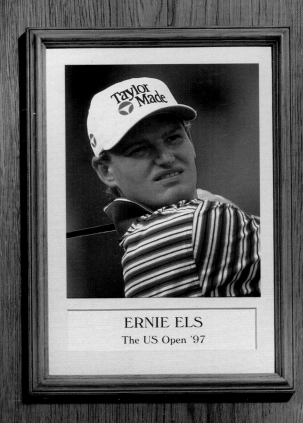

ERNIE ELS
The US Open '97

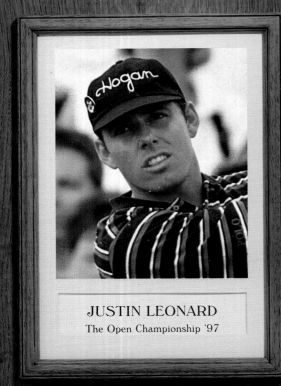

JUSTIN LEONARD
The Open Championship '97

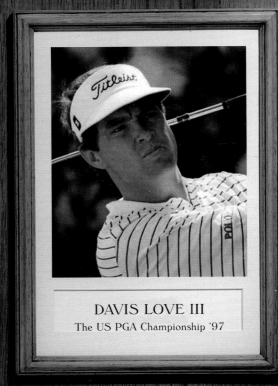

DAVIS LOVE III
The US PGA Championship '97

WE CONGRATULATE THEM ON THEIR MAJORS. AND THANK THEM FOR OUR GRAND SLAM.

Perhaps it's no coincidence that all four 1997 Major Champions play Titleist. After all, 7 out of 10 Pro's worldwide choose the same.* Tiger Woods got the ball rolling in record breaking and dramatic style at Augusta. Then, in the US Open, a last day leaderboard developed comprised entirely of Titleist players. It was Ernie Els who came home first.

The next Major winner, Texan Justin Leonard, also relied on Titleist's advanced wound ball technology. And he too headed a Titleist top three. Lastly, in the US PGA Championship at Winged Foot, a decisive victory for Davis Love III took our unbroken string of major victories to seven. Of course, we're not saying that you have to play Titleist to win. It just seems that way.

And as for the Grand Slam, who else but the No. 1 ball in golf could claim that?

Titleist®
Nº1 ball in golf.

Titleist, St Ives, Cambs PE17 4LS
http://www.titleist.com

* Source: Sports Marketing Surveys Ltd.

Contents

Europe reigns in Spain

In another thrilling finish, Europe won the

first Ryder Cup by Johnnie Walker

match to be staged in Spain

T eam Europe did it again! If Oak Hill was a miracle, what superlatives were there left for Valderrama, 1997?

Yul Brynner and Frankie Dettori both had their Magnificent Sevens, but Severiano Ballesteros brought his Magnificent Twelve into town and gunned down the Americans.

If you had written the movie script, back it would have come with a rejection slip and the words 'Too fanciful'. The self-same one point victory as 1995 against a side with a combined world ranking 260 spots higher than that of Europe, a team that contained a modern phenomenon,

Tiger Woods, and three of the year's major championship winners. Win? Pull the other one.

Some 'experts' said Europe's greatest names were too old, past their best. Too many were out of form. But what do 'experts' know? The bookmakers' odds said it was a hopeless case, too. One punter had £30,000 on the USA, another £12,000. Punters 0, bookies 2. They all reckoned without the pride and passion of Europe's heroes. Nine nations, one aim. To retain the Ryder Cup? Not a bit of it – that was not enough for Ballesteros in the first match to be played on Spanish soil,

to be played in front of his King, Juan Carlos. Only outright victory would be good enough in the greatest showdown in the world of sport.

And outright victory it was, though not without a few scares on the way, before Colin Montgomerie, top points-scorer on either side, fittingly wrapped it up with an immaculate tee shot and arrow-straight nine iron that shut out American captain Tom Kite's dream of equality.

A dead-heat would at least have spared some of the American pain in Spain and sent their much-heralded team, rated the best since the Nicklaus-Watson-Trevino-Irwin-Kite-Floyd platoon that turned Walton Heath 1981 into a rout, home with heads held high after a superlative 31 under par singles comeback.

But the Europeans had done too much damage in the four-balls and four-somes, taking a five-point lead (10½-5½) into the 12 singles. And the beauty of the week was that every European, from the experienced to the five rookies, was a winner. Carve all their names with pride, none more so than the incredibly brave José Maria Olazábal who less than 12

months earlier was unable to walk because of a crippling foot condition that baffled all the experts. He could walk all right, though, at Valderrama, playing in all five series of matches. It even seemed he would produce the fairytale finish, snatching the winning point that the legion of Spanish golf fans who braved the freak storms yearned for. Sadly, it was not to be. Lee Janzen, his opponent, had not read the script and won the last three holes.

Yet it remained a great triumph for Spain, who defied all the prophets of gloom and doom by staging the Ryder Cup by Johnnie Walker brilliantly, even in

the most trying of the unexpected conditions.

The foresight of Jaime Ortiz-Patiño, the Club President, in spending £8 million on drainage since he acquired his beloved Valderrama, paid timely dividends. Probably no other course in Spain would have been able to get the Ryder Cup through by Sunday afternoon after what Patiño reckoned was the first rain in the third week of September for a decade. And what rain. To believe it, you simply had to be there. Thunder, lightning, rivers of water, cars stuck in the mud, the lot. But Valderrama, not just a pretty face, coped with it all like the thoroughbred

champion Patiño believed her to be.

Delays of 100 minutes on the first day, 110 on the second, both forcing an overspill of uncompleted foursomes matches to the following morning, were, of course, a major inconvenience, anywhere else a nightmare.

Certainly, the daily crowds of 30.000, many of them armed with BBC Radio Five's special service which kept them fully abreast of match positions on course, as well as all the changes and rescheduling, had no trouble in remaining in the best of spirits. It was Ballesteros' big week and, boy, did he make the most of it, haring around, buggying hither and thither,

7

The American Team

Back row left to right: Justin Leonard, Jeff Maggert, Tiger Woods, Brad Faxon, Tom Lehman, Scott Hoch, Fred Couples, Mark O'Meara. Front row left to right: Jim Furyk, Davis Love III, Tom Kite (captain), Lee Janzen, Phil Mickelson

coaching, coaxing, cajoling, bringing out the refreshments, a real Captain Marvel of a leader, reaching parts of the course that others had never reached before. As one Pressroom wag wrote: 'Seve was so conspicuous, he was almost beside himself.'

Presented with the Cup by the Infanta Maria, daughter of the Spanish King, an almost breathless Ballesteros declared: 'That was my best win ever. I have won five majors, six orders of merit, a lot of great tournaments around the world, but I have felt nothing like this. I am the happiest man in the world. This will go down in history because I am the first non-British captain to win the Ryder Cup both as a captain and as a player. The players in

my team played with heart and that is why we won. I don't believe the Americans lost, I believe Europe won. Our team spirit has been fantastic. I have 12 heroes, 12 great champions, and 12 great guys. I don't think I could ever have more.'

The champagne flowed, grown men wept floods of tears of unashamed joy. The Press are a hard-bitten lot, but even they had their hankies out when it came to Olazábal's turn to speak at the post-match conference. 'Every time you play in the Ryder Cup it is special,' he said. 'But for me, this one is very special. A year ago I could not even walk...' His voice trailed off, the tears welled up but he just held

them in. Then Bernhard Langer and Costantino Rocca cradled him in their arms and everyone felt incredibly proud and humble.

So nothing was more appropriate than that Olazábal, in company with Rocca, should post Europe's first point of the 1997 Ryder Cup and that the Spaniard should play the shot which turned the match round against Davis Love III and Phil Mickelson. To a deafening roar, he holed a 133-yard pitching wedge to eagle the 14th. It inspired Rocca to birdie the next, and when Love missed from seven feet and Mickelson from five on the last green, it was first blood to Europe.

Elsewhere Fred Couples and Brad

The European Team

Back row left to right: Per-Ulrik Johansson, Ignacio Garrido, Jesper Parnevik, Colin Montgomerie, Lee Westwood, José Maria Olazábal, Costantino Rocca, Ian Woosnam. Front row left to right: Bernhard Langer, Thomas Bjorn, Severiano Ballesteros (captain), Nick Faldo, Darren Clarke

Faxon were staging a storming counter-attack to overturn the early lead of Nick Faldo and Lee Westwood.

The longest match in the history of the biennial contest came next, all five hours and 43 minutes of it. But the result, when it eventually came, made all the waiting worth while, so long as you were European. Jesper Parnevik holed from 20 feet on the 17th and even more bravely from ten feet on the last to give him and fellow Swede Per-Ulrik Johansson a one up win over Tom Lehman and Jim Furyk.

But with neither an off-form Montgomerie nor trusty Langer producing a single birdie between them in the tricky wind, it was parity at two points each

going into the second session, debutant Woods and experienced Mark O'Meara, easily the best player of the four on the day, taking the honours by 3 and 2.

Time for a Ballesteros masterstroke. He gambled and won, guessing that Kite would keep Woods and O'Meara together for the afternoon foursomes, and in the bottom match. Despite their morning flop, or the fact that the likes of Ian Woosnam, Darren Clarke and Thomas Bjorn were champing at the bit for an outing, Ballesteros asked Montgomerie and Langer to go right back and avenge their defeat in the more demanding form of golf. It was of the utmost importance to prove early on that Woods was beatable.

To have their number one brought down on the opening day would certainly undermine American confidence. So it proved, with the Scottish-German alliance far too good this time, romping home by 5 and 3. 'I took a risk and I was right,' said Ballesteros with relish – and the Americans were never the same force again.

With Olazábal and Rocca going down on the last green to debutant Scott Hoch and Janzen in the only other match to be completed before dusk, it was deadlock at three points apiece. Europe, though, were on the brink of victory in one of the unfinished matches. It was going to be harder, far harder than the Americans had expected.

The next morning, in a blink of an eye, it was Europe ahead. Faldo and Westwood, two up with three to play overnight against Justin Leonard and Jeff Maggert, made the first of what would, uniquely, be three Saturday appearances together. Just one putt, from Westwood, from ten feet for birdie at the 16th, was required to clinch that point, an historic

America, the first day they had never won a match. Five wins and two halves to Europe. No wonder a shell-shocked Kite could only say: 'It's not an insurmountable lead but something needs to happen in the three unfinished matches for us to have a chance.'

Something certainly did happen but it wasn't what the American captain had in

rubbing salt into the wound at the last by asking the young Masters champion to hole from two feet to save the match. As Sky's roving reporter, Ken Brown, put it: 'There are no Jack Nicklauses round this green – that's for certain', alluding to that most golden of Ryder Cup moments, at Royal Birkdale in 1969, when the great man conceded a longer putt to Tony

Ian Woosnam (left) misses: Per-Ulrik Johansson (right) exults: Seve Ballesteros (centre) watches for Europe.
Nailed to the flag: Patriotic manicure from Swedish supporter (opposite).

one in more ways than one. It gave the 25-year-old the first of what will surely be many and cemented a second great landmark for Faldo, who, by playing in the contest for an 11th time, was already a record-breaker. This, however, was his 24th point, overtaking the 23½ of Billy Casper – and all without touching a ball.

That first point opened the floodgates on perhaps the most amazing day in Ryder Cup history. It started at 3-3, ended at 9-4, the blackest of Black Saturdays for

mind. Olazábal and Rocca, one up overnight, trampled World Cup-winning duo Couple and Love by 5 and 4, and Parnevik and the boyish Ignacio Garrido, whose father Antonio had played in the first Europe v USA match in 1979, clung on for an unexpected half against major champions Woods and Leonard, the Swede, as he had done on day one, sinking a crucial late putt. This time it was from eight feet for an improbable birdie at the 17th after a wicked drive, and then

Jacklin and the match was tied. Back to Saturday, glorious Saturday, at Valderrama. Despite the jump-start of Westwood's early victory and Faldo's record, the early exchanges when the second series of four-balls eventually got under way around 10.50, looked ominous. First, Leonard holed a wedge shot to eagle the fourth during an astonishing five under par burst that seemed certain to disembowel Woosnam and Bjorn, both finally drafted into the fray.

11

Threequarters of an hour later, it was the turn of Couples, holing a 119-yard second shot to bag an eighth-hole eagle just as Montgomerie was trying to nurse Clarke through his baptism of fire. Yet, amazingly, the Europeans were to fight back and win both matches. At one stage, the USA led in three, were square in the other. It could have been a landslide. It was a landslide... for Europe.

Ballesteros' ploy of not playing Woosnam, Clarke or Bjorn on day one turned out

**Mark O'Meara (above) was in top form.
European joy (below).**

to be another winner for here they were, playing like unleashed tigers thirsting for American blood, and getting it. Montgomerie and Clarke 1 up over Couples and Love, Woosnam and Bjorn 2 and 1 over Leonard and Faxon, and five Westwood birdies in a whirlwind eight-hole spell that left Woods and O'Meara gasping.

Westwood's four iron second shot from 207 yards to just eight feet behind the hole at the great amphitheatre of the 17th shook Woods so much that, in striving too hard for the eagle which might have kept his side in the match, he thumped the ball right off the green and into the water. So excited were the huge crowds that even HRH The Duke of York, from his privileged position inside the ropes, was told in no uncertain manner to 'get out of the way, mate, you're blocking the view.'

With Garrido, this time with compatriot Olazábal as his partner, snatching his second consecutive half against Lehman and Mickelson, producing a birdie from a bunker shot at the 17th with the water yawning in front of him that Lehman rated 'the second greatest I've ever seen' it was 3½ to Europe, ½ to the US. But still Europe wasn't finished for the day.

In the only afternoon match to be completed, the top foursomes between Montgomerie-Langer and Janzen-Furyk, finished, albeit in near darkness at 8.23pm, The Europeans, one up with one to go, were given the break they needed after missing the final green in two. Janzen, asked to get down in two from 50 feet to square it, blasted his putt through the gloom to 12 feet past the hole. Furyk missed the one back. More despair in the American locker room.

If the position in the three incomplete matches stayed as they were, 1 up, all square and 1 down, Europe would go into the singles with a five-point advantage. Shades of Muirfield Village 1987 – and Europe only just

Mark O'Meara, Tom Kite and Tiger Woods discuss tactics (above).
Lee Westwood gets out of trouble (below).

hung on to win there 15-13.

This time it was to be even closer. The three foursomes did stay as they were with Hoch partnering another of the supposed lesser lights, Maggert, to a surprise win over Faldo and Westwood, the only blip for Europe. But you cannot have everything, even if your name is Ballesteros, and there was the real bonus of that half from Parnevik-Garrido against mighty Woods-Leonard. Asked after his marathon three-match stint on Saturday whether he felt weary, Garrido replied memorably: 'The crowd carry us in their arms. I could have played a hundred holes.'

Sunday dawned, mercifully dry, and the main worry for Europe was how ageing legs would stand up to being sent into battle for the fifth time in three hectic days on a hilly, tiring, rain-softened course. It was a justifiable concern because not one of the four players used for every series was able to post a singles win. Three of them lost, as did the only American to play all five, Woods.

It was the sole non-loser, Montgomerie, who, batting at number ten and hoping for nothing more than 'a stroll in the park', was suddenly pitchforked into a cauldron of drama as one by one the flowers of Europe were beheaded.

No shame in that, as the Americans, now with very little to lose, relaxed and began shaping up with the sort of golf that had been expected of them. An eagle

13

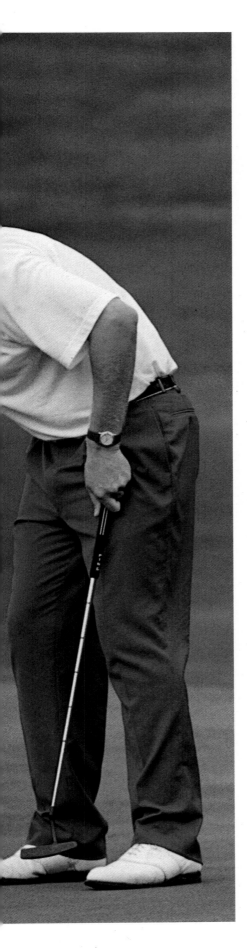

Europeans make
a decent fist of it:
Nick Faldo
(far left),
Colin Montgomerie
(left) and Jesper
Parnevik (right).

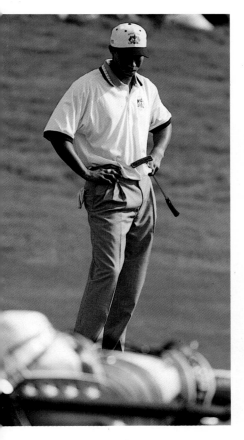

SHOT OF THE WEEK

Plenty of contenders here with understandable support for two great Spanish shots in the first Spanish Ryder Cup: Olazábal's 133-yard pitch for eagle at the 370-yard 14th that turned his first-day four-ball round Europe's way; Garrido's nerveless bunker shot at the 17th that set up the birdie and halved match with Lehman and Mickelson on day two. Westwood's 207-yard four iron to eight feet at the same hole that brought Woods and O'Meara to heel was also pretty awesome. But the vote went to Montgomerie's tee shot at the 18th in the final singles against Hoch when Europe required the Full Monty to get them past the winning post. A par four on the 397-yard finale was the minimum task and the Scot found all the answers.

Bad day at the office for Tiger Woods (above). Tom Lehman (left) goes airborne after holed chip.

Ignacio Garrido and José Maria Olazábal find success is bonding (above).

and five birdies from Couples. Result: Woosnam, only one over par, dispatched 8 and 7 and still without a Ryder singles victory after eight attempts. Eight birdies from Maggert who shook hands on the 16th with Westwood needing a 4-4 finish for 63. Faultless O'Meara, seven under in taming Parnevik 5 and 4. Lehman, taking out his frustration on the luckless Garrido, also out in 31 on the way to the proverbial dog-licence margin, 7 and 6.

When Leonard opened with three birdies to take a vice-like grip on rookie Bjorn, it began to look serious. At four down, skipper Ballesteros gave up exhorting the young Dane and zoomed off elsewhere in his chariot of fire. Result: Bjorn picked up five holes, climaxed by a brute of an eight feet birdie putt on the 17th to

go one up that had Ballesteros roaring back to clap home his young hero. It was a rare Ballesteros bloomer, for Bjorn followed one bad shot with another on the last and Leonard, who had a dreadful Cup debut for an Open champion, got out of jail with only his second half-point of the week.

For Europe's sake it was as well that not all the visitors were rising to the occasion. Woods ran into one of the heroes of the week, the magnificent Rocca, and

became a notable first Ryder Cup singles scalp for the lovable Italian, who needed nothing more than work-manlike figures to ease home 3 and 2 against the devastated 21-year-old, for whom 1 point out of 5 represented, in his perfectionist book, not so much the ceiling caving in on him as the entire Empire State Building doing so.

If Woods was woe, Love was bleeding too, a picture of abject misery as the USPGA champion slumped to his fourth consecutive defeat (only player on either side not to gain a point) by 3 and 2 against the Cup's only Mr 100 Per Cent, Johansson (2 from 2). And though Clarke was finding Mickelson too much of a handful, Europe's strongly-packed 'tail' still looked to have a point or two in hand with Langer edging ahead of Faxon in a high-scoring match, Olazábal seeming to have Janzen's measure, Faldo taking an

THE COURSE

Valderrama, 6,734 yards, par 71. 'They keep saying it's an American-style course, but it's not,' said US skipper Tom Kite. 'I wish we had a few like this in the States. The ones they're making now aren't in this league.' The controversial 17th provided all the drama expected of it, the short holes were all class, the drive at the 18th sorted the men from the boys. And how it was so wonderfully playable so quickly after the torrential rain will forever remain a miracle of draining power. Well played, Jimmy Patiño. Remodelled by Robert Trent Jones, with a little bit of help from S. Ballesteros, this deservedly ranks as a premier course in continental Europe. Exquisitely difficult, but low scores are possible. Ask Jeff Maggert.

early lead off Furyk and Montgomerie going one ahead after 14 against Hoch. Then it all started to go badly wrong. Janzen took the last two holes off Olazábal, and the match, with birdies, Furyk chipped in to match Faldo at the short 15th, and Hoch, the only undefeated American, produced a devastating pitch from the rough at the 17th for a gimme

birdie to go to the last all square with Montgomerie.

The panic buttons were well and truly flashing, but cool Langer, one of the stars of the week, delivered his third point from four, and the Ryder Cup, by halving the 17th in five for a 2 and 1 triumph over Faxon.

With 14 points on the board, Europe

couldn't lose now... but could they win? Cometh the hour, cometh the man, and all the rain might well have been champagne as Montgomerie, needing a half at the 18th to repeat the Oak Hill scoreline, split the fairway with an eye-of-the-needle tee shot on one of the toughest driving holes on the course. It was the shot of a champion, and how appropriate it was to

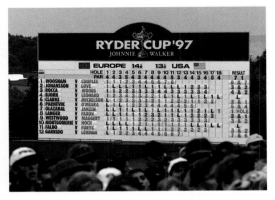

Costantino Rocca and José Maria Olazábal (top) happy in the rain. The final scoreboard (centre). Uncontained joy from the European wives (above).

victorious Americans at Walton Heath in 1981, might well have said in his colourful, homespun way about this David and Goliath confrontation: 'And the lamb got up and bit the butcher'. That, at least, is what another great Ryder Cup player, Peter Alliss, thought would have been Marr's verdict in a moving tribute to the 1965 USPGA champion shortly after his death. It was a line we would all liked to have delivered.

Kite, the 1997 US captain, had no such *bon mots* for us, but, gracious to the end, he thanked the clearly partisan crowds for 'the fair play you showed at all times to my players' and congratulated the European golfers for 'chipping better and putting much better' than his own men.

With the King of Spain phoning through his congratulations to Ballesteros, and Prince Andrew, Prince Bernhard of the Netherlands, George Bush, European Commission President Jacques Santer and Juan Antonio Samaranch, President of the International Olympic Committee, just the tip of the iceberg of the great and good supporting this magnificent production, aided and abetted by Turespana, Spain's greatest golf backer, Sotogrande SA, who provided the massive car-parking facilities, and the Junta de Andalucia, without whose mass of volunteers this demanding event simply could not have taken place, this was, as Ballesteros said: 'A win for Spain, for Europe and the whole world of golf'.

And so say all of us. Roll on The Country Club, Brookline, Massachusetts, 1999.

Jeremy Chapman

have the European number one to play it. He followed it with another, an arrow-straight approach to 22 feet to which Hoch, unable to make the green in two, had no answer. The American's pitch to 15 feet was hardly enough to have Montgomerie shaking in his boots, and the relieved Scot calmly putted up dead, then, encouraged by his captain, walked across to Hoch to concede the half. With the green enveloped by the madding crowd who had followed Montgomerie up the 18th as if he were the Pied Piper of Hamelin, there was no way Hoch could have taken the putt away.

It was a fitting sporting gesture to a perfect sporting occasion, and, as a beaming Montgomerie raised his arms aloft, mouthing 'thank you, thank you' to the wildly cheering and uncaringly drenched crowd, there was no better place on earth to be.

As the late Dave Marr, captain of the

VALDERRAMA GOLF CLUB, SPAIN, SEPTEMBER 26TH - 28TH, 1997

• CAPTAINS: SEVERIANO BALLESTEROS (EUROPE), TOM KITE (USA) •

EUROPE		USA	
DAY ONE			
Four-balls: Morning			
JM Olazábal & C Rocca (1 hole)	1	D Love III & P Mickelson	0
N Faldo & L Westwood	0	F Couples &B Faxon (1 hole)	1
J Parnevik & P-U Johansson (1 hole)	1	T Lehman & J Furyk	0
B Langer & C Montgomerie	0	T Woods & M O'Meara (3&2)	1
Europe	2	USA	2

EUROPE		USA	
Foursomes: Afternoon			
JM Olazábal & C Rocca	0	S Hoch &L Janzen (1 hole)	1
B Langer & C Montgomerie (5&3)	1	T Woods & M O'Meara	0
N Faldo & L Westwood (3&2)	1	J Leonard & J Maggert	0
I Garrido & J Parnevik (halved)	½	P Mickelson & T Lehman (halved)	½
Europe	4½	USA	3½

EUROPE		USA	
DAY TWO			
Four-balls: Morning			
C Montgomerie & D Clarke (1 hole)	1	F Couples & D Love III	0
I Woosnam & T Björn (2 & 1)	1	J Leonard & B Faxon	0
N Faldo & L Westwood (2 & 1)	1	T Woods & M O'Meara	0
JM Olazábal & I Garrido (halved)	½	P Mickelson & T Lehman (halved)	½
Europe	8	USA	4

EUROPE		USA	
DAY TWO continued			
Foursomes: Afternoon			
C Montgomerie & B Langer (1 hole)	1	L Janzen & J Furyk	0
N Faldo & L Westwood	0	S Hoch & J Maggert (2 & 1)	1
I Garrido & J Parnevik (halved)	½	T Woods & J Leonard (halved)	½
JM Olazábal & C Rocca (5&4)	1	F Couples & D Love III(1 hole)	0
Europe	10½	USA	5½

EUROPE		USA	
DAY THREE			
Singles			
I Woosnam	0	F Couples (8&7)	1
P-U Johansson (3 & 2)	1	D Love III	0
C Rocca (4 & 2)	1	T Woods	0
T Björn (halved)	½	J Leonard (halved)	½
D Clarke	0	P Mickelson (2 & 1)	1
J Parnevik	0	M O'Meara (5 & 4)	1
JM Olazábal	0	L Janzen (1 hole)	1
B Langer (2 & 1)	1	B Faxon	0
L Westwood	0	J Maggert (3&2)	1
C Montgomerie (halved)	½	S Hoch (halved)	½
N Faldo	0	J Furyk (3&2)	1
I Garrido	0	T Lehman (7 & 6)	1
Final Score Europe 14½		USA 13½	

Individual performances
Europe

	P	W	L	H	Pts
C Montgomerie	5	3	1	1	3½
C Rocca	4	3	1	0	3
B Langer	4	3	1	0	3
JM Olazábal	5	2	2	1	2½
L Westwood	5	2	3	0	2
N Faldo	5	2	3	0	2
J Parnevik	4	1	1	2	2
P-U Johansson	2	2	0	0	2
I Garrido	4	0	1	3	1½
T Björn	2	1	0	1	1½
D Clarke	2	1	1	0	1
I Woosnam	2	1	1	0	1

A handshake to end a great sporting contest.

Individual performances
USA

	P	W	L	H	Pts
S Hoch	3	2	0	1	2½
F Couples	4	2	2	0	2
P Mickelson	4	1	1	2	2
M O'Meara	4	2	2	0	2
L Janzen	3	2	1	0	2
J Maggert	3	2	1	0	2
T Lehman	4	1	1	2	2
T Woods	5	1	3	1	1½
B Faxon	3	1	2	0	1
J Leonard	4	0	2	2	1
J Furyk	3	1	2	0	1
D Love III	4	0	4	0	0

JOHNNIE WALKER AND THE RYDER CUP

The Ryder Cup, first played for in 1927, has become the world's most prestigious team golf event now contested by the top professionals from Europe and the USA.

More glory to come

The 1997 European Tour saw playing standards
rise to a new peak as more players reached
a new level of excellence

As European tour-nament golf heads towards the millennium there is a growing, almost tangible, awareness that a new and even greater chapter in its history is about to unfold. The signs were self-evident during 1997.

Throughout the season there was a brisk sense of purpose about the style of its cast of characters as they pursued success in various parts of the world that have now become regular venues on the European Tour pilgrimage. Moreover, there was a gathering pace at every level of the game as players achieved their respective milestones and in the process gave the Tour an increasing momentum that shows no signs of slowing down.

Not since those valiant golf missionaries left Scottish shores to give the game to the world, and then dominate it at the beginning of this century, has there been such widespread respect for the European game. It has bounced back from the intervening years of decline and not only caught up but now stands close to becoming the dominant force again.

The Famous Five – Severiano Ballesteros, Bernhard Langer, Nick Faldo,

Sandy Lyle and Ian Woosnam – restored the game to the world standard and José Maria Olazábal and Colin Montgomerie followed on in that tradition. Now, however, a new generation of campaigners, brought up since childhood in that atmosphere of excellence, has arrived and is impatient to get started. More than this, it is about to break out and take on the

world.

At the beginning of the 1997 season Ken Schofield, the Executive Director of the PGA European Tour, outlined the task ahead for the European game. He declared: 'The challenge is to maintain the progress achieved over the Tour's first 25 years which saw the development of a nucleus of champions who reached, matched and then set the highest international standards of play around the world.'

In that context therefore, must the European Tour 1997 be judged, and the good news is that the end-of-term report makes impressive reading because personal playing standards have continued to rise and the volume of players reaching the highest level has also increased. Not quite ten-out-of-ten, perhaps, but certainly no need to scribble 'Must try harder' in the margin either.

The established stars turned in vintage performances to confirm that they had not lost the knack or desire. Their immediate successors demonstrated encouraging signs of stamina and longevity. And the newcomers – not all of them fresh-faced – marched in cool certainty to claim their

HOYO	JUGADOR	+ − PAR	RESULTADO
54	WESTWOOD	−1	6
4	HARRINGTON	−1	3
4	OLAZABAL	−1	2
4	KARLSSO	−1	1
4	McNULTY	−1	0
4	OMALLE	−1	0
4	SJOLAN	−1	0

**Colin Montgomerie and Lee Westwood at the Volvo Masters (above).
Bernhard Langer (left) at the Benson and Hedges International Open.**

first victories in Europe.

The world at large was given fair warning of the impending force that is now about to emanate from Europe. First, there was the inspired leadership of Ballesteros who took a European squad, making its transition to the new order, to a compelling victory against the best American golf could offer in the Ryder Cup by Johnnie Walker.

Before that, there was the showdown for the US Open championship between two European Tour members at the Congressional Club in Washington when Ernie Els pipped Colin Montgomerie. Earlier in the season, Nick Faldo made a decisive assault on the US Tour and won the Nissan top prize while Lee Westwood travelled eastwards to capture the Malaysian Open title and another Tour member, Vijay Singh, won in South Africa and twice in the United States.

There is now general agreement that the exhaustive globe-trotting lifestyle of European Tour players, who visit 16 countries in the course of their season, has turned them into world-beaters who have developed an ability to adapt and excel wherever they find themselves. Their shared pilgrimage for success has bred a camaraderie that makes them collectively a consistent world force.

Any suspicious that disparate nationalities might undermine essential team spirit have long since been laid to rest by a succession of Ryder Cup victories and the fact that the Tour has sustained an inte-

23

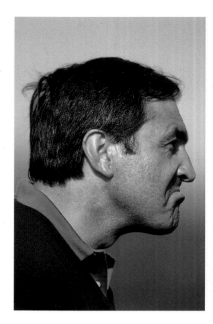  

Seve Ballesteros (left) is determined, Costantino Rocca and José Maria Olazábal (centre) are cheeky chappies, Ernie Els (right) is on a new diet
and Robert Karlsson is overwhelmed after victory at the BMW International Open (below).

grated growth, and in 1997 attracted players from 20 different countries on a full-time basis, confirms the point.

To a man, all of them rejoiced when José Maria Olazábal returned to tournament play at the Dubai Desert Classic after more than a year of crippling illness during which there were fears he might never walk again. This was to be a comeback story that had all the drama of a Hollywood epic because within three weeks of his return, the Spanish professional had captured the Turespana Masters-Open de Canarias against an impressive field, and by the end of this year was to play a major role in Europe's Ryder Cup success.

There was a heartening moment too, for England's Ross McFarlane, who toiled for ten years without victory but had built such a depth of competitive experience that when the chance came his

way he knew how to handle it and held on to win the Deutsche Bank Open – TPC of Europe title and thus remind all those other campaigners, who may have thought their own chances had slipped by, that there is always hope.

The most obvious scenario at the start of the year focused on Colin Montgomerie and his assault on a record-breaking fifth successive Volvo Ranking title. Yet, the Scottish professional left the early running to others as Ernie Els took the Johnnie Walker Classic in Queensland and challenged in the Dimension Data Pro-Am and the Alfred Dunhill South African PGA Championship (both won by Nick Price) to top the money list for fifteen weeks until Bernhard Langer won the Benson and Hedges International Open in May at The Oxfordshire to displace him.

It was the prelude to a

24

remarkable season by the German who went on to win the Conte of Florence Italian Open, the Chemapol Trophy Czech Open and the Linde German Masters. Even so there had been quite definite early signs that this contest for the Volvo Ranking title would be closely fought and involve a number of contenders who would certainly have to battle all the way to the end-of-season Volvo Masters to decide the outcome.

Langer had been on top for only three weeks when Ian Woosnam bounced back to form and won the Volvo PGA Championship at Wentworth to take over the leading spot. Woosnam held it for most of the summer until the unmistakable figure of Montgomerie came into view at the Canon European Masters in the Swiss resort of Crans-sur-Sierre and while not winning the event (Costantino Rocca took the title) earned enough cash to dislodge the Welshman.

And there Montgomerie stayed, closely pursued by Langer as well as Ulsterman Darren Clarke, whose sheer consistency had kept him high in the money list all season without actually winning and took him close to the Open title at Royal Troon, with Ian Woosnam in fourth place until the showdown at the Volvo Masters. Westwood completed an outstanding season with victory at Montecastillo and Montgomerie was crowned number one for the fifth time. It was testimony indeed, of the narrow margin that now separates the

**Transports of delight:
Darren Clarke with his Ferrari,
Per-Ulrik Johansson afloat at
the Alamo English Open,
Greg Norman drops into
the Open, Tom Kite in
transit at Valderrama.**

very best players and it also demonstrated the complete self-assurance and ability of the new generation with Clarke, Ignacio Garrido, Westwood and Robert Karlsson all ranked among Europe's top money winners so early in their careers.

Montgomerie has quite clearly reached that stage in his career on the European Tour when he is not only the man to beat but stands also as the player against whom all others judge themselves. He snapped up the Compaq European Grand Prix at Slaley Hall a week before narrowly missing out to Els in the US Open. He then successfully defended the Murphy's Irish Open at Druids Glen, setting a course record 62 in the final round. He also established a course record 63 at the Forest of Arden during the One 2 One British Masters but finished runner-up to New Zealander Greg Turner, who was the model of calm consistency.

Per-Ulrik Johansson was another multiple winner during the season, taking the Alamo English Open at the Marriott Hanbury Manor and later retaining the Smurfit European Open at the K Club, south of Dublin. Fellow Swede Michael Jonzon followed his first-time European Tour win in the Portuguese Open with more success – albeit shared

25

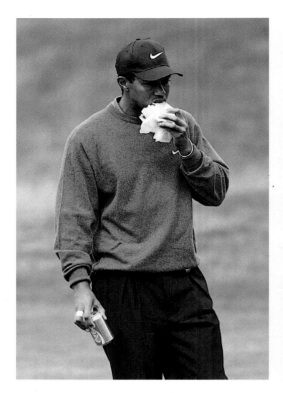

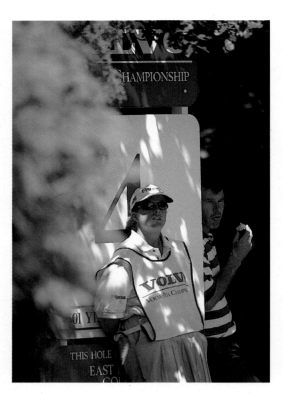

Tiger Woods (left) and Nick Faldo (right) in snacking mode.
For a few birdies more: Sam Torrance (below) does his Clint Eastwood impression.

- in the Open Novotel Perrier with Anders Forsbrand.

The forceful Swedish presence was completed by Joakim Haeggman winning the Volvo Scandinavian Masters while Robert Karlsson took the BMW International Open and non-European Tour member Jesper Parnevik finished joint runner-up in the Open Championship and later justified captain Ballesteros' judgement as a personal Ryder Cup choice.

There were six first-time winners on Tour during 1997 and they were Justin Leonard (Open Championship), Richard Green (Dubai Desert Classic in a play-off with Greg Norman and Ian Woosnam), South African Clinton Whitelaw (Moroccan Open), Stuart Cage (Europe 1 Cannes Open), Ignacio Garrido (Volvo German Open) and Ross McFarlane (Deutsche Bank-TPC of Europe).

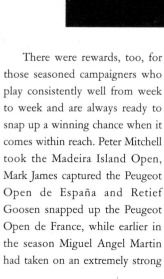

There were rewards, too, for those seasoned campaigners who play consistently well from week to week and are always ready to snap up a winning chance when it comes within reach. Peter Mitchell took the Madeira Island Open, Mark James captured the Peugeot Open de España and Retief Goosen snapped up the Peugeot Open de France, while earlier in the season Miguel Angel Martin had taken on an extremely strong

Glittering comeback for José Maria Olazábal (above).

26

field to win the Heineken Classic in Australia.

Irishman Paul McGinley passed a personal and lucrative milestone by winning the OKI Pro-Am in Spain and pushed his career earnings over £1 million while Sven Strüver added to his growing reputation by winning the Sun Microsystems Dutch Open at Hilversum.

Quite apart from the Open trophy at Royal Troon, some other prized possessions found their way into American hands as Tom Lehman took the Gulfstream Loch Lomond World Invitational a week before his Open title defence and later in the season Mark O'Meara made off with the Trophée Lancome from Saint-Nom-la-Bretéche.

As if to underline the international strength of golf in Europe, Vijay Singh beat Ernie Els for the Toyota World Match-Play Championship at Wentworth. The Fijiian professional, who won the South African Open early in the year, is quite clearly on the threshold of great things and his US victories in the Memorial Tournament and the Buick Open confirm that he is now a major force on both sides of the Atlantic.

Ernie Els has already proved that fact about himself and led South Africa to victory over Sweden in the Alfred Dunhill Cup at St Andrews. Such evidence suggests beyond question that Europe is now the hub of world golf and can claim to be the most effective and influential force within the game. There is much more glory to come. And not too far away either.

Michael McDonnell

Montgomerie's high five

Colin Montgomerie's record of achievement
reached a new peak with his fifth consecutive
Volvo Ranking title

*I*t was the height of irony that when the glittering climax to Colin Montgomerie's European season arrived he was required merely to sit around in the Montecastillo clubhouse while outside the rain ruined the final day's play of the Volvo Masters.

In golf, of course, the one thing you cannot vouchsafe is the weather and in Spain during this final week the storms had the final say, a water-logged course rebuffing all efforts to wring it out. So Montgomerie's dream of a record fifth Volvo Ranking title was ultimately realised in the most relaxed manner possible.

His edginess over the previous three days, however, betrayed just how much achieving this record meant to Montgomerie. Even for a man who wears his emotions on both sleeves most of the time, he was in a highly nervous state over the early rounds.

His instinct is to reveal instantly and publicly exactly how he is feeling, although sometimes even he admits he goes a smidgeon too far: 'My wife soon lets me know about it when I get home,' he says. It is, for the most part, a good thing that one of the European Tour's most recognisable faces is also a very human one.

In any case, the abiding image of Montgomerie from 1997 is once again a very large grin. By overtaking Peter Oosterhuis, who was top European Golfer four times consecutively between 1971 and 1974, Montgomerie has set a new and startling benchmark. It is, viewed from any angle, a prodigiously impressive achievement.

Few men ever dominate a game like this. It is a record that is as unlikely as Bjorn Borg's Wimbledon pre-eminence or, more recently, Frankie Dettori's outrageous charge through the Ascot card. These sorts of sporting achievements are outstanding because, logically, they simply should not happen. The odds against such success are so mountainous that optimistic punters should consider wearing crampons before attempting to place a bet. When you build into the equation the fact that in golf there are also so many outside variables – from weather, to bounce, to obstructive spike-mark for example – then

Montgomerie's record takes on an even glossier sheen.

When Montgomerie tied Oosterhuis' quartet of victories in 1996, the tall Englishman graciously insisted that the Scot's achievement was the greater because the standard of play on Tour these days is so much higher. Now to have added a fifth title eloquently underlines Montgomerie's soaring, natural talent. 'I have had to improve year by year,' he explained. 'If I had stood still I would have been overtaken. The standard has increased and I have increased with it. When I played in the Volvo Masters I had not missed a halfway cut in any event anywhere in the world in 1997 and I've never done that before.'

This consistency, in a sport that by its very nature enthusiastically encourages inconsistency, is the cornerstone of Montgomerie's golf. He rarely practises much, preferring to rely on a natural swing, a keen intelligence and what he admits is 'an incredible desire to succeed'. Certainly his ambition remains huge.

After much thought over the autumn he decided to remain a European Tour player, a decision based on loyalty to the organisation which has helped him to make the bulk of his fortune and also on family considerations as a father to two young children with a third expected in

May. His reason for playing more in the USA is simple enough: at 34 he has Europe at his feet but his inability so far, to win a major remains an insufferable frustration.

In 1997 he once again came close to breaking the mould when he narrowly lost out to Ernie Els in the US Open. This is the second time in three years that the South African has thwarted him in the US Open and again it seems that Els' more sanguine approach to the game was the decisive factor at the Congressional Club just outside Washington.

Significantly, when the pair met again during the Alfred Dunhill Cup in October, Els was eager to record that his opponent seemed genuinely relaxed. 'If he had been like that in the US Open then he would have stood a much better chance of winning it,' said Els.

Maybe, but what is beyond doubt is that no one will be more committed to take this or any of the year's other three major titles in 1998. Having established his European record, having starred in the Ryder Cup by Johnnie Walker, where he recovered from a hesitant start to emerge as Europe's top points gatherer, and having taken his European Tour tournament tally to 14 in eight years, more records still beckon.

In 1997 he played 19 European events, won twice (the Compaq European Grand Prix and the Murphy's Irish Open), was 177 under par for the 75 rounds played and inevitably led the stroke average table with 69.37. He also led the Guardian Insurance 'Better than Par' statistics with his total of 325 birdies and 13 eagles in Europe.

This is prodigious stuff. It is, however, just the bones of the story. To flesh out Montgomerie you need to see him in the real as he pursues yet another unlikely target such as his nine under par 62 in the last round of the Murphy's Irish Open when he overhauled Lee Westwood.

His refusal to concede, and his ability then to move his game on to a new and higher plane on these occasions, is a quality shared by very few other professionals. And like all genuine champions if he cannot win then he grafts as hard as he can to finish as high as possible. Thus, three weeks before the Volvo Masters, Montgomerie covered the final back nine of the Linde German Masters in 32 strokes which in turn moved him from seventh to second place and meant an extra £65,000. 'That is where I won my fifth consecutive Volvo Ranking title,' he smiled. He is, of course, wrong. Colin Montgomerie won his fifth title, as he did the previous four, because of an ambition forged many years ago. And that is simply to be the best.

Bill Elliott

COLIN MONTGOMERIE 1997 TOURNAMENT RECORD

Tournament	Posn		R1	R2	R3	R4	Agg	Par	Winnings £	Cumalative £
Johnnie Walker Classic	15	T	71	74	73	67	285	-3	10080	10080
Heineken Classic	22	T	70	72	72	67	281	-7	5934	16014
Dubai Desert Classic	6	T	65	72	68	71	276	-12	19652	35667
Benson and Hedges Int	59	T	70	71	76	81	298	10	2030	37697
Alamo English Open	12	T	72	68	70	67	277	-11	9091	46788
Volvo PGA Championship	5		69	69	76	64	278	-10	46640	93428
Compaq EGP	1		69	68	68	65	270	-18	108330	201758
Peugeot Open de France	11	T	66	70	73	69	278	-10	10320	212078
Murphy's Irish Open	1		68	70	69	62	269	-15	113636	325715
Gulfstream Loch Lomond	10	T	69	70	70	67	276	-8	15360	341075
126th Open Golf Championship	24	T	76	69	69	70	284	0	10362	351437
Volvo Scandinavian Masters	8	T	72	71	69	66	278	-10	16830	368267
Smurfit European Open	22	T	64	69	72	75	280	-8	9180	377447
BMW International Open	3		65	67	67	66	265	-23	46940	424387
Canon European Masters	10	T	65	72	64	70	271	-13	15360	439747
Trophée Lancôme	22	T	71	72	69	69	281	-3	7560	447307
One 2 One British Masters	2		72	74	67	63	276	-12	83320	530627
Linde German Masters	2		71	68	66	68	273	-15	83320	613947
Volvo Masters	8		65	71	71	-	207	-9	25000	638947
*Volvo Bonus Pool	1		-	-	-	-	-	-	160000	798947

Rounds: 75 — Strokes: 5203 — Stroke Average: 69.37 — Total Par: −177

ROLL OF HONOUR

	1993	1994	1995	1996	1997
Volvo Ranking Position	1	1	1	1	1
Volvo Ranking Money	£613,682	£762,719	£835,051	£875,146	£638,947
Tounaments	24	21	20	18	19
Wins	2	3	2	3	2
Top Tens	9	13	14	8	11
To Par	-65	-160	-146	-87	-177
Stroke Average	70.81	69.60	69.70	70.26	69.37
Total Money	£798,145	£920,647	£1,038,708	£1,034,752	£981,719

Colin Montgomerie is congratulated by Mel Pyatt of Volvo.

The finishing touches

Once again, Apollo Week provided a solid grounding for aspiring Tour newcomers

Denmark's Thomas Björn, Scotland's Raymond Russell and Ireland's Padraig Harrington emphasised in 1996 the benefits of attending Apollo Week – the European Tour Training School – with their superb victories in the Loch Lomond World Invitational, Air France Cannes Open and Peugeot Open de España respectively.

At Apollo Week all players are given ample time to work on their swings, and all aspects of their game, and John Jacobs, Tommy Horton, Denis Pugh, Harold Swash and John O'Leary are among the coaches to have given guidance and tuition. Graduates also gain a superb insight into all aspects of life on the European Tour by attending a variety of lectures.

Harrington and Russell came through the Qualifying School Finals to attend the 1996 Apollo Week, and Björn emerged from the European Challenge Tour.

'The experience of listening to all the coaches at Apollo Week helped me greatly in my preparation for the season,' Harrington said. 'I would thoroughly recommend all eligible golfers to attend in future years.'

Indeed Harrington, who returned by special invitation to the 1997 Apollo Week which was once again held at San Roque, went on to finish his rookie sea-

Coaching foursome of Harold Swash, John Jacobs, Denis Pugh and Tommy Horton.

son in 11th place in the 1996 Volvo Ranking. On his return to Apollo Week he found himself much in demand by players, all seeking advice about what to expect on the European Tour.

The 1997 Apollo Week was voted the best-ever by the regular attendees — coaches, fitness advisers, lecturers, golf writers, radio and TV reporters, European Tour staff and executives of Apollo Sports Technologies, which came under new ownership last year.

Managing Director Andy Taylor, who was at San Roque with the owner of Apollo Sports Technologies Ltd, Jim Probst, and his wife Renee, spoke with pride about the three 1996 Apollo Week graduates who went on to win tournaments in their first European Tour season — Björn, Russell and Harrington. And he staggered this year's intake by announc-

ing: 'Players who have attended Apollo Week since it all began nine years ago have gone on to win £25m between them.

'Last year's Apollo Week graduates did us proud on the European Tour, the best results since Apollo Week began nine years ago in 1989, and it's no coincidence that 19 out of 36 European Tour winners last season played Apollo golf shafts.

'Apollo Week is about the transfer of experience and we were delighted to welcome back to San Roque as our special guest Padraig Harrington, whose insights into life on the European Tour were invaluable to the 1997 graduates.'

George O'Grady, Deputy Executive Director of the PGA European Tour, said at the farewell dinner at San Roque that the 1996 season had been the most successful to date for Apollo Week graduates. They won more than £3m in prize money and three of the 22 won tournaments. He impressed on the players that they were now part of the European Tour family and explained how their Board of Directors formulated Tour policy and how their Tournament Committee represented their interests on all playing matters.

O'Grady was one of three people who helped to found Apollo Week, the others being Andy Taylor and Doug

Tony Adamson, George O'Grady, Steve Webster and Andy Taylor are ready for the pro-am (above). Guy Delacave in the 3M physio unit (right).

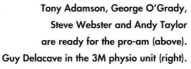

John Paramor rules OK (above). Harold Swash and John Jacobs with Christian Cevaer (left).

Billman, Joint Managing Director of European Tour Productions. It was developed from an original Young Professionals' School started by former Ryder Cup player Tommy Horton and later involving John Jacobs, who was Director General of the European Tour in its formative years. Tommy Horton has coached at Apollo Week since the start and John Jacobs has attended for the last few years. Also attending as coaches in January were Denis Pugh, principal tutor at the Warren Golf Academy, and Harold Swash, an expert on putting technology.

Apart from playing golf at San Roque and Valderrama and taking advantage of daily coaching sessions, lectures are held most mornings and evenings to help prepare players for life on the European Tour. These include instruction on the Rules of Golf by John Paramor, the then European Tour's Director of Operations and Chief Referee, and by José Maria Zamora, a Spanish amateur international and a member of the European's Tour's vastly experienced refereeing and tournament administration team. John Paramor also gives a comprehensive and revealing talk entitled 'Inside the European Tour'

which explains the structuring and operational side of the Tour. Other insights are provided by Marketing Director Scott Kelly, who explains about sponsorship and the European Tour, and Doug Billman, whose European Tour Productions provides the golf tournament pictures for TV stations around the world, including Sky TV.

Former Ryder Cup player John O'Leary, a member of the PGA European Tour's Board of Directors, talks at each Apollo Week to the players about course management while leading sports psychologist Alan Fine and one of the world's foremost fitness instructors, Ted Pollard, conduct daily sessions dealing with the mental and physical preparation necessary for playing successfully on the European Tour. Guy Delacave explains how the 3M Physiotherapy Unit works, and Jean-Luc Pannier was on hand this year to advise

on the important subject of 'Golf and Nutrition.' Rupert Hampel, General Manager of European Tour Productions, organised the 1997 Apollo Week and chaired lectures.

Apollo's Graeme Horwood and Mike Perry conducted an hour-long discussion in January on the role of the golf shaft — and during the week they re-shafted many of the players' clubs — while the European Tour's Mark Watson, a former travel company representative, told the players about travelling on Tour. Advice was on hand about the advantages and pitfalls of client management, given by Colin Montgomerie's manager, Guy Kinnings, from International Management Group, while another member of the IMG staff, David Lumley, explained the importance of financial management.

As Padraig Harrington concluded: 'Apollo Week gives you a good insight into what to expect on the European Tour and it's a good chance to get to know the faces you'll be seeing during the season. The evenings are pretty informal and allow you the opportunity to mix. You come away feeling you have learned something from everyone.'

Mitchell Platts

Els starts with a flourish

Ernie Els launched the
1997 European Tour
with victory in Australia

Ew year, new challenges, new hopes. And for the start of the 1997 European Tour season, newIMAGES as well.

An initiative from the British government to promote its links with Australia in a year-long programme of events called 'newIMAGES' resulted in the Johnnie Walker Classic breaking fresh ground. After previously being staged in Hong Kong, Bangkok, Singapore, Phuket, Manila and then Singapore again, the tournament moved out of Asia and set up camp on Queensland's Gold Coast. At the appropriately named Hope Island.

Never had the European Tour begun so far from home. But, as Colin Mongomerie said, if the choice was between no golf in Europe or golf 12,000 miles away, the co-sanctioned events such as this were the right way to go. Never mind the jet-lag, feel the sun and taste the competition.

A star-studded cast gathered, not simply from the European and Australasian Tours, but also United States-based draw-cards Ernie Els, John Daly, Vijay Singh and previous winners Nick Faldo and Fred Couples. In Els, Faldo, Couples and Montgomerie, beginning his bid, of course, for a record-breaking fifth successive Volvo Ranking title, the tournament boasted four of the world's current top six.

Ken Schofield, the PGA European Tour Executive Director, spoke in the Tour's weekly newsletter of this being 'a year of challenge for all' and had proffered the opinion that the Tour had in its ranks 'the largest, brightest, best crop of emerging, fresh talent' ever produced. As the starting gun was fired there was keen anticipation inside and outside the ropes to see which of them would deliver.

Two such were 24-year-old David Carter and 21-year-old David Howell, and they set about the task of slaying the Goliaths with no delay. Carter, runner-up to another bright prospect Raymond Russell in the 1996 Air France Cannes Open, and winner of the Indian PGA championship in December, set the stan-

THE COURSE

Five times Open champion Peter Thomson designed Hope Island Golf Club with his partner Mike Wolveridge and they have brought to Queelsand's Gold Coast a taste of British links golf. Undulating fairways and small strategically-placed bunkers test driving ability, but the biggest challenge comes in the approach shots to well-guarded, plateau greens. Water comes into play on nearly half the holes too, and the fact that nobody scored lower than 67 throughout the Johnnie Walker Classic tells its own story.

dard — not bettered all week — with a five under par 67 highlighted by an eagle putt from 18 feet on the long 17th. Howell raced to six under with four to play, only to drop three strokes over the closing stretch.

That left Carter to share the pace at the end of the first day with Australians Steve Conran and Anthony Painter and another unexpected figure in 23-year-old Indian, Arjun Atwal. But none of the four could break par in the second round and it was all change at the top, a second successive 68 from New Zealander Michael Long (he finished eagle-birdie) lifting him two clear of South African Els and another

David Howell (right) amid Hope Island's flora. Peter Lonard (opposite) cuts one up from the fairway.

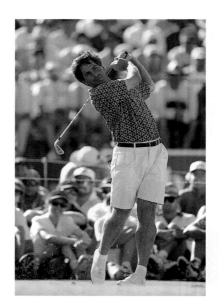

Fred Couples was a shorts hitter.

SHOT OF THE WEEK

He made it look so easy that it was easy to overlook, but the chip which Ernie Els played to save his par at the 153-yard 14th in the final round came at a crucial time and kept him on course for the title. The South African had bogeyed the previous hole to allow his lead to be cut to a single stroke and when he missed the green with his next tee shot he needed to get his act together quickly. The shortest of Hope Island's par threes had caused its fair share of problems, but Els judged his chip superbly, up and over the slope and then rolling to within two feet of the flag.

Vijay Singh views some new clubs.

Australian, Peter Lonard.

Among those making early departures were Daly, rounds of 77 and 79 being a big disappointment after his seventh place finish in America the previous week-end, Ian Baker-Finch, who despite victory in the pro-am was still a million miles from the form which made him the 1991 Open champion, and Andrew Coltart, the Scot who had lost a play-off to Ian Woosnam 12 months earlier.

Surviving was one thing. Being a contender was another. Woosnam had left himself too much ground to make up and Montgomerie's second round 74 knocked him back sufficiently enough to put him out of the running. The same looked true of Couples when he managed only a 76, but a 67 followed and with a round to play he was lying fifth, two behind Els and four in arrears of joint leaders Long, Painter and Lonard. Faldo was just one further back, his move made before he went off to cuddle some koalas.

Couples and Faldo, paired together for the final round, closed the gap some more on the front nine, but after an inter-

ruption for rain and the threat of lighting both crashed to not-so-magnificent sevens on the 548-yard 11th and left the issue to be fought out by Long, Lonard and Els.

The South African produced a burst of four birdies in six holes from the fifth to lead by two, but a little edginess crept into his play as he bogeyed the 13th and then had to work hard for his par on the next. He missed the green at the 15th as well, but the vital moment came when

Long prepared to attempt his long birdie putt. As the Kiwi addressed his ball he — and nobody else — spotted that it moved a tiny fraction. 'It's something that I would not wish on anyone,' he said later, 'but it happens and when it does you've got to be honest with yourself and own up. That's the game we play.'

Long called a penalty stroke on himself, two-putted for bogey and then saw Els hole from 35 feet on the 16th. There was only one winner after that, although the final gap was just one, courtesy of a closing bogey from the 1994 US Open champion.

Long tried not to think of what it meant in cash terms — just as well really since Lonard holed from 45 feet on the last to deny him outright second place. His chance of victory and £116,660 may have gone in that split-second, but he could hold his head high. 'Gentlemen play this game,' said Els. 'In tennis you his it close to the lines and it's in the hands of a line judge or umpire, but in golf we take it on ourselves.'

Mark Garrod

HOPE ISLAND, QUEENSLAND, AUSTRALIA, JANUARY 23-26, 1997 · YARDAGE 7074 · PAR 72

Pos	Name	Country	Rnd 1	Rnd 2	Rnd 3	Rnd 4	Total	Prize Money £
1	Ernie ELS	(SA)	70	68	71	69	278	116660
2	Peter LONARD	(Aus)	69	69	69	72	279	60795
	Michael LONG	(NZ)	68	68	71	72	279	60795
4	Anthony PAINTER	(Aus)	67	73	67	75	282	29713
	Fred COUPLES	(USA)	68	76	67	71	282	29713
	Nick FALDO	(Eng)	70	72	70	70	282	29713
7	Michael CAMPBELL	(NZ)	70	71	74	68	283	14900
	Peter O'MALLEY	(Aus)	73	68	74	68	283	14900
	David HOWELL	(Eng)	69	72	75	67	283	14900
	Bernhard LANGER	(Ger)	73	72	69	69	283	14900
	Robert ALLENBY	(Aus)	73	73	70	67	283	14900
	Stephen LEANEY	(Aus)	69	72	75	67	283	14900
	Marc FARRY	(Fr)	72	70	72	69	283	14900
14	Ian WOOSNAM	(Wal)	74	70	71	69	284	10710
15	Joakim HAEGGMAN	(Swe)	72	71	70	72	285	10080
	Colin MONTGOMERIE	(Scot)	71	74	73	67	285	10080
	Chia Yuh HONG (AM)	(Tai)	72	74	70	69	285	
17	Craig JONES	(Aus)	68	76	72	70	286	9053
	Alexander CEJKA	(Ger)	73	67	73	73	286	9053
	Phillip PRICE	(Wal)	76	70	68	72	286	9053
20	Paul BROADHURST	(Eng)	74	70	72	71	287	7770
	Gary ORR	(Scot)	71	75	70	71	287	7770
	David CARTER	(Eng)	67	75	72	73	287	7770
	Steve ALKER	(NZ)	68	73	73	73	287	7770
	Stephen AMES	(T&T)	72	74	72	69	287	7770
	Steve CONRAN	(Aus)	67	75	73	72	287	7770
	Raymond RUSSELL	(Scot)	74	69	73	71	287	7770
27	Frank NOBILO	(NZ)	70	73	72	73	288	6615
	Padraig HARRINGTON	(Ire)	71	73	73	71	288	6615
	Anders FORSBRAND	(Swe)	74	72	73	69	288	6615
	Andrew SHERBORNE	(Eng)	71	73	75	69	288	6615
31	Lucas PARSONS	(Aus)	69	77	70	73	289	5903
	André BOSSERT	(Swi)	70	74	74	71	289	5903
	Rick GIBSON	(Can)	68	76	72	73	289	5903
34	Arjun ATWAL	(Indo)	67	78	72	73	290	4900
	Lian-Wei ZHANG	(Chi)	69	75	71	75	290	4900
	David GILFORD	(Eng)	70	76	73	71	290	4900
	Jon ROBSON	(Eng)	72	74	72	72	290	4900
	Richard GREEN	(Aus)	71	73	73	73	290	4900
	Richard BOXALL	(Eng)	72	74	73	71	290	4900
	Paul DEVENPORT	(NZ)	71	75	70	74	290	4900
	Shane ROBINSON	(Aus)	72	72	75	71	290	4900
	Jean VAN DE VELDE	(Fr)	70	69	76	75	290	4900
	Paul EALES	(Eng)	69	70	77	74	290	4900
	Katsuyoshi TOMORI	(Jap)	74	72	73	71	290	4900
45	Darren CLARKE	(N.Ire)	72	73	74	72	291	3780
	Barry LANE	(Eng)	71	71	77	72	291	3780
	Mike HARWOOD	(Aus)	74	71	74	72	291	3780
	Thomas GÖGELE	(Ger)	71	72	72	76	291	3780
	Fabrice TARNAUD	(Fr)	72	70	73	76	291	3780
50	Kaname YOKOO	(Jap)	72	74	73	73	292	2940
	Jonathan LOMAS	(Eng)	73	72	71	76	292	2940
	Greg CHALMERS	(Aus)	71	73	73	75	292	2940
	Ross MCFARLANE	(Eng)	72	73	75	72	292	2940
	Bob SHEARER	(Aus)	74	71	73	74	292	2940
	Ali KADIR	(Mal)	70	73	76	73	292	2940
	Miles TUNNICLIFF	(Eng)	69	73	76	74	292	2940
57	Taichi TESHIMA	(Jap)	72	73	76	72	293	2310
	Carl SUNESON	(Sp)	75	67	77	74	293	2310
59	Scott LAYCOCK	(Aus)	69	75	77	73	294	2135
	Gary EVANS	(Eng)	73	71	75	75	294	2135
61	Peter BAKER	(Eng)	71	74	73	77	295	1995
	Guan-Soon CHUA	(Sing)	75	70	78	72	295	1995
63	Felix CASAS	(Phil)	68	75	79	74	296	1890
64	Rodger DAVIS	(Aus)	70	75	76	77	298	1820
65	Klas ERIKSSON	(Swe)	72	73	78	76	299	1750

Defending champion Ian Woosnam.

Martin foils Couples

Miguel Angel Martin's second Tour win

was achieved in the face

of strong opposition

*T*here was a certain air of inevitability about Ernie Els winning the season-opening Johnnie Walker Classic once the tournament reached its closing holes. With all due respect to Michael Long and Peter Lonard, he was the one with the world-class pedigree, the proven track record, and when he pressed the accelerator and had his four birdies in six holes midway through the final round for a two-stroke lead, no bets were being placed on any other outcome.

A week later Fred Couples appeared to have timed his run even better at the Heineken Classic, played over the immaculate Vines course just outside Perth. Couples, winner of the first

SHOT OF THE WEEK

Miguel Angel Martin fell two behind Fred Couples when he, like Katsuyoshi Tomori just before him, failed to get out of a fairway bunker on the 12th. He could not afford another mistake if he was going to win and a drive into more sand three holes later spelt danger. But this time the Spaniard no only got out, he sent a four iron to the heart of the green. Without that shot the ultimate triumph might not have been possible.

two events on the European Tour in 1995, was bang on line for another successful raid when he began the last nine holes with a hat-trick of birdies and had two more at the 14th and 16th. From four behind the American charged two ahead. An engraver might have felt safe to start applying his name to the trophy.

The man he overtook was Spain's Miguel Angel Martin, winner of just one title since joining the European Tour in 1983. Martin had almost lost his card in 1993 and 1995 and his start to 1997 had hardly caused shockwaves. He missed the halfway cut at Hope Island by six shots. There was a reason for that, though. 'It's the first time I've come to Australia.' he said. 'There is nine hours' difference. I felt very bad. It felt like the holes and the bunkers were moving. I wanted to sleep in the middle of the course.'

But once the holes and the bunkers stopped moving Martin began finding the former and missing the latter. In the first three rounds in Perth he did not have a single bogey — 'my best golf ever' he reck-oned — and even when Couples came

Ernie Els reaches for the sky.

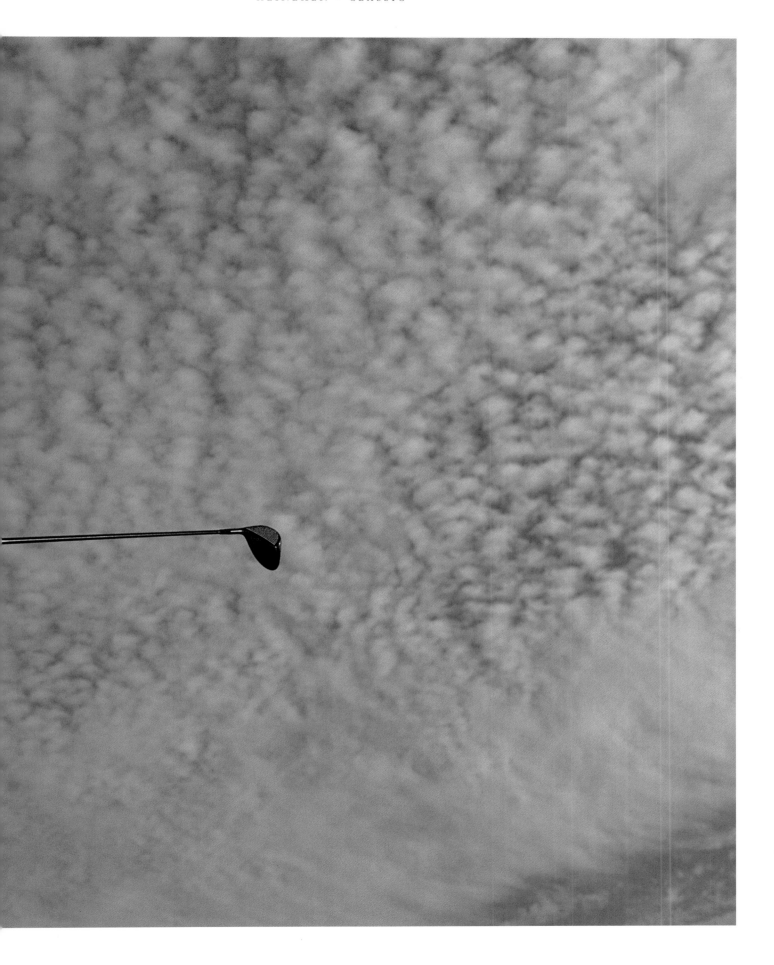

French connection: Marc Farry and Jean Van de Velde (above) in tête à tête. (Below) Padraig Harrington's scorecard for his course record-breaking 63.

racing past him the 34-year-old refused to lie down meekly.

As Couples pushed a nine iron into sand and bogeyed the 17th, the Spaniard rolled in a birdie putt on the 14th. And as the world number six found another bunker off the tee at the 517-yard last and could only par, Martin stayed on terms. It came down to the classic equation of a birdie on the 18th to win. Ian Woosnam had done it a year before with a drive and five iron to ten feet and two putts. Martin had to work harder. His four wood second sailed into a back bunker, but from there he splashed out to eight feet and the putt, like so many others in this week to remember, was perfectly judged.

'I thought this game was for big guys – but sometimes the small guy can win,' said the 5ft 6in champion. The £107,546 cheque was reason enough to celebrate, but added to his runner-up finish in the One 2 One British Masters (he lost a play-off to Robert Allenby) he was now second in the Ryder Cup points table and commented: 'This is the best win of my career. To beat the players here this week gives me a great feeling. I couldn't be happier.'

Martin had opened quietly with a two under par 70, five behind New Zealander Greg Turner, and although he then added a 67 he was still four off the pace since Ireland's Padraig Harrington shaved two shots off the course record with a nine-birdie 63. 'I had trouble counting up how many under par I was.' stated the Dubliner. 'You very rarely get into the zone but that's exactly how it was.'

It was as the temperature climbed to a mind-blowing – almost literally – 44 degrees Centigrade on the Saturday that Martin came to the fore. Woosnam found his clubs nearly too hot to handle and Paul Eales described it was like somebody opening an oven door above their heads, but Martin locked himself into a cocoon of concentration, shot 65 and opened up a three-stroke advantage.

Come Sunday, Martin was trying his heart out for only the second victory of his Tour career. Martin came under threat first from Katsuyoshi Tomori, the Japanese Tour star who had come through the European Tour Qualifying School, and then from Allenby, the man who had denied him at Collingtree Park the previous August.

They faded as Couples made his move. But Martin didn't and when Couples opened the door he stepped right in.

Mark Garrod

The Vines Resort, Perth, Australia, January 30-February 2, 1997 • Yardage 7101 • Par 72

Pos	Name	Country	Rnd 1	Rnd 2	Rnd 3	Rnd 4	Total	Prize Money £
1	Miguel Angel MARTIN	(Sp)	70	67	65	71	273	107546
2	Fred COUPLES	(USA)	68	70	69	67	274	60943
3	Frank NOBILO	(NZ)	66	69	70	70	275	30969
	Jean VAN DE VELDE	(Fr)	69	69	69	68	275	30969
	Marc FARRY	(Fr)	72	66	69	68	275	30969
6	Ian WOOSNAM	(Wal)	72	69	69	66	276	20314
	Wayne RILEY	(Aus)	71	66	69	70	276	20314
8	Katsuyoshi TOMORI	(Jap)	69	68	69	71	277	16291
	Ernie ELS	(SA)	73	71	68	65	277	16291
	Robert ALLENBY	(Aus)	70	68	71	68	277	16291
11	Greg TURNER	(NZ)	65	71	72	70	278	11113
	Greg CHALMERS	(Aus)	70	72	71	65	278	11113
	Paul EALES	(Eng)	70	69	67	72	278	11113
	Padraig HARRINGTON	(Ire)	70	63	73	72	278	11113
	Rodney PAMPLING	(Aus)	68	73	66	71	278	11113
16	Peter O'MALLEY	(Aus)	68	69	71	71	279	8185
	Rodger DAVIS	(Aus)	71	72	68	68	279	8185
18	David CARTER	(Eng)	71	69	70	70	280	6639
	Ken DRUCE	(Aus)	71	69	72	68	280	6639
	Peter SENIOR	(Aus)	69	71	70	70	280	6639
	Roger CHAPMAN	(Eng)	70	69	73	68	280	6639
22	Colin MONTGOMERIE	(Scot)	70	72	72	67	281	5934
	Andrew COLTART	(Scot)	71	72	69	69	281	5934
	Stephen LEANEY	(Aus)	72	71	69	69	281	5934
25	Darren CLARKE	(N.Ire)	70	69	71	72	282	4884
	Darren COLE	(Aus)	73	71	68	70	282	4884
	Thomas BJORN	(Den)	69	70	74	69	282	4884
	Paul BROADHURST	(Eng)	70	69	70	73	282	4884
29	Shane TAIT	(Aus)	71	70	73	69	283	3689
	Wayne GRADY	(Aus)	67	72	73	71	283	3689
	Rick GIBSON	(Can)	70	70	70	73	283	3689
	Miles TUNNICLIFF	(Eng)	67	72	72	72	283	3689
	Jon ROBSON	(Eng)	72	67	70	74	283	3689
	Paul MCGINLEY	(Ire)	72	65	69	77	283	3689
	Stuart CAGE	(Eng)	69	73	71	70	283	3689
	Carl SUNESON	(Sp)	69	72	71	71	283	3689
37	David SMAIL	(NZ)	73	68	71	72	284	2927
	David HIGGINS	(Ire)	71	67	76	70	284	2927
	Fabrice TARNAUD	(Fr)	77	67	69	71	284	2927
	Martyn ROBERTS	(Wal)	71	72	69	72	284	2927
41	Andrew SHERBORNE	(Eng)	72	71	69	73	285	2449
	Mathew GOGGIN	(Aus)	72	70	69	74	285	2449
	Peter MCWHINNEY	(Aus)	70	71	69	75	285	2449
	Peter LONARD	(Aus)	71	71	71	72	285	2449
45	Lee WESTWOOD	(Eng)	71	73	72	70	286	2031
	Stephen AMES	(T&T)	69	73	73	71	286	2031
	Michael CAMPBELL	(NZ)	69	68	72	77	286	2031
48	Wayne SMITH	(Aus)	74	69	72	72	287	1672
	Stephen COLLINS	(Aus)	69	75	73	70	287	1672
	Stephen SCAHILL	(NZ)	73	71	72	71	287	1672
51	Thomas GÖGELE	(Ger)	72	70	76	70	288	1342
	Justin COOPER	(Aus)	71	72	72	T3	288	1342
	David BRANSDON	(Aus)	69	72	72	75	288	1342
	Daniel CHOPRA	(Swe)	71	72	70	75	288	1342
	Peter MITCHELL	(Eng)	72	69	73	74	288	1342
	Stewart APPLEBY	(Aus)	73	69	76	70	288	1342
	Carl MASON	(Eng)	71	73	75	69	288	1342
58	Tim ELLIOTT	(Aus)	69	72	77	71	289	1260
	Lyndsay STEPHEN	(Aus)	72	72	74	71	289	1260
60	Jay TOWNSEND	(USA)	74	70	73	73	290	1242
61	Elliot BOULT	(NZ)	70	69	80	72	291	1230
62	Michael LONG	(NZ)	72	71	79	70	292	1218
63	Raymond RUSSELL	(Scot)	69	72	75	77	293	1206
64	Lucas PARSONS	(Aus)	69	75	74	77	295	1194
65	John DALY	(USA)	70	73	83	76	302	1183

THE COURSE

A superb test of golf, the Graham Marsh-designed Vines is a half-hour drive from Perth along the Swan Valley. Accuracy off the tee is the key to good scoring — ask John Daly, who once he abandoned the policy of keeping his driver in his bag crashed to a third round 83. Still, there was plenty of wildlife, kangaroos included, for him to enjoy as he ventured off the straight and narrow. The huge greens were softer this time and that contributed to the winning total coming down from Ian Woosnam's 11 under par to Miguel Angel Martin's 15 under.

Singh gets down to business

The abandonment of the long putter
helped Vijay Singh record his
first victory for 18 months

Vijay Singh, the tall, ice-cool Fijian, recorded the seventh European Tour victory of his career when he won the South African Open Championship at the Glendower Golf Club in Johannesburg.

A big partisan crowd supported the finest of southern Africa's players as they put him under last-round pressure but he held on to his nerve to return a 69 for an aggregate total of 270, 18 under par, to beat Zimbabwe's Nick Price (68) by one stroke. Ernie Els (70), Mark McNulty (69) and Fulton Allem (67) shared third place on 275. Ian Woosnam (66-75-69-69) and David Gilford (69-66-74-70) were the best of the European contingent and finished tied for seventh place on 279.

Singh had used a broomstick putter for most of last year but when he failed to win anything with it, his wife persuaded him to go back to the smaller tradi-

Wayne Westner (left) finds sand and Fulton Allem (above) finds the bush.

tional model. He also had to borrow a driver from fellow competitor, Bruce Vaughan, when he cracked his own on the range shortly before starting his first round. Collecting the winner's cheque of £71,476, Singh said: 'After 18 months without a victory I was getting very frustrated. I had played well for three rounds and I felt I could win if I could maintain it. I didn't make any mistakes.'

Price looked as though he might draw level on the par five 17th. Two behind, he was on in three, only ten feet from the hole and Singh was 15 feet away for four, after tangling with thick rough on the

THE COURSE

Glendower is a superb parkland course and a nature reserve. It is long and tight with water and thick rough waiting to punish poor shots. Its greens are slick too, and these are the qualities which have earned it a rating of fourth among South Africa's 400 courses. It was designed by an Englishman, Charles Hugh Allison, a contemporary of Harry Colt, and was opened in 1937.

49

way. But Vijay calmly holed out, Price missed and the chance was gone. Former Open champion Price had had pre-tournament doubts about low scoring but his pessimism was certainly unfounded on the first day when 71 of the 156 players returned par or better.

Pride of place went to little known South African, Wayne Bradley who had nine birdies in a round of 65. He put his score down to a brand new driver he had acquired only the previous evening and an old Arnold Palmer blade putter he had brought 'out of retirement' the previous week. Four players were tied for second place on 66 — Errnie Els and Fulton Allem of South Africa, Thomas Bjorn of Denmark, and Ian Woosnam of Wales.

Els, the 1994 US Open champion was only one under after 12 but then burst into life, going birdie, birdie, eagle, birdie. 'I lost my concentration for a couple of holes but overall I hit the ball well. I had finished 68-65 in Australia last weekend and it was good to bring that form here,' he said.

Allem eagled the 522-yard 17th (his eighth) when he hit a five wood to ten feet and then caught fire coming home, birdieing five of the first six holes. Woosnam's round was bogey free but he admitted: 'Tee to green it was my worst round of the season, but I putted really

SHOT OF THE WEEK

South Africa's Justin Hobday started his first round at 7.30am with a spectacular eagle two. His 275-yard drive at the first hole, rated by members to be the second hardest on the course, had left him with 185 yards to go. He hit a seven iron from semi-rough which bounced 30 yards short and rolled in. He never saw it drop.

well.' His touch deserted him in the second round when he returned a disappointing 75.

Rain and threats of lightning wiped out play in the afternoon with half the field still out on the course, but not before Bjorn had finished a round of 69 to tie Bradley (70) for the lead on 135; nine under par.

The second round was completed mid-Saturday morning with Singh and David Gilford posting 66s to join the leaders. But of the four out front, only Singh withstood the third-round pressure as the players brought the course to its knees. In all, the field recorded 230 birdies and ten eagles during the day, impressive scoring on a course rated among the toughest in the country.

Eamonn Darcy, Adam Hunter and Price all shared the lead for a time. Singh, however, was rock solid and a four-birdie burst over the last five holes gave him a 66 for 201, 15 under par, and a two-shot cushion. A 65 by Price put him into second place with Els (67) a further two strokes behind.

With Mark McNulty and Fulton Allem still within striking distance, the leaderboard for the final day promised plenty of drama — and Singh emerged from it all a worthy winner.

Frank Clough

Ernie Els has an arboreal experience.

GLENDOWER GOLF CLUB, JOHANNESBURG, FEBRUARY 6-9, 1997 · YARDAGE 7408 · PAR 72

Pos	Name	Country	Rnd 1	Rnd 2	Rnd 3	Rnd 4	Total	Prize Money £
1	Vijay SINGH	(Fij)	69	66	66	69	270	71476
2	Nick PRICE	(Zim)	72	66	65	68	271	52023
3	Ernie ELS	(SA)	66	72	67	70	275	24066
	Mark MCNULTY	(Zim)	69	69	68	69	275	24066
	Fulton ALLEM	(SA)	66	71	71	67	275	24066
6	Retief GOOSEN	(SA)	72	67	72	67	278	16014
7	Ian WOOSNAM	(Wal)	66	75	69	69	279	12236
	David GILFORD	(Eng)	69	66	74	70	279	12236
9	Sven STRÜVER	(Ger)	70	71	71	68	280	8911
	Clinton WHITELAW	(SA)	74	66	74	66	280	8911
	Jean VAN DE VELDE	(Fr)	68	69	73	70	280	8911
12	Andrew MCLARDY	(SA)	72	71	69	69	281	6932
	Gary EVANS	(Eng)	68	72	72	69	281	6932
	Wayne WESTNER	(SA)	69	70	73	69	281	6932
	Eamonn DARCY	(Ire)	67	69	73	72	281	6932
16	Francis QUINN	(USA)	69	72	72	69	282	6242
	Hennie OTTO (AM)	(SA)	74	68	68	72	282	
17	Trevor DODDS	(Nam)	72	70	71	71	284	5790
	Adam HUNTER	(Scot)	71	68	70	75	284	5790
	Thomas BJORN	(Den)	66	69	75	74	284	5790
20	Ignacio GARRIDO	(Sp)	70	73	71	71	285	5247
	Wayne BRADLEY	(SA)	65	70	75	75	285	5247
22	Ashley ROESTOFF	(SA)	74	68	72	72	286	4749
	Warren SCHUTTE	(SA)	74	69	72	71	286	4749
	André BOSSERT	(Swi)	73	69	73	71	286	4749
	Bobby LINCOLN	(SA)	71	69	72	74	286	4749
	Phillip PRICE	(Wal)	71	68	76	71	286	4749
27	Warrick DRUIAN	(SA)	70	74	70	73	287	4274
	Padraig HARRINGTON	(Ire)	72	73	73	69	287	4274
29	Thomas GÖGELE	(Ger)	71	71	80	66	288	3950
	Anders FORSBRAND	(Swe)	70	72	70	76	288	3950
	Justin HOBDAY	(SA)	72	68	73	75	288	3950
32	Malcolm MACKENZIE	(Eng)	71	72	76	70	289	3438
	Wallie COETSEE	(SA)	69	74	77	69	289	3438
	Raymond BURNS	(N.Ire)	70	74	74	71	289	3438
	Paul BROADHURST	(Eng)	71	71	72	75	289	3438
	David FROST	(SA)	70	72	73	74	289	3438
	Miguel Angel MARTIN	(Sp)	72	70	77	70	289	3438
	Ian PALMER	(SA)	76	65	74	74	289	3438
	Kevin STONE	(SA)	70	70	75	74	289	3438
40	Steve WOODS	(USA)	68	74	74	74	290	2578
	Gary ORR	(Scot)	73	70	70	77	290	2578
	Bruce VAUGHAN	(USA)	72	71	70	77	290	2578
	David CARTER	(Eng)	69	75	70	76	290	2578
	Peter BAKER	(Eng)	70	74	75	71	290	2578
	Steve VAN VUUREN	(SA)	73	71	70	76	290	2578
	Jon ROBSON	(Eng)	73	71	71	75	290	2578
	Jamie SPENCE	(Eng)	69	75	74	72	290	2578
	Wimpie BOTHA	(SA)	72	72	72	74	290	2578
	Robert KARLSSON	(Swe)	69	72	75	74	290	2578
	Nico VAN RENSBURG	(SA)	69	72	75	74	290	2578
51	Stephen AMES	(T&T)	72	72	75	72	291	1900
	Daniel CHOPRA	(Swe)	70	74	74	73	291	1900
	Michael CAMPBELL	(NZ)	75	70	75	71	291	1900
	Craig KAMPS	(SA)	71	71	76	73	291	1900
	Trevor IMMELMAN (AM)	(SA)	72	72	71	76	291	
55	Chris DAVISON	(Eng)	70	74	73	75	292	1520
	Anders HANSEN	(Den)	76	69	76	71	292	1520
	David HIGGINS	(Ire)	71	74	71	76	292	1520
	Dean VAN STADEN	(SA)	73	72	74	73	292	1520
	Sammy DANIELS	(SA)	71	70	77	74	292	1520
60	Michael ARCHER	(Eng)	69	74	72	78	293	1357
61	Brett LIDDLE	(SA)	74	71	75	74	294	1266
	Marc FARRY	(Fr)	70	75	74	75	294	1266
	Marco GORTANA	(It)	74	67	76	77	294	1266
64	Patrik SJÖLAND	(Swe)	71	72	74	78	295	1130
	Michael DU TOIT	(SA)	73	72	76	74	295	1130
	Carl SUNESON	(Sp)	73	69	77	76	295	1130
67	Richard KAPLAN	(SA)	70	75	76	75	296	1040

Nick Price in double vision.

Price lifts the gloom

In fading light at Sun City,

Nick Price ended a 15-month

spell without victory

Nick Price ended a frustrating 15 months' victory famine by strolling home with eight strokes to spare in the Dimension Data Pro-am at Sun City — and the moon and the stars were out to shine on his big day.

After a total of six hours and 20 minutes were lost to lightning, Tournament Director Andy McFee and his staff had all on to get the tournament finished on schedule, but they made it — just.

It looked odds on the champagne staying on ice overnight when the siren sounded to suspend play just as Price and Padraig Harrington and their two amateurs completed nine holes in exactly three hours, but they stepped on the gas to come home in two hours 15 minutes.

Price explained: 'Padraig and I in the last match were given the option on the 17th of coming back in the morning but neither of us fancied that, so we got our skates on — it was virtually dark when I knocked in a putt to par the last. I felt sorry for young Padraig, who bogeyed the last two holes in the gathering gloom to lose a lot of money.'

A 20 below par 268 tally left him eight ahead of South African David Frost with Denmark's Thomas Bjorn a stroke behind him and Harrington, after a closing 75, defending champion Mark McNulty, Wayne Westner, American Ronnie McCann and Trinidad and Tobago's Stephen Ames two further back.

Price revived memories of his record breaking 24 under par 12 strokes victory in the Million Dollar Challenge over the same Gary Player Country Club course by shooting 67 (at nearby Lost City), 66,66, and 69 to leave his rivals chasing shadows, not that there were many as the blazing African sun nudged temperatures at the spectacular resort complex up into the 90s.

It was quite a way to celebrate his 40th birthday a fortnight before and the former world number one admitted: 'It was a terrific relief to get the monkey of not winning since the 1995 Zimbabwe Open off my back.

'A victory was always on the cards after I ended 1996 with a run of top fives, including finishing a stroke behind when Colin Montgomerie beat Ernie Els in a play-off in December's Million Dollar and then starting 1997 with third place in Pheonix, where I shot 64 and 65, and second place to Vijay Singh in the South African Open, where I finished 66,65,68,'

Price went 54 holes without a bogey from his sixth in round one and never once three-putted in the tournament: 'The key was my long putting, for which I give myself full marks. I've been lacking confidence on the greens but my pace and line

THE COURSE

The Gary Player course, over which the pros played three rounds, and the panoramic Lost City layout were both designed by Gary, the former being longer (7,484 yards to 7,326) and less hilly than the latter, which is sited in an extinct volcano beside the Pilanesburg Mountains and whose short 13th is flanked by a pool which serves as home to 38 crocodiles (bottom right).

were spot on all week.'

Using a special nasal spray to contain the sinus problems that dogged him for most of 1996, Price went into round four five strokes clear on 199 after back-to-back 66s reminiscent of the form which earned him 13 worldwide titles, including the Open and a second USPGA, in 1993 and 1994, when he was twice US number one.

Patience proved a virtue for the genial Zimbabwean in an event in which amateurs were scheduled to play all four days but, because of the weather delays, stepped aside in round three.

Frost, three times winner of the Million Dollar title at Sun City, and youngsters Bjorn and Harrington also stayed cool, calm and collected.

A first day 67, best by two on the more demanding Gary Player course, left Costantino Rocca among nine players two behind surprise leader McCann, one of three South African-born golfing stepsons of top teaching professional Phil Ritson who grew up in America.

When the second round was suspended overnight after two 2½ hour

SHOT OF THE WEEK

The second putt for a four at the par five fourth (his 13th) by Nick Price on day one at Lost City. He had just been told two penalty strokes imposed on him and five other pros for taking a buggy ride from the 14th (his fifth) tee, had been rescinded and recalls: 'It was effectively a double eagle.'

Local man Desvonde Botes (above left). Nick Price tries to help Seve Ballesteros.

lighting hold-ups, Frost was sharing the clubhouse lead with 28-year-old Melbourne professional John Wade, making his Tour debut after finishing third at the European Tour Qualifying School.

Both fired 65s and Bjorn and Britain's Gary Evans also completed 65s next morning. But Price completed a homeward 31 to edge a stroke clear on 133,

then went out in 32 in round three.

Sadly Severiano Ballesteros, after running up four sevens in an opening 82 at Lost City, missed the cut by ten after adding a 72, and Darren Clarke, fourth in the Ryder Cup rankings, and Ricky Willison, joint second to McNulty in the 1996 event with Price, also went out.

Gordon Richardson

GARY PLAYER & LOST CITY COURSES, SOUTH AFRICA, FEBRUARY 13-16, 1997 · YARDAGE 7484/7326 · PAR 72

Pos	Name	Country	Rnd 1	Rnd 2	Rnd 3	Rnd 4	Total	Prize Money £
1	Nick PRICE	(Zim)	67	66	66	69	268	63384
2	David FROST	(SA)	69	65	71	71	276	46155
3	Thomas BJORN	(Den)	67	67	71	72	277	27765
4	Mark MCNULTY	(Zim)	71	66	69	73	279	14455
	Wayne WESTNER	(SA)	72	66	70	71	279	14455
	Stephen AMES	(T&T)	69	69	70	71	279	14455
	Padraig HARRINGTON	(Ire)	70	66	68	75	279	14455
	Ronnie MCCANN	(USA)	65	73	71	70	279	14455
9	Desvonde BOTES	(SA)	69	67	70	74	280	8293
	Tony JOHNSTONE	(Zim)	67	71	70	72	280	8293
11	Lee WESTWOOD	(Eng)	70	69	71	72	282	6263
	Daniel CHOPRA	(Swe)	72	67	71	72	282	6263
	Costantino ROCCA	(It)	67	72	73	70	282	6263
	Hugh BAIOCCHI	(SA)	72	68	73	69	282	6263
	Ian GARBUTT	(Eng)	69	72	68	73	282	6263
	Paul MCGINLEY	(Ire)	68	72	72	70	282	6263
17	Chris WILLIAMS	(Eng)	69	69	70	75	283	5208
	Iain PYMAN	(Eng)	70	67	74	72	283	5208
	Retief GOOSEN	(SA)	71	68	72	72	283	5208
20	Des SMYTH	(Ire)	73	68	71	72	284	4727
	Trevor DODDS	(Nam)	69	72	70	73	284	4727
22	Chris DAVISON	(Eng)	74	67	75	69	285	4407
	Anders HANSEN	(Den)	67	74	70	74	285	4407
	Katsuyoshi TOMORI	(Jap)	71	68	77	69	285	4407
25	Phil GOLDING	(Eng)	71	68	73	74	286	3859
	Peter BAKER	(Eng)	73	71	69	73	286	3859
	Roger WESSELS	(SA)	73	71	70	72	286	3859
	Brett LIDDLE	(SA)	67	77	69	73	286	3859
	Eamonn DARCY	(Ire)	70	74	73	69	286	3859
	Sven STRÜVER	(Ger)	70	68	74	74	286	3859
31	Sean PAPPAS	(SA)	74	70	69	74	287	3325
	Marco GORTANA	(It)	70	72	71	74	287	3325
	Stephen SCAHILL	(NZ)	74	67	72	74	287	3325
	Callie SWART	(SA)	73	70	71	73	287	3325
	Brad OTT	(USA)	72	71	75	69	287	3325
36	Gary EVANS	(Eng)	69	65	78	76	288	2764
	Hendrik BUHRMANN	(SA)	72	70	74	72	288	2764
	Bruce VAUGHAN	(USA)	72	71	69	76	288	2764
	John WADE	(Aus)	69	65	76	78	288	2764
	Malcolm MACKENZIE	(Eng)	69	74	73	72	288	2764
	Gary CLARK	(Eng)	68	71	75	74	288	2764
	Brenden PAPPAS	(SA)	68	74	72	74	288	2764
	Gary EMERSON	(Eng)	73	71	73	71	288	2764
	Alberto BINAGHI	(It)	71	69	70	78	288	2764
45	Paul FRIEDLANDER	(Swa)	74	69	71	75	289	2163
	Paul AFFLECK	(Wal)	69	71	74	75	289	2163
	Francis QUINN	(USA)	73	66	74	76	289	2163
	Bobby LINCOLN	(SA)	68	75	78	68	289	2163
	Warren SCHUTTE	(SA)	68	74	72	75	289	2163
	Andrew COLTART	(Scot)	70	73	75	71	289	2163
51	Michael CAMPBELL	(NZ)	73	69	77	71	290	1802
	Jonathan LOMAS	(Eng)	70	74	74	72	290	1802
	Warrick DRUIAN	(SA)	71	71	72	76	290	1802
54	Dean VAN STADEN	(SA)	68	73	76	74	291	1522
	Bob MAY	(USA)	71	71	75	74	291	1522
	Allan MCLEAN	(Eng)	70	70	75	76	291	1522
	Graeme VAN DER NEST	(SA)	67	71	77	76	291	1522
58	Stephen GALLACHER	(Scot)	74	70	74	74	292	1262
	Ignacio GARRIDO	(Sp)	70	72	75	75	292	1262
	Andrew SHERBORNE	(Eng)	74	69	73	76	292	1262
	Jeff HAWKES	(SA)	71	73	72	76	292	1262
62	Jannie LE GRANGE	(SA)	70	74	75	74	293	1141
	Donald GAMMON	(SA)	68	75	72	78	293	1141
64	Wayne BRADLEY	(SA)	71	73	78	72	294	1081
65	Mark MURLESS	(SA)	69	68	79	79	295	821
	Robbie STEWART	(SA)	71	70	79	75	295	821
67	Desmond TERBLANCHE	(SA)	72	72	75	77	296	597
	Michael JONZON	(Swe)	72	70	77	77	296	597
	John BICKERTON	(Eng)	73	71	78	74	296	597
70	Greg PETERSEN	(USA)	71	73	77	76	297	591
	Fredrik ANDERSSON	(Swe)	72	71	75	79	297	591
	Max ANGLERT	(Swe)	71	73	75	78	297	591

Padraig Harrington

The difference is evident

The *Levington* DIFFERENCE

Levington products are chosen by professionals looking for the very best results: the PGA European Tour recommend Levington Professional turfcare products such as those used at the Wentworth Club. The All England Lawn Tennis and Croquet Club, Wimbledon, also uses Levington products on its famous courts.

Levington is dedicated to producing the best for the gardener too. 1997 has seen the introduction of Stimulex® into our range of composts. Stimulex is a beneficial micro–organism which colonises plant root to give improved growth, root development and resistance to disease. Levington has also launched Evergreen® Easy, for scorch–free, season long lawn feeding, and Evergreen Grass Seed, three varieties of high quality grass seed that can actually improve lawn germination by up to 20%.

If you would like to see the difference for yourself, look out for Levington garden products at your local garden centre. As always, we are so confident of their performance that we will offer you your money back if you use our products as recommended and are not completely satisfied. And if you want help or advice about any of our products just call our FREECALL garden advice line on 0500 888558.

Levington Horticulture Ltd., Paper Mill Lane, Bramford, Ipswich, Suffolk IP8 4BZ. Tel: 01473 830492.

EVERGREEN, STIMULEX, LEVINGTON and THE LEVINGTON DIFFERENCE are registered Trade Marks of Levington Horticulture Ltd.

© Levington Horticulture Ltd. 1997.

Double for Price

Victory over David Frost made
Nick Price the first man to win twice
on the 1997 European Tour

*D*avid Frost made up two shots a round on Nick Price in the Alfred Dunhill South African PGA Championship, and it still wasn't enough. After finishing a distant second eight strokes behind Price in the Dimension Data Pro-Am at Sun City, Frost tied with his rival at Houghton only to lose on the first hole of a sudden-death play-off. For the 37-year-old South African, it was a sad conclusion to a determined effort to end a title drought which had lasted since November 1994.

Having set a course-record 63 on the second day, Frost went into the final round with a three-stroke lead and, more significantly, five clear of Price. But his own words after his third-round 66 — 'No lead is ever big enough' — proved as prophetic as the local weather forecasters' predictions of thunder.

A 90-minute delay for just this reason meant that play finished in darkness on day three, but Frost lifted the gloom by distributing 600 pairs of second-hand golf shoes among caddies, young players and underprivileged professionals. 'I wrote to my fellow US tour pros asking for their spare shoes and the response was unbelievable,' said Frost. 'I got five pairs from Jack Nicklaus and Arnold Palmer sent an autographed pair. Eventually I told the guys not to send me any more because I had so many at my home in Dallas.'

It would have been a popular victory if Frost had claimed the winner's £50,000 cheque, but it was not to be. In the rarefied atmosphere — Johannesburg is 6,000ft above sea level — balls fly vast distances and someone always shoots a low score. On the final day, that man was Price. The 40-year-old Zimbabwean carded a six under par 66 while Frost dropped four shots in his first five holes, including a double-bogey six after visiting water at the fifth. He then played the last

SHOT OF THE WEEK

The highlight of Massimo Scarpa's first-round 65 came at the 13th when he chipped in from 20 yards, left-handed. The ball floated over a mound, landed softly and rolled straight into the cup. 'I'm naturally left-handed,' said the 26-year-old Italian. 'I now play and putt right-handed but I still chip left-handed. I carry two left-handed clubs — a sand-wedge and nine iron.'

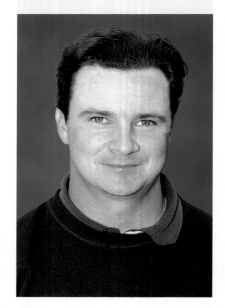

13 in five under, highlighted by a heroic birdie three from 15 feet at the 18th.

Ironically, the 18th proved Frost's undoing in the play-off. After driving into the left rough, he failed to reach the green with his second, chipped six feet short and missed the putt to leave Price needing to tap in from 18 inches for a regulation par.

It was the tenth time Price had broken 70 in 12 rounds (he was second to Vijay Singh in the South African Open a fortnight earlier), and he confessed: 'I'm really tired. This has been a hard three weeks and I feel like I've been ten rounds with Mike Tyson.'

Price, second in the PGA five times, thought his chance of going one better had gone when he three-putted the third green after a birdie three at the second. 'That was a wake-up call. It made me really angry with myself because I knew I couldn't afford to make a single mistake. But I bounced back with two birdies and then I eagled the seventh from 25 feet. After that I felt I had a chance.' After becoming the first player to exceed R1million in one season on the South African Tour, Price flew home to Florida in his JetStar, formerly owned by Greg Norman. The 23-hour journey took

David Frost (above) was thwarted in the play-off. Wayne Westner (left) lets go on the 14th tee.

him via Libraville in Gabon, Daker in Senegal, the Azores and Bermuda.

For a while during the final round, though, the highest flier was local pro Nico van Rensburg, who led by two strokes after racing to the turn in 31. But the 30-year-old ran out of inspiration over the back nine and finished a shot out of the play-off. His compatriot, Retief Goosen was fourth, a further two strokes back while the Swedes, Niclas Fasth and Max Anglert were the leading Europeans in joint eighth, a stroke clear of the 1996 champion Sven Strüver. Before his final round, the 29-year-old German said he

61

THE COURSE

Designed in 1926 by A. P. Copland, the club's first professional, this jewel of the High Veldt is one of South Africa's most attractive and respected courses. With water on eight holes, Houghton could almost double up as a bird sanctuary. The ball flies further at altitude, but tangly kikuyu grass, lightning-fast greens and a bewildering variety of trees provide considerable protection.

needed to repeat the 63 which swept him to that astonishing triumph. He only managed a 70, but his prediction was spot on — a 63 would have put him one shot clear of Price and Frost.

The northern hemisphere challenge was overshadowed by Severiano Ballesteros's seven-shot failure to survive the cut on a course he had last played as a 17-year-old. The guillotine fell, incredibly, on four under par, a figure matched or bettered by 77 of the 158-strong field.

Scotland's Gordon Sherry holed in

Halfway leader Retief Goosen.

one during the pro-am with a 145-yard wedge at the short 17th (his eight hole) and nearly repeated the feat when he hit

the pin with a nine iron from 155 yards at the third. The day before, Zimbabwe's Tony Johnstone, who missed a six-inch putt on the 71st hole at Sun City, put 'the most embarrassing moment of my golfing life' behind him to win the Canon Shoot-Out foursomes in partnership with Goosen.

Ultimately, though, the shoot-out which mattered came in glorious sunshine on the final afternoon. And while Frost melted, Price stayed cool.

Paul Trow

HOUGHTON GOLF CLUB, JOHANNESBURG, SOUTH AFRICA, FEBRUARY 20-23, 1997 • YARDAGE 7035 • PAR 72

Pos	Name	Country	Rnd 1	Rnd 2	Rnd 3		Total	Prize Money £
1	Nick PRICE	(Zim)	67	66	70	66	269	47319
2	David FROST	(SA)	69	63	66	71	269	34457
3	Nico VAN RENSBURG	(SA)	68	68	66	68	270	20728
4	Retief GOOSEN	(SA)	65	66	70	71	272	14716
5	Marco GORTANA	(It)	70	67	67	69	273	10618
	Greg PETERSEN	(USA)	71	69	65	68	273	10618
	Wayne WESTNER	(SA)	68	66	71	68	273	10618
8	Max ANGLERT	(Swe)	68	67	69	70	274	6288
	Mathew GOGGIN	(Aus)	69	69	69	67	274	6288
	Katsuyoshi TOMORI	(Jap)	67	67	67	73	274	6288
	Niclas FASTH	(Swe)	66	69	68	71	274	6288
12	Greg CHALMERS	(Aus)	70	68	71	66	275	4725
	Craig KAMPS	(SA)	68	68	68	71	275	4725
	Sven STRÜVER	(Ger)	71	69	65	70	275	4725
15	Desvonde BOTES	(SA)	68	72	67	69	276	4032
	Bob MAY	(USA)	66	68	72	70	276	4032
	Tony JOHNSTONE	(Zim)	70	69	67	70	276	4032
	Trevor DODDS	(Nam)	68	72	68	68	276	4032
	Ignacio GARRIDO	(Sp)	69	69	67	71	276	4032
20	Van PHILLIPS	(Eng)	70	64	74	69	277	3290
	Mark MCNULTY	(Zim)	69	69	67	72	277	3290
	Paul MCGINLEY	(Ire)	71	67	71	68	277	3290
	Gordon SHERRY	(Scot)	69	68	71	69	277	3290
	Fulton ALLEM	(SA)	69	69	69	70	277	3290
	Carl WATTS	(Eng)	69	69	69	70	277	3290
	Michael ARCHER	(Eng)	68	68	74	67	277	3290
27	Ian HUTCHINGS	(Eng)	67	71	68	72	278	2757
	James KINGSTON	(SA)	69	71	71	67	278	2757
	Brad OTT	(USA)	68	69	67	74	278	2757
	Mark MURLESS	(SA)	66	69	69	74	278	2757
	Ashley ROESTOFF	(SA)	67	70	69	72	278	2757
32	John MELLOR	(Eng)	69	70	70	70	279	2422
	Warrick DRUIAN	(SA)	69	70	69	71	279	2422
	John MASHEGO	(SA)	69	70	73	67	279	2422
	Malcolm MACKENZIE	(Eng)	69	68	70	72	279	2422
	Brian DAVIS	(Eng)	72	67	72	68	279	2422
37	Justin HOBDAY	(SA)	70	69	68	73	280	2063
	Hugh BAIOCCHI	(SA)	69	68	70	73	280	2063
	Thomas GÖGELE	(Ger)	64	68	71	77	280	2063
	Desmond TERBLANCHE	(SA)	69	68	72	71	280	2063
	Andrew COLTART	(Scot)	69	69	74	68	280	2063
	Daniel CHOPRA	(Swe)	70	69	73	68	280	2063
	Paul LAWRIE	(Scot)	69	66	74	71	280	2063
44	Klas ERIKSSON	(Swe)	73	67	68	73	281	1675
	Gary EMERSON	(Eng)	67	67	72	75	281	1675
	Massimo SCARPA	(It)	65	68	69	79	281	1675
	Clinton WHITELAW	(SA)	68	67	74	72	281	1675
	Bradford VAUGHAN	(SA)	68	70	69	74	281	1675
	David CARTER	(Eng)	74	64	71	72	281	1675
50	Allan MCLEAN	(SA)	66	71	70	75	282	1375
	Ian GARBUTT	(Eng)	70	68	69	75	282	1375
	Wayne BRADLEY	(SA)	68	70	71	73	282	1375
	Jannie LE GRANGE	(SA)	72	67	71	72	282	1375
54	Nicolas VANHOOTEGEM	(Bel)	69	69	70	75	283	1106
	Carlos DURAN	(Swi)	70	69	72	72	283	1106
	Padraig HARRINGTON	(Ire)	69	71	71	72	283	1106
	Rolf MUNTZ	(Hol)	67	72	75	69	283	1106
	Andrew BEAL	(Eng)	70	69	72	72	283	1106
59	Ross MCFARLANE	(Eng)	72	68	73	71	284	912
	Dean VAN STADEN	(SA)	70	69	74	71	284	912
	Ronnie MCCANN	(USA)	67	73	70	74	284	912
	André CRUSE	(SA)	69	71	72	72	284	912
63	Paul FRIEDLANDER	(Swa)	71	68	73	73	285	663
	Stephen GALLACHER	(Scot)	68	71	75	71	285	663
	Callie SWART	(SA)	73	67	74	71	285	663
	Bobby LINCOLN	(SA)	69	70	72	74	285	663
	David HIGGINS	(Ire)	69	70	73	73	285	663
68	Sammy DANIELS	(SA)	70	70	74	72	286	443
	Raphaël JACQUELIN	(Fr)	71	67	77	71	286	443
	David TAPPING	(Eng)	70	70	72	74	286	443
71	Michael JONZON	(Swe)	70	68	75	74	287	438
	Alan TAIT	(Scot)	73	66	76	72	287	438
73	Gary CLARK	(Eng)	68	69	75	76	288	435
74	John NELSON	(SA)	66	71	81	71	289	433
75	Christian CÉVAER	(Fr)	69	71	74	77	291	431
76	Russell FLETCHER	(SA)	69	71	75	77	292	429
77	Gordon J BRAND	(Eng)	70	70	76	77	293	427

Sven Strüver defended strongly.

It's Green in the desert

Richard Green mastered a strong
international field to win his
first European Tour title

*I*f a golf course is judged by the winners of the tournaments played upon it, the honours board at the Emirates club in Dubai is an impressive advertisement for the miracle course sculpted out of the desert. The names of Severiano Ballesteros, Ernie Els, Fred Couples and Colin Montgomerie were already there and if Ian Woosnam or Greg Norman thought of joining that list, they were to be disappointed.

Again the Emirates brought the cream to the top, with Montgomerie, Norman and Bernhard Langer all within three shots of Woosnam at the top of the leaderboard going into the final day. Richard Green then timed his upset to perfection.

You have to have your first wins somewhere and the young left-handed Australian had twice won the New Caledonian Open. Now it was time for a bigger stage. By winning a play-off at the first extra hole against Norman and Woosnam, Green became the first south-paw to win on the European Tour since

Bob Charles at the 1974 Swiss Open.

'Greg has been a huge idol of mine since I was young and to win against guys like him and Ian is an unbelievable feeling,' Green said, after wiping away both his tears and those of his wife, Anita, who was caddieing for him. 'To hole a putt on the 18th to get into the play-off was spe-

Come-back of the year for José Maria Olazábal.

cial, but I was so nervous that my heart was pumping.'

Green, 26, whose mentor at the Huntingdale club in Melbourne is another Aussie great, Norman von Nida, played his way onto the European Tour as an affiliate member in 1996 and finished 45th on the Volvo Ranking that year after finishing runner-up to Marc Farry in the BMW International Open. He started the final round in Dubai a stroke behind Woosnam after the Welshman had finished his third round four under par for the last four holes.

At the first and only play-off hole, the 17th, Richard Green had an 106-yard sand-wedge shot for his approach. While Ian Woosnam and Greg Norman both saw their second shots hop through to the back, Green's stopped within 12 feet of the pin. 'Ian and Greg hit their shots to about the same spot as mine, but they didn't have the spin,' Green said. 'I just tried a three-quarter sand-iron to put some spin on it.'

Montgomerie, the defending champion, never threatened and twice found the water at the ninth and 18th greens which he cleared so magnificently the year before. Langer, showing a return to confidence with his long-handled putter, led briefly but did not recover after a bogey six at the 13th. When Woosnam picked up his fourth birdie in six holes at the 17th, where he had holed out with a wedge the day before, he was in front by two.

But at the last, the Welshman, unbelievably, failed to clear the water with his 73-yard pitch shot. 'All I had to do was hit

67

Headgear in place for Greg Norman (left), Severiano Ballesteros (centre), and Bernhard Langer (right) but not for Colin Montgomerie (below).

a little sand-wedge on to the last green but I must have caught it heavy,' he rued.

Now his certain victory was anything but. Norman, playing his first 72-hole tournament for three months and improving in every round, had already birdied the last to get to 16 under. Green, having chipped badly from the back of the putting surface, then holed from 20 feet to match his countryman. 'As soon as I missed the chip I thought I was behind the eight-ball.' Green admitted, 'but I said to myself, 'don't give up, give it another go'.' That meant Woosnam had to hole his putt from ten feet for a bogey six just

to get in the play-off. Which was a short-lived affair.

While both Norman and Woosnam went through to the back fringe of the 17th, the first extra hole, Green spun his approach to 12 feet and, as he had done

seemingly all week on the smoothest of putting surfaces, holed the putt. 'This is my first really big win, but I have big aspirations. I think I can compete against the top players,' Green said.

He showed that, but the week also saw the welcome return to the Tour after an 18-month break of José Maria Olazábal. The Spaniard may not have won, but by finishing in 12th place, including a third round 65, he showed that he, too, will be back to compete against the best after being virtually crippled with his foot injuries.

Andrew Farrell

THE COURSE

Over one million gallons of desalinated water are pumped onto the Emirates course a day to maintain the green oasis in the desert. But it is not just an engineering miracle. The course, designed by Karl Litten, is rated one of the best layouts on the Tour. Many players would like to take the greens round with them each week.

EMIRATES GC, FEBRUARY 27-MARCH 2, 1997 · YARDAGE 7102 · PAR 72

Pos	Name	Country	Rnd 1	Rnd 2	Rnd 3	Rnd 4	Total	Prize Money £
1	Richard GREEN	(Aus)	70	68	66	68	272	116660
2	Ian WOOSNAM	(Wal)	69	67	67	69	272	60795
	Greg NORMAN	(Aus)	71	68	67	66	272	60795
4	Bernhard LANGER	(Ger)	66	70	68	69	273	35000
5	Thomas GÖGELE	(Ger)	69	72	68	66	275	29640
6	Raymond BURNS	(N.Ire)	68	69	69	70	276	19652
	Malcolm MACKENZIE	(Eng)	69	71	66	70	276	19652
	Paul MCGINLEY	(Ire)	69	71	67	69	276	19652
	Colin MONTGOMERIE	(Scot)	65	72	68	71	276	19652
10	Angel CABRERA	(Arg)	73	72	70	63	278	13440
	Costantino ROCCA	(It)	70	69	71	68	278	13440
12	Klas ERIKSSON	(Swe)	68	71	67	73	279	10605
	Joakim HAEGGMAN	(Swe)	72	71	65	71	279	10605
	Phillip PRICE	(Wal)	70	73	69	67	279	10605
	Roger CHAPMAN	(Eng)	69	71	70	69	279	10605
	Jean VAN DE VELDE	(Fr)	67	75	67	70	279	10605
	José Maria OLAZABAL	(Sp)	69	74	65	71	279	10605
18	Robert COLES	(Eng)	69	70	69	72	280	8855
	Andrew OLDCORN	(Scot)	69	70	73	68	280	8855
20	Prayad MARKSAENG	(Thai)	68	71	68	74	281	7980
	Domingo HOSPITAL	(Sp)	65	69	74	73	281	7980
	Mark JAMES	(Eng)	66	75	69	71	281	7980
	José COCERES	(Arg)	70	73	69	69	281	7980
	Per-Ulrik JOHANSSON	(Swe)	69	73	68	71	281	7980
25	Mats HALLBERG	(Swe)	68	73	73	68	282	7140
	Wayne WESTNER	(SA)	72	69	69	72	282	7140
	Des SMYTH	(Ire)	74	71	65	72	282	7140
28	Jeev Milkha SINGH	(Ind)	69	71	70	73	283	6206
	Carl SUNESON	(Sp)	70	74	64	75	283	6206
	Darren CLARKE	(N.Ire)	73	70	70	70	283	6206
	Padraig HARRINGTON	(Ire)	66	72	71	74	283	6206
	Van PHILLIPS	(Eng)	73	72	65	73	283	6206
	Robert LEE	(Eng)	69	74	68	72	283	6206
34	Ross DRUMMOND	(Scot)	71	71	71	71	284	5460
	Daniel CHOPRA	(Swe)	69	75	73	67	284	5460
	Ian GARBUTT	(Eng)	71	71	73	69	284	5460
37	Silvio GRAPPASONNI	(It)	71	73	69	72	285	4970
	Gary ORR	(Scot)	72	73	67	73	285	4970
	Miguel Angel JIMÉNEZ	(Sp)	72	72	70	71	285	4970
	Massimo FLORIOLI	(It)	71	73	72	69	285	4970
41	Emanuele CANONICA	(It)	73	72	71	70	286	4340
	Miguel Angel MARTIN	(Sp)	70	69	72	75	286	4340
	Marc FARRY	(Fr)	71	74	68	73	286	4340
	Fernando ROCA	(Sp)	73	72	70	71	286	4340
	Derrick COOPER	(Eng)	72	69	75	70	286	4340
46	Dean ROBERTSON	(Scot)	71	71	71	74	287	3500
	Christy O'CONNOR JNR	(Ire)	71	73	71	72	287	3500
	Mark MOULAND	(Wal)	70	74	68	75	287	3500
	Peter MITCHELL	(Eng)	70	73	72	72	287	3500
	Andrew COLTART	(Scot)	73	72	70	72	287	3500
	Philip WALTON	(Ire)	72	70	71	74	287	3500
	Steven BOTTOMLEY	(Eng)	75	70	72	70	287	3500
53	Miles TUNNICLIFF	(Eng)	70	73	74	71	288	2660
	Michael JONZON	(Swe)	72	73	68	75	288	2660
	David HOWELL	(Eng)	69	72	71	76	288	2660
	Peter BAKER	(Eng)	69	74	73	72	288	2660
	Robert WILLIS	(Aus)	68	73	75	72	288	2660
58	Jon ROBSON	(Eng)	70	74	73	72	289	2205
	Eamonn DARCY	(Ire)	66	77	74	72	289	2205
60	David HIGGINS	(Ire)	73	71	75	71	290	1960
	Tse-Peng CHANG	(Tai)	70	72	75	73	290	1960
	Paolo QUIRICI	(Swi)	71	74	72	73	290	1960
	Ricky WILLISON	(Eng)	72	72	72	74	290	1960
	Richard BOXALL	(Eng)	72	73	73	72	290	1960
65	Gary EVANS	(Eng)	71	74	73	73	291	1223
	Wayne RILEY	(Aus)	74	70	76	71	291	1223
	David GILFORD	(Eng)	69	73	73	76	291	1223
	Barry LANE	(Eng)	72	71	72	76	291	1223
69	Lian-Wei ZHANG	(Chi)	71	73	72	76	292	1044
70	Anders FORSBRAND	(Swe)	71	74	72	76	293	1042
71	Rolf MUNTZ	(Hol)	74	71	74	76	295	1040

Thomas Gögele in verdant surroundings.

Whitelaw breaks through

South Africa's Clinton Whitelaw took the Moroccan Open for his first title on the European Tour

The Meteorological Office supply weather forecasts for all European Tour events during the season but their predictions for the annual Moroccan Open in Agadir broke all records. For the first time in memory, the Met Office issued a six-day forecast from the Birmingham Weather Centre which was identical in every respect on all six days. 'Tuesday: Dry and sunny, surface winds easterly 10 mph becoming westerly 15 mph by mid-afternoon, maximum temperature 33 Celsius, minimum temperature 9 Celsius. Ditto Wednesday, ditto Thursday, ditto Friday, ditto Saturday and ditto Sunday.'

And the good men from the Met Office were proved to be correct. Glorious, hot and sunny weather blessed the Open daily, resulting in some low scoring and big crowds, though it has to be said that many of the families who came to watch at the Royal Golf Links d'Agadir were also taking the rare opportunity to stroll in the grounds of King Hassan II's palace.

Most European Tour events provide an abundance of good, interesting stories and the seventh playing of the Moroccan Open was no exception as a wide range of

players, from 'veterans' of the European Tour to players recently graduated from the European Tour Qualifying School Finals, took centre stage in an exciting week.

David A Russell, now happily recovered after a two-year battle with lymphatic cancer, made the first-day headlines by scoring a three-under-par first round of 69,

having never seen the course before, though it was a young Australian of Scottish parentage, Stephen Allan, who led the field with a 67.

Russell took up the front-running on day two and by the end of the third round, there was a logjam at the top of the leader board — Russell, without a tournament win to his name in 20 seasons on the European Tour, was tied with Phillip Price, Jon Robson and former South African Open champion Clinton Whitelaw. Russell, a Man of Kent, now lives mainly in Los Angeles and he was offered a late place in the tournament, but the journey from LA to the seaside town of Agadir took him 51 hours and he arrived in the early hours of Thursday, too late to practise on the tough Robert Trent Jones course. But he put together a fine 69 which included a hole-in-one, the 14th of his career.

The nearest Russell had come to winning in his 20 years on Tour was in 1987 when he finished second in the Dutch Open and there were plenty of people willing him on in Morocco. The same applied to Nairobi-born Englishman Roger Chapman, 15 years on Tour without a win, whose cv includes five

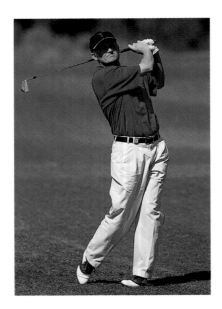

Another second place for Roger Chapman.

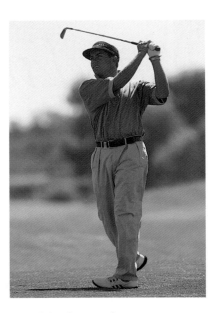

Solid performance from Brian Davis.

through healthwise in the past two years, his Moroccan Open week was, in fact, quite wonderful.

Australian Darren Cole, nine shots behind the leaders starting the final round, set the tournament target with a closing 64, the best of the week, which included 29 shots for the last nine holes and required only 11 putts. It was not the first time he had scored a 29, he said, but he

SHOT OF THE WEEK

It was the shot everybody was talking about, not so much for its execution but for the description afforded it by its perpetrator, Domingo Hospital: 'I had 100 yards to the flag at the ninth hole but I hit miles behind the ball. The divot reached the green but the ball did not. In fact, the divot overtook the ball in flight. I feel I qualified for a Mulligan.'

runner-up spots. In fact, when Chapman took the outright lead on ten under par with a birdie on the 17th hole in the final round, hardened pressmen walked the quarter of a mile to the 18th green in the hope of seeing him achieve his dream. But it was not to be — he bogeyed the hole.

Then Russell, who had started poorly on the final afternoon, took up the running on ten under par with three holes to play but as the pressmen were about to trek to the 18th once again word came through that he had dropped a shot at the short 16th. Ten minutes later, he dropped another at the 17th and his victory chance was gone. But he conceded after finishing fifth that after everything he had been

doubted that his nine under par 279 would be good enough to win. Another Australian, Wayne Riley, expressed the same opinion after joining him on nine under and Chapman, on the same mark, just knew that he was destined to finish runner-up for a sixth time.

But the title still had to be won and Clinton Whitelaw, a graduate of the 1996 European Tour Qualifying School, proved to be the man do to it. He was one shot behind pacesetters Riley, Cole and Chapman with three holes to play but then staged a spectacular birdie-eagle-par finish for a round of 69, an 11-under-par total of 277 and a two-stroke victory.

Richard Dodd

THE COURSE

The Royal Golf Links d'Agadir is a superb Moroccan Open venue. Built in the grounds of King Hassan II's summer palace, it was designed by Robert Trent Jones and sweeps grandly down to the sea. Strangely, there is no clubhouse and the locker rooms, restaurants and tournament offices are all housed in tents.

GOLF ROYAL D'AGADIR, MARCH 6-9, 1997 • YARDAGE 6657 • PAR 72

Pos	Name	Country	Rnd 1	Rnd 2	Rnd 3	Rnd 4	Total	Prize Money £
1	Clinton WHITELAW	(SA)	68	71	69	69	277	58330
2	Darren COLE	(Aus)	72	74	69	64	279	26096
	Wayne RILEY	(Aus)	72	72	67	68	279	26096
	Roger CHAPMAN	(Eng)	74	68	70	67	279	26096
5	David A RUSSELL	(Eng)	69	68	71	72	280	14830
6	Per-Ulrik JOHANSSON	(Swe)	72	73	67	69	281	9830
	Brian DAVIS	(Eng)	70	68	71	72	281	9830
	Robert KARLSSON	(Swe)	70	71	70	70	281	9830
	Jon ROBSON	(Eng)	73	65	70	73	281	9830
10	Eduardo ROMERO	(Arg)	72	69	71	70	282	5787
	Tony JOHNSTONE	(Zim)	71	72	71	68	282	5787
	Katsuyoshi TOMORI	(Jap)	72	71	70	69	282	5787
	Andrew COLTART	(Scot)	68	73	68	73	282	5787
	José COCERES	(Arg)	71	67	72	72	282	5787
	Diego BORREGO	(Sp)	73	71	66	72	282	5787
	Paul BROADHURST	(Eng)	70	71	71	70	282	5787
17	Niclas FASTH	(Swe)	70	72	72	69	283	4375
	Gary ORR	(Scot)	71	73	70	69	283	4375
	Costantino ROCCA	(It)	69	71	69	74	283	4375
	Sam TORRANCE	(Scot)	74	71	68	72	285	2961
	Ross DRUMMOND	(Scot)	73	68	72	72	285	2961
35	Peter O'MALLEY	(Aus)	73	72	68	73	286	2660
	Santiago LUNA	(Sp)	71	71	72	72	286	2660
	Raymond BURNS	(N.Ire)	71	71	73	71	286	2660
38	Padraig HARRINGTON	(Ire)	69	75	74	69	287	2450
	Antoine LEBOUC	(Fr)	69	70	74	74	287	2450
	Mark ROE	(Eng)	72	70	73	72	287	2450
41	John BICKERTON	(Eng)	73	72	74	69	288	2310
42	Juan Carlos PIÑERO	(Sp)	69	78	67	75	289	2205
	Stephen ALLAN	(Aus)	67	76	73	73	289	2205
44	Bob MAY	(USA)	68	75	72	75	290	1890
	Fabrice TARNAUD	(Fr)	73	74	71	72	290	1890
	Silvio GRAPPASONNI	(It)	73	70	73	74	290	1890
	Andrew SANDYWELL	(Eng)	76	68	71	75	290	1890
	Carl WATTS	(Eng)	73	71	71	75	290	1890
	Daniel CHOPRA	(Swe)	75	71	71	73	290	1890
	Ronan RAFFERTY	(N.Ire)	76	70	71	73	290	1890
51	Paul EALES	(Eng)	74	73	70	74	291	1540
	Ben TINNING	(Den)	73	71	75	72	291	1540
	David TAPPING	(Eng)	72	74	71	74	291	1540

Costantino Rocca heads out to sea.

Pos	Name	Country	Rnd 1	Rnd 2	Rnd 3	Rnd 4	Total	Prize Money £
	Wayne WESTNER	(SA)	69	71	75	68	283	4375
	Russell CLAYDON	(Eng)	77	66	70	70	283	4375
22	Alex CEJKA	(Ger)	74	70	66	74	284	3622
	Miguel Angel MARTIN	(Sp)	73	68	68	75	284	3622
	Jim PAYNE	(Eng)	70	71	71	72	284	3622
	Joakim HAEGGMAN	(Swe)	69	73	70	72	284	3622
	Carl SUNESON	(Sp)	74	71	70	69	284	3622
	Domingo HOSPITAL	(Sp)	69	71	71	73	284	3622
	Phillip PRICE	(Wal)	72	66	70	76	284	3622
	Max ANGLERT	(Swe)	75	72	67	70	284	3622
30	Anders FORSBRAND	(Swe)	71	75	67	72	285	2961
	Adam HUNTER	(Scot)	71	69	75	70	285	2961
	Mark JAMES	(Eng)	71	67	73	74	285	2961
54	Van PHILLIPS	(Eng)	71	75	74	72	292	1400
55	Roger WESSELS	(SA)	73	71	70	79	293	1330
56	Gordon SHERRY	(Scot)	74	72	73	75	294	1190
	Francisco VALERA	(Sp)	73	72	78	71	294	1190
	Dennis EDLUND	(Swe)	75	69	73	77	294	1190
59	Daniel WESTERMARK	(Swe)	76	69	71	79	295	1015
	Massimo FLORIOLI	(It)	75	72	75	73	295	1015
	Peter HEDBLOM	(Swe)	74	68	82	71	295	1015
	Jeff HAWKES	(SA)	73	72	72	78	295	1015
	Craig HAINLINE	(USA)	71	74	72	78	295	1015
64	Duncan MUSCROFT	(Eng)	76	69	74	77	296	910
65	Manuel PIÑERO	(Sp)	75	71	74	77	297	700
	Daren LEE	(Eng)	75	72	73	77	297	700
67	Joe HIGGINS	(Eng)	76	71	76	76	299	523

Jonzon stays cool

Michael Jonzon remained calm
to capture his first European Tour title

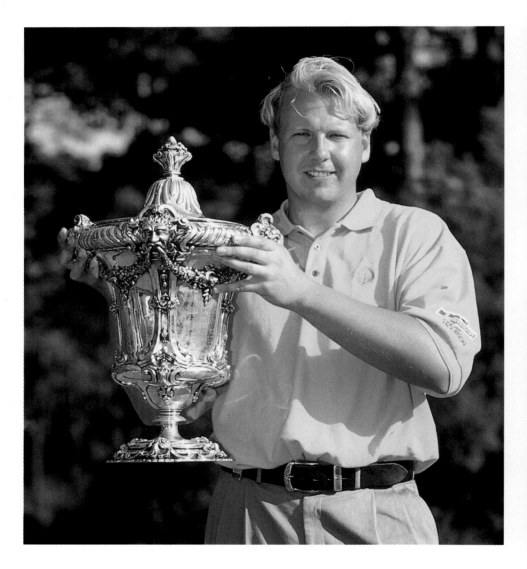

Michael Jonzon fits the template marked 'Typical Swedish Tournament Professional Golfer'. He is tall, blond, talented and very, very cool. The first two characteristics did not help him much, frankly, in the Portuguese Open. But the last two did, and then some.

Imagine the scene for a moment. Here he was, in the last group on the course on the final day, going for his maiden European Tour victory. The man standing alongside him on the tee was a hero to countless millions, the winner of a major championship, acknowledged as one of the best golfers on the planet who was playing in the second tournament in an emotional return to the game after 18 tortured months out of action. The man was José Maria Olazábal; if MORI had conducted an opinion poll at that moment asking the gallery who they wanted to win, Jonzon would probably not have reached double figures.

Olazábal had been made the pre-tournament 14-1 favourite to win this, the second Portuguese Open to be held on the pleasant Aroeira course near Lisbon. The Spaniard had chuckled when told of

José Maria Olazábal (left) and
José Rivero (above) led the Spanish assault.

THE COURSE

Aroeira is not your typical Iberian layout. It is a lush green course that weaves its way between thousands of tall, gracious trees and is uncannily like one of the better British inland courses — a Portuguese Berkshire, if you like. Improved weather in the early part of the year left it in much better condition than it had been in for its debut as a European Tour venue the year before, when three months' incessant rain had left its owners with problems. In 1997 it was seen at its best — and that made it as good as most.

Early challenge from Van Phillips.

the bookies' faith in him. 'They are a little bit insane,' he said. Now, as he readied himself to take on the ice-cold Swede, the Honest Joes with the milk crates and the big brown satchels did not look so daft after all.

Olazábal was at pains all week to insist that he was not yet ready to win, and ultimately he was proved correct. Not, though, before he had subjected the 6ft 2in Swede to a searching examination of his visceral fortitude that he passed in a canter.

It was not classic golf that brought victory to Jonzon with a final round of 69 and a total of 269, 19 under par. It was, rather, the golf of a man on a mission, an unemotional, Frigidaire-frosty performance that was as remorseless to watch as it was impressive.

Jonzon admitted when it was all over and he had beaten a charging Ignacio Garrido, who came from nowhere with a 65, by three strokes, Paul Broadhurst by six and Olazábal and three others by

seven, that if he had not been able to win himself he would have loved the £58,330 first prize to have gone to Ollie. 'José Maria is a hero of mine,' he said. 'I have always admired his attitude and the way he always goes right at the flag. I know most people wanted him to win.' And then added, chillingly, 'But I was focused on my own game. I couldn't afford to think about anybody else.'

Olazábal started the final day two strokes behind Jonzon, a brilliant 65 in the third round equalling the lowest round of

the tournament. One of those he equalled was Jonzon himself, who produced his in the second round to take the lead going into the weekend.

Peter O'Malley led with another 65 on the first day to put himself a shot ahead of Max Anglert and two ahead of Jonzon, Van Phillips and Domingo Hospital. Olazábal bided his time with a 70.

As Jonzon made his big move on Friday to lead by two from Wayne Riley, the defending champion, and O'Malley, with Broadhurst and Phillips a further shot behind, Olazábal improved to a 67 but was still five strokes behind.

Ominously, Olazábal continued to assess his form at about 70 per cent of his best. He had had one eagle, eight birdies and only two bogeys in 36 holes; people were already quaking at the prospect of his return to full efficiency. If Friday was 70 per cent, then Saturday was surely more like 90. He was the man to beat, there was no question about it.

77

Aroeira, Lisbon, March 21-24, 1996 · Yardage 6685 · Par 72

Pos	Name	Country	Rnd 1	Rnd 2	Rnd 3	Rnd 4	Total	Prize Money £									
										José Maria CAÑIZARES	(Sp)	69	73	69	70	281	2765
										André BOSSERT	(Swi)	70	73	69	69	281	2765
1	Michael JONZON	(Swe)	67	65	68	69	269	58330	37	Paul LAWRIE	(Scot)	68	70	74	70	282	2310
2	Ignacio GARRIDO	(Sp)	69	71	67	65	272	38880		Gary EVANS	(Eng)	72	69	68	73	282	2310
3	Paul BROADHURST	(Eng)	68	67	67	73	275	21910		Russell CLAYDON	(Eng)	71	72	70	69	282	2310
4	José Maria OLAZABAL	(Sp)	70	67	65	74	276	13770		Eduardo ROMERO	(Arg)	72	69	67	74	282	2310
	Darren CLARKE	(N.Ire)	70	71	68	67	276	13770		Massimo FLORIOLI	(It)	73	70	68	71	282	2310
	Wayne RILEY	(Aus)	68	66	71	71	276	13770		Mike MCLEAN	(Eng)	71	71	69	71	282	2310
	Stephen ALLAN	(Aus)	69	73	67	67	276	13770		Paul MCGINLEY	(Ire)	72	71	70	69	282	2310
8	Richard BOXALL	(Eng)	70	71	67	69	277	8750		Ariel CAÑETE	(Arg)	69	73	72	68	282	2310
9	Silvio GRAPPASONNI	(It)	71	65	70	72	278	6376		Andrew SANDYWELL	(Eng)	70	70	70	72	282	2310
	Peter O'MALLEY	(Aus)	65	69	72	72	278	6376	46	Angel CABRERA	(Arg)	72	71	71	69	283	1960
	Mark JAMES	(Eng)	70	66	70	72	278	6376	47	Gary ORR	(Scot)	71	72	71	70	284	1715
	José COCERES	(Arg)	71	69	69	69	278	6376		Tony JOHNSTONE	(Zim)	70	72	74	68	284	1715
	Raymond RUSSELL	(Scot)	69	69	68	72	278	6376		António SOBRINHO	(Port)	67	73	69	75	284	1715
	Mark MOULAND	(Wal)	72	69	69	68	278	6376		Domingo HOSPITAL	(Sp)	67	71	74	72	284	1715
15	John WADE	(Aus)	68	70	72	69	279	4297		Mathew GOGGIN	(Aus)	71	69	68	76	284	1715
	Mark DAVIS	(Eng)	69	69	67	74	279	4297		Alberto BINAGHI	(It)	70	72	75	67	284	1715
	José RIVERO	(Sp)	71	69	69	70	279	4297	53	Santiago LUNA	(Sp)	71	69	72	73	285	1400
	Alex CEJKA	(Ger)	69	70	69	71	279	4297		Peter MITCHELL	(Eng)	70	70	70	75	285	1400
	Van PHILLIPS	(Eng)	67	68	70	74	279	4297		Bob MAY	(USA)	72	71	70	72	285	1400
	Robert LEE	(Eng)	71	68	67	73	279	4297	56	Andrew BEAL	(Eng)	73	70	70	73	286	1163
	Ronan RAFFERTY	(N.Ire)	73	69	70	67	279	4297		Gordon BRAND JNR.	(Scot)	75	68	71	72	286	1163
	Jean VAN DE VELDE	(Fr)	73	69	66	71	279	4297		Darren COLE	(Aus)	72	71	71	72	286	1163
	Katsuyoshi TOMORI	(Jap)	72	70	66	71	279	4297		Gary CLARK	(Eng)	69	71	74	72	286	1163
	Adam HUNTER	(Scot)	71	68	71	69	279	4297	60	John BICKERTON	(Eng)	73	69	71	74	287	997
	Paul AFFLECK	(Wal)	69	69	70	71	279	4297		Scott HENDERSON	(Scot)	70	73	71	73	287	997
26	Pedro LINHART	(Sp)	68	71	72	69	280	3255		Ignacio FELIU	(Sp)	71	68	76	72	287	997
	Daniel CHOPRA	(Swe)	72	68	71	69	280	3255		Fernando ROCA	(Sp)	74	69	73	71	287	997
	Miguel Angel MARTIN	(Sp)	70	70	68	72	280	3255	64	Stephen GALLACHER	(Scot)	73	69	73	73	288	770
	Stephen MCALLISTER	(Scot)	71	71	71	67	280	3255		Marc FARRY	(Fr)	70	73	73	72	288	770
	Jon ROBSON	(Eng)	72	70	68	70	280	3255		Steve WEBSTER	(Eng)	72	70	74	72	288	770
	Diego BORREGO	(Sp)	69	70	68	73	280	3255	67	Mark ROE	(Eng)	68	71	76	75	290	522
	Max ANGLERT	(Swe)	66	74	71	69	280	3255		Mats HALLBERG	(Swe)	71	68	80	71	290	522
33	Paul CURRY	(Eng)	70	71	70	70	281	2765	69	Miguel Angel JIMÉNEZ	(Sp)	69	68	79	75	291	519
	Paolo QUIRICI	(Swi)	70	69	71	71	281	2765	70	Daniel SILVA	(Port)	70	72	77	76	295	517

SHOT OF THE WEEK

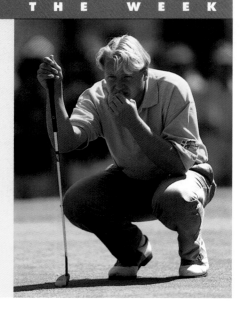

Not a searing drive, nor a raking long-iron shot, nor yet a superbly feathered wedge to a foot. No, this shot of the week was a putt for a bogey. It was hit by Jonzon on the par five tenth hole in the last round. He had already lost a ball off the tee and was still 20 feet from the pin and looking at a double-bogey seven. Olazábal, meanwhile, had a putt for a birdie. Olazábal missed and Jonzon rolled his putt in for as good a bogey six as he will ever get. Only one stroke lost, a nasty moment averted. Jonzon was never again in serious trouble.

So Jonzon did just that. He weathered Olazábal's birdie on the second that brought the Spaniard to within a shot, and hit back with birdies of his own at the fourth, fifth, seventh and ninth to turn five ahead. There might have been a three-shot swing at the tenth, but Jonzon survived the moment of crisis. After that, with Olazábal tiring perceptibly to finish with a 74, his only above-par round of the tournament, it was plain sailing.

Jonzon had a couple of bogeys on the back nine, but still had the tournament won, his birdie on the 16th was a massive irrelevance. The hot favourite had failed to melt the ice man. The bookies, at last, could breath again.

Mel Webb

THE ULTIMATE SUIT FOR THE ULTIMATE COMPETITION.

The Ryder Cup suit is the lightest weight suit in the ProQuip range. Meticulously designed to provide maximum ease of movement, it's the most comfortable suit on the market.

The Ryder Cup suit is fully waterproof and comes with a 2 year guarantee. So whilst you can never rely on the weather you can always rely on ProQuip.

The suit is made from Porelle Ultra, an exceptionally breathable outer fabric exclusive to ProQuip. The special UltraLite design with its unique Porelle Ultra fabric ensures maximum air movement without bagginess.

Whether you are facing the pressure of a critical approach shot at Valderamma's 18th hole or preparing to tee-off against howling wind and lashing rain in your Club's monthly medal you can be sure of one thing. The UltraLite performance suit from ProQuip won't let you down.

Designed for the heat of world class competition, ProQuip's new UltraLite suit offers you the ultimate in comfort and protection. It's the most lightweight, breathable and waterproof performance suit on the market. So when you have to rise to the challenge of the elements and the game, make sure your waterproofs are the best. UltraLite.

PROQUIP

MASTERS OF WEATHERWEAR

ProQuip International Limited, Wisloe Road, Cambridge, Gloucestershire GL2 7AF, England.
Tel: (01453) 890707 Fax: (01453) 890826

Olazábal's glorious return

José Maria Olazábal made an emotional

return to the winner's circle in only

his third tournament of the season

S ome people said he'd never play again. The doom and gloom merchants practically had him at death's door. Think of a dread disease and the rumours of the day afflicted him with it.

But José Maria Olazábal is a Basque; one of a group of hardy, outdoor people who are closely bound to the forests, the hills and the rugged coastline of their native land. Their language is a mystery

with no known or clearly identifiable roots. There are hidden depths to the Basques; they have something magical; something enduring and, above all, they simply never give up. Never say die is the

THE COURSE

Campo de Golf Maspalomas was designed by Mackenzie Ross on the initiative of the Count of Le Vega Grande, owner of the land. The course is located in the Maspalomas resort in an area surrounded by sand dunes and palm trees.

Eduardo Romero gives it everything.

phrase which could have been invented for them. It certainly fits Olazábal and he used that particular Basque trait to overcome what, in the Spring of 1995, had been diagnosed as rheumatoid arthritis in his feet.

At first he responded to medication but suddenly things got worse. So much worse that between April and September of 1996 he never touched a golf club. He was couch-ridden; on the point of sending for a wheelchair catalogue. During the long pain-filled months he was besieged by well-wishers and witch doctors. He tried everything (almost) until he was persuaded to go to Munich where he met doctor Hans Wilhelm Muller-Wolfhart and found daylight. The new diagnosis was a back hernia, the remedy, injections of minerals to build up his

muscles and, above all, exercises for his feet.

By March 1997 he had returned to the European Tour and a few weeks later in the Canaries, the 'fortunate islands', after only his third tournament he was back in the winners' circle. For Olazábal victory in the Turespaña Masters Open Canarias was a highly charged emotional affair. This very private man, self-controlled to the point of introspection, was simply over-

Lee Westwood amid the palms (below) en route to his course record 63 (above).

come. He played well at Maspalomas but was the first to admit that his game was far from its best. His driving was erratic, well below par, and before the tournament he had said: 'Until I get my long game sorted out I won't be in a position to win.'

But somehow Olazábal just got carried along on the crest of a wave of goodwill as the Tour's family spirit once again came to the fore. There was an underlying current bubbling beneath the surface of the tournament and even some of the most veteran, tournament-toughened caddies were willing him on. He opened with a tidy 70 and was third, followed that up with a 67 to be second and had a 68 in the third round to start in third place on Sunday.

Lee Westwood and José

José Cóceres gets to grips with nature.

Cóceres would accompany Olazábal on the final circuit of the pretty Maspalomas course. They were two stokes ahead of the Basque thanks to a superb second round 63 by the Englishman and a third round 65 from the Argentinian but by the fourth hole on Sunday their advantage had melted away in the warm spring sunshine.

Westwood and Cóceres were simply swept along with a tide that had turned in favour of the Spanish player. Olazábal was simply irresistible over the front nine which he covered in 32 strokes and when he birdied the 11th to match Westwood's birdie from 35 feet it was clear that it was to be his day.

'There was a very special moment when I had three putts to win on the 18th. I was overcome by a host of memories,' said Olazábal choking back the tears. 'The hard, bad times I've been through came into my head. Just the thought that I might never play again and then this situation after only three weeks back playing has been very special.'

'It's nice to lose against such a good player,' said Westwood later and, summing up the feelings expressed by many other Tour players, 'he had to win some day, it's wonderful that his comeback victory should be in Spain.'

Jeff Kelly

SHOT OF THE WEEK

José Maria Olazábal's three iron to the 18th green at Maspalomas during the final round was as important a shot as he has had to make since claiming victory at the Volvo PGA Championship at Wentworth in 1994. He took a one iron off the tee for accuracy and was now 230 yard short. From the middle of the fairway he struck his three iron approach, away from the bunker, to the right hand side of the green. The title was his for the asking.

MASPALOMAS, MARCH 20-23, 1997 • YARDAGE 7021 • PAR 72

Pos	Name	Country	Rnd 1	Rnd 2	Rnd 3	Rnd 4	Total	Prize Money £
1	José Maria OLAZABAL	(Sp)	70	67	68	67	272	61964
2	Lee WESTWOOD	(Eng)	72	63	68	71	274	41302
3	Paul BROADHURST	(Eng)	69	72	67	68	276	20932
	Eduardo ROMERO	(Arg)	70	70	67	69	276	20932
5	David GILFORD	(Eng)	70	69	70	68	277	14383
	José COCERES	(Arg)	67	71	65	74	277	14383
7	Diego BORREGO	(Sp)	70	72	68	68	278	11154
8	Ignacio FELIU	(Sp)	73	69	70	67	279	8346
	Ignacio GARRIDO	(Sp)	70	71	71	67	279	8346
	Retief GOOSEN	(SA)	69	71	69	70	279	8346
11	Domingo HOSPITAL	(Sp)	71	71	68	70	280	6072
	Ian GARBUTT	(Eng)	73	70	69	68	280	6072
	Massimo FLORIOLI	(It)	72	69	68	71	280	6072
	Peter MITCHELL	(Eng)	68	73	69	70	280	6072
	Scott HENDERSON	(Scot)	69	71	71	69	280	6072
16	Andrew SANDYWELL	(Eng)	71	67	72	71	281	5128
	Paolo QUIRICI	(Swi)	74	64	70	73	281	5128
18	Daniel CHOPRA	(Swe)	71	73	70	68	282	4703
	Francisco CEA	(Sp)	71	71	70	70	282	4703
20	Neal BRIGGS	(Eng)	68	70	73	72	283	3959
	Fabrice TARNAUD	(Fr)	70	73	71	69	283	3959
	Alex CEJKA	(Ger)	70	74	70	69	283	3959
	Andrew COLTART	(Scot)	71	71	70	71	283	3959
	Robert COLES	(Eng)	73	69	71	70	283	3959
	Stephen ALLAN	(Aus)	70	70	70	73	283	3959
	Dennis EDLUND	(Swe)	72	68	70	73	283	3959
	Katsuyoshi TOMORI	(Jap)	68	72	71	72	283	3959
	Miguel Angel JIMÉNEZ	(Sp)	69	70	70	74	283	3959
	Andrew OLDCORN	(Scot)	72	71	71	69	283	3959
30	Miguel Angel MARTIN	(Sp)	71	72	69	72	284	3104
	Mark DAVIS	(Eng)	69	73	72	70	284	3104
	Padraig HARRINGTON	(Ire)	72	69	71	72	284	3104
	Adam HUNTER	(Scot)	67	73	73	71	284	3104
	Joakim HAEGGMAN	(Swe)	70	69	72	73	284	3104
	Jonathan LOMAS	(Eng)	69	69	72	74	284	3104
36	Michael JONZON	(Swe)	69	74	69	73	285	2602
	Michael CAMPBELL	(NZ)	70	73	69	73	285	2602
	Brian DAVIS	(Eng)	66	77	71	71	285	2602
	Sven STRÜVER	(Ger)	72	71	73	69	285	2602
	Roger CHAPMAN	(Eng)	73	71	69	72	285	2602
	José RIVERO	(Sp)	67	75	71	72	285	2602
	Des SMYTH	(Ire)	70	70	72	73	285	2602
43	Peter BAKER	(Eng)	67	76	70	73	286	2082
	Pedro LINHART	(Sp)	73	70	74	69	286	2082
	Santiago LUNA	(Sp)	72	71	74	69	286	2082
	Christian CÉVAER	(Fr)	71	73	74	68	286	2082
	Jim PAYNE	(Eng)	70	72	72	72	286	2082
	Ross DRUMMOND	(Scot)	72	70	70	74	286	2082
	Juan Carlos PIÑERO	(Sp)	70	69	71	76	286	2082
50	Mathew GOGGIN	(Aus)	74	69	71	73	287	1673
	Jean VAN DE VELDE	(Fr)	70	74	72	71	287	1673
	Carl SUNESON	(Sp)	72	70	74	71	287	1673
	Mats HALLBERG	(Swe)	67	71	73	76	287	1673
54	Bob MAY	(USA)	72	71	74	71	288	1338
	Jon ROBSON	(Eng)	75	69	71	73	288	1338
	Andrew BEAL	(Eng)	69	75	71	73	288	1338
	Max ANGLERT	(Swe)	72	72	70	74	288	1338
	Patrik SJÖLAND	(Swe)	70	70	71	77	288	1338
59	Richard BOXALL	(Eng)	71	72	74	72	289	1152
60	David HIGGINS	(Ire)	72	71	72	75	290	1078
	Mark MOULAND	(Wal)	71	72	73	74	290	1078
	Daren LEE	(Eng)	69	74	73	74	290	1078
63	Stephen FIELD	(Eng)	71	72	77	71	291	1003
64	Raymond RUSSELL	(Scot)	71	72	79	70	292	948
	Joakim GRÖNHAGEN	(Swe)	73	71	74	74	292	948
66	Warren BENNETT	(Eng)	69	75	74	75	293	556
	Raphaël JACQUELIN	(Fr)	71	73	77	72	293	556
68	Duncan MUSCROFT	(Eng)	74	70	75	75	294	553

Lee Westwood has a taste of paradise.

Mitchell's final thrust earns victory

With a stunning second shot to the final hole
Peter Mitchell held on in Madeira

Madeira, a tiny island in the Atlantic Ocean famous for its wine and orchids, cuisine and climate, hosted its fifth European Tour event with typical friendliness and efficiency in a week when low cloud did its best to make golfing life difficult on the spectacular Santo da Serra GC course.

The Madeira Island Open, a popular stop on the European Tour, saw three past winners return for another tilt at the title — Mats Lanner, Santiago Luna and defending champion Jarmo Sandelin — but it was England's Peter Mitchell who emerged triumphant after a testing four days which resulted in only three rounds being played.

Santo da Serra boasts some of the most spectacular golf holes in Europe but there was precious little to view on the first day of the tournament. The course is 2,300 feet above sea level and low cloud delayed play for three hours on the opening morning. When play eventually began, high winds sprang up and with the leading groups having played only eight holes, Tournament Director David Probyn was forced to suspend play when balls began moving on the greens. And then the cloud descended again.

Prospects of any further play that day were slim but all the players and their caddies, officials and helpers sat around chatting good-naturedly and hoping for a quick resumption. It was not to be, the club President Miguel de Sousa suspected as much. He invited all 150 players to join him for lunch in the Sponsors' Marquee, a generous gesture which was gratefully accepted.

At 4.30pm, David Probyn abandoned play for the day and that left him with a headache of trying to catch up. The second day was spent completing the first round and getting the second round under way but with more low cloud swirling around and a bad weather forecast for the weekend, it was announced on Friday afternoon that the tournament would be decided over 54 holes.

So that was the scene for the 1997 Madeira Island Open, which was a great shame because the island is truly delightful with a normally temperate climate.

SHOT OF THE WEEK

Peter Mitchell came to the 385-yard finishing hole at Santo da Serra needing a birdie three to secure his second European Tour win. He hit what he described as a chip-and-run drive 'just to get it down the fairway' and then hit a wedge which pitched on the front of the green, stopping the ball dead on the second bounce 12 inches behind the hole. The tournament was won.

Fredrik Jacobson (above) came close. (Opposite) Peter Mitchell's second round scorecard.

Scotland's Andrew Coltart, a past winner of the Australian PGA Championship but still seeking his first win on the European Tour, played only nine shots of his first round on Thursday but returned on Friday morning and his first shot of the day was a chip to the third green, which resulted in a birdie and set him on his way to the first round lead on 66, six under par.

Happily, there were no further inter-ruptions to play and with the Santo da Serra course in its best-ever condition for the tournament, Mitchell began his victory march with a second round of 63, a course record by two shots and including seven birdies and an eagle. It beat the previous record of 65 set by Jeff Hall in the inaugural Madeira Island Open in 1993 and equalled on the second day, this time by Andrew Sherborne.

It was not the lowest round of

THE COURSE

For this fifth Madeira Island Open, the two nines were reversed to provide a grandstand finish for spectators, and they were not disappointed. Santo da Serra has some of the most spectacular golf holes in Europe and the 220-yard fourth is probably the most stunning with magnificent sea and ravine views.

Santo da Serra GC, March 27-30, 1997 · Yardage 6606 · Par 72

Pos	Name	Country	Rnd 1	Rnd 2	Rnd 3	Rnd 4	Total	Prize Money £
1	Peter MITCHELL	(Eng)	70	63	71		204	50000
2	Fredrik JACOBSON	(Swe)	68	73	64		205	33330
3	Andrew COLTART	(Scot)	66	72	68		206	18780
4	Andrew SHERBORNE	(Eng)	72	65	70		207	15000
5	Carl SUNESON	(Sp)	70	72	66		208	10733
	José COCERES	(Arg)	73	67	68		208	10733
	David TAPPING	(Eng)	70	68	70		208	10733
8	Thomas GÖGELE	(Ger)	71	67	71		209	7500
9	Malcolm MACKENZIE	(Eng)	69	73	68		210	5842
	Padraig HARRINGTON	(Ire)	73	69	68		210	5842
	Paul AFFLECK	(Wal)	72	69	69		210	5842
	Dean ROBERTSON	(Scot)	71	67	72		210	5842
13	Jean VAN DE VELDE	(Fr)	69	74	68		211	4515
	Anders FORSBRAND	(Swe)	69	73	69		211	4515
	John BICKERTON	(Eng)	72	70	69		211	4515
	Heinz P THÜL	(Ger)	70	68	73		211	4515
17	Robert COLES	(Eng)	72	71	69		212	3880.
	Gordon J BRAND	(Eng)	73	71	68		212	3880
	Bob MAY	(USA)	69	73	70		212	3880
20	David HOWELL	(Eng)	72	71	70		213	3240
	Philip WALTON	(Ire)	74	70	69		213	3240
	Des SMYTH	(Ire)	72	73	68		213	3240
	Van PHILLIPS	(Eng)	73	70	70		213	3240
	Mark MOULAND	(Wal)	71	71	71		213	3240
	Andrew SANDYWELL	(Eng)	69	73	71		213	3240
	Paul LAWRIE	(Scot)	71	71	71		213	3240
	Ross MCFARLANE	(Eng)	68	73	72		213	3240
	Russell CLAYDON	(Eng)	69	71	73		213	3240
29	Duncan MUSCROFT	(Eng)	72	71	71		214	2512
	Rolf MUNTZ	(Hol)	67	77	70		214	2512
	Scott HENDERSON	(Scot)	69	75	70		214	2512
	Richard BOXALL	(Eng)	70	75	69		214	2512
	Michel BESANCENEY	(Fr)	72	71	71		214	2512
	Paul BROADHURST	(Eng)	70	72	72		214	2512
	Santiago LUNA	(Sp)	70	71	73		214	2512
	John WADE	(Aus)	72	69	73		214	2512
37	Mark ROE	(Eng)	69	74	72		215	2010
	Ignacio FELIU	(Sp)	72	72	71		215	2010
	Stuart CAGE	(Eng)	69	75	71		215	2010
	Mike WEIR	(Can)	73	72	70		215	2010
	Kalle VAINOLA	(Fin)	72	70	73		215	2010
	John MCHENRY	(Ire)	72	70	73		215	2010
	Peter HEDBLOM	(Swe)	71	71	73		215	2010
	Ignacio GARRIDO	(Sp)	68	73	74		215	2010
45	Ariel CAÑETE	(Arg)	71	72	73		216	1650
	Mathew GOGGIN	(Aus)	71	72	73		216	1650
	Andrew OLDCORN	(Scot)	73	71	72		216	1650
	Phillip PRICE	(Wal)	73	71	72		216	1650
49	Martin GATES	(Eng)	70	73	74		217	1290
	Craig HAINLINE	(USA)	71	73	73		217	1290
	Raphaël JACQUELIN	(Fr)	72	73	72		217	1290
	Joe HIGGINS	(Eng)	76	69	72		217	1290
	Michael WATSON	(Eng)	72	71	74		217	1290
	Justin HOBDAY	(SA)	73	69	75		217	1290
	Peter BAKER	(Eng)	71	71	75		217	1290
	Fredrik LARSSON	(Swe)	70	72	75		217	1290
57	Juan Carlos PIÑERO	(Sp)	74	69	75		218	952
	Stephen MCALLISTER	(Scot)	70	75	73		218	952
	Brian DAVIS	(Eng)	74	71	73		218	952
	Fabrice TARNAUD	(Fr)	71	74	73		218	952
61	André BOSSERT	(Swi)	75	70	74		219	855
	Francisco VALERA	(Sp)	70	72	77		219	855
63	Fredrik ANDERSSON	(Swe)	72	72	76		220	795
	Iain PYMAN	(Eng)	71	73	76		220	795
	Alexandre HENRIQUES (AM)	(Port)	74	70	76		220	
65	Jim PAYNE	(Eng)	74	71	76		221	549
	Antoine LEBOUC	(Fr)	73	72	76		221	549
	Carl WATTS	(Eng)	75	70	76		221	549

Match: 24 Time: 17.50
28 Mar 97 Round: 2
Peter MITCHELL Eng
Tee:10 70. 63. 133.

5º OPEN DA MADEIRA DE GOLFE
27 a 30 de MARÇO 1997

Hole	1	2	3	4	5	6	7	8	9	Out
Metros	371	378	431	391	383	487	138	319	384	3082
Par	4	4	4	4	4	5	3	4	4	36
Score	4	3	3	3	4	4	2	3	4	30

Hole	10	11	12	13	14	15	16	17	18	In	Total
Metros	323	501	382	418	317	172	460	182	362	3077	6039
Par	4	5	4	4	4	3	4	3	4	36	72
Score	4	5	4	3	5	3	4	3	3	33	63.

Mitchell's career — he twice scored a 62 in winning the 1992 Austrian Open, his only previous European Tour victory — but it gave him a four-stroke lead over the field on 133 (11 under par). His nearest challenger was Sherborne on 137 and there were five other players on 138, Coltart, who had a second round of 72, Thomas Gögele (67), Dean Robertson (67), Heinz Peter Thül (68) and David Tapping (68), who graduated from the 1996 European Tour Qualifying School.

With just the third and final round to play, the weather improved and most of Sunday afternoon was bathed in welcome sunshine. Mitchell increased his lead to five strokes with an opening birdie and victory was there for the taking. Nobody seemed to be making a move but suddenly the tournament sprang into life.

Swede Fredrik Jacobson, a 1996 European Challenge Tour graduate, made a strong claim for victory with a closing round of 64 to set a clubhouse target of 205, 11 under par, at which point Mitchell was on the same mark with three holes to play. Sherborne and Coltart both moved to within a shot of Mitchell and Carl Suneson mounted a strong challenge with six birdies and an eagle in his first 11 holes.

But none was able to catch clubhouse leader Jacobson and that left Mitchell in a win, lose or draw situation. He was still level with Jacobson standing on the 18th tee and to the delight of the crowds he hit his second shot to within 12 inches of the hole to secure a winning birdie. 'This has been a great week and it was nice to have been leading the tournament and then actually win it,' said Mitchell. 'That means a lot to me.'

Richard Dodd

Cage opens the door for victory

With four rounds under 70 Stuart Cage coasted to his maiden Tour victory by five shots

Stuart Cage, the former Walker Cup golfer from Leeds, romped to his first European Tour victory by winning the Europe 1 Cannes Open by five shots with a 14 under par total of 270.

Yet perhaps the greatest triumph was gained by David Carter, who finished joint second with Paul Broadhurst less than eight weeks after being found unconscious in his hotel room in Dubai with fluid and inflammation on his brain.

Cage, the only player to break 70 in all four rounds, was tied second with a 68 after the first round, one shot behind New Zealander Stephen Scahill, but he

THE COURSE

The Royal Mougins golf course is only 6,594 yards long, short by professional standards, but it has undulating fairways and greens, a number of tight holes where it is advisable to take irons off the tee, and water comes into play on 11 holes, with particular difficulty at the last.

SHOT OF THE WEEK

Stuart Cage played the shot of the tournament at the 566-yard 18th hole when, from 108 yards, he hit a blind nine iron over the water guarding the green to within four feet of the flag. It enabled him to birdie the hole and take a three-shot lead going into the last round.

would have been outright leader had he not four-putted the 17th green.

It made little difference, however, for Cage took the lead with a birdie three at the 16th hole in the second round and, though level with Spaniard Santiago Luna after seven holes of the third round, was never headed again.

He shot 67 to lead the field by one shot after the second round, went three strokes clear following a third round 69 and then, after Broadhurst and Paul Eales had closed to just one shot at the turn in the final round, Cage simply drew away to end with a 66 and five shots clear.

As he said later: 'This is a big breakthrough for me, a dream come true. You play and practice all the time just to try and win on the European Tour. And now I've done it. When you first come out on

93

Another day at the rock face for Steven Bottomley (top).
Jamie Spence (above) fired an astonishing final round (right).

Tour you think some of the guys are unbeatable but now I know they are not. What makes my win really pleasing is that I caught a stomach bug in South Africa and it took me a long time to get over it. I'd missed the cut in four of my last five tournaments so to win an event is almost unbelievable.'

Carter could hardly have been less pleased than Cage. He was in hospital for three weeks after being found in his hotel room by golfing friends, Iain Pyman and Roger Wessels, two days before the Dubai Desert

Classic began in February.

Fluid had to be drained from his brain, he had no idea where he was for two weeks and he was still having problems with his short-term memory when he arrived in Cannes.

Yet he shot a 68 in the first round to be joint second and, though falling back to tied 23rd after two further rounds of 74 and 71, had an incredible 62 on the final day to close with a nine under par 275.

Little wonder Carter should say: 'I'm ecstatic. I was just hoping to make the

ROYAL MOUGINS, APRIL 17-20, 1997 • YARDAGE 6594 • PAR 71

Pos	Name	Country	Rnd 1	Rnd 2	Rnd 3	Rnd 4	Total	Prize Money £
1	Stuart CAGE	(Eng)	68	67	69	66	270	50000
2	Paul BROADHURST	(Eng)	68	70	69	68	275	26055
	David CARTER	(Eng)	68	74	71	62	275	26055
4	Paul EALES	(Eng)	72	65	70	69	276	13850
	Jamie SPENCE	(Eng)	74	72	69	61	276	13850
6	Paul MCGINLEY	(Ire)	72	68	70	68	278	9750
	Clinton WHITELAW	(SA)	71	71	68	68	278	9750
8	Neal BRIGGS	(Eng)	71	69	70	69	279	6427
	Carl SUNESON	(Sp)	73	69	69	68	279	6427
	Andrew SANDYWELL	(Eng)	76	67	67	69	279	6427
	Andrew COLTART	(Scot)	71	70	69	69	279	6427
12	Ben TINNING	(Den)	72	68	73	67	280	4747
	Philip WALTON	(Ire)	70	73	66	71	280	4747
	Andrew SHERBORNE	(Eng)	69	74	72	65	280	4747
	Santiago LUNA	(Sp)	70	66	73	71	280	4747
16	Ronan RAFFERTY	(N.Ire)	74	70	67	70	281	3894
	Francisco VALERA	(Sp)	72	69	74	66	281	3894
	Michael JONZON	(Swe)	72	71	69	69	281	3894
	Barry LANE	(Eng)	75	69	67	70	281	3894
	Paul CURRY	(Eng)	72	72	68	69	281	3894
21	Pierre FULKE	(Swe)	74	70	69	69	282	3195
	Howard CLARK	(Eng)	70	75	69	68	282	3195
	Domingo HOSPITAL	(Sp)	74	70	67	71	282	3195
	Pedro LINHART	(Sp)	71	73	73	65	282	3195
	Mathias GRÖNBERG	(Swe)	71	71	66	74	282	3195
	Rolf MUNTZ	(Hol)	68	73	69	72	282	3195
	David HOWELL	(Eng)	72	72	71	67	282	3195
	Adam MEDNICK	(Swe)	75	70	72	65	282	3195
29	Thomas BJORN	(Den)	71	68	73	71	283	2745
	Des SMYTH	(Ire)	72	69	75	67	283	2745
31	Peter MITCHELL	(Eng)	73	70	71	70	284	2404
	Katsuyoshi TOMORI	(Jap)	76	69	67	72	284	2404
	Fernando ROCA	(Sp)	72	75	70	67	284	2404
	Daniel WESTERMARK	(Swe)	71	73	68	72	284	2404
	David GILFORD	(Eng)	79	67	67	71	284	2404
	Niclas FASTH	(Swe)	73	68	72	71	284	2404
	Ariel CAÑETE	(Arg)	71	75	69	69	284	2404
38	Mark MOULAND	(Wal)	73	72	70	70	285	1950
	Sven STRÜVER	(Ger)	74	71	69	71	285	1950
	John MELLOR	(Eng)	72	72	73	68	285	1950
	Steven BOTTOMLEY	(Eng)	70	70	75	70	285	1950
	Fabrice TARNAUD	(Fr)	73	73	69	70	285	1950
	Joakim HAEGGMAN	(Swe)	83	63	72	67	285	1950
	Ross MCFARLANE	(Eng)	70	72	74	69	285	1950
	Derrick COOPER	(Eng)	73	70	72	70	285	1950
46	Bob MAY	(USA)	72	73	71	70	286	1620
	Stephen FIELD	(Eng)	74	73	69	70	286	1620
	Ignacio GARRIDO	(Sp)	75	72	72	67	286	1620
49	Dennis EDLUND	(Swe)	77	70	71	69	287	1500
50	Klas ERIKSSON	(Swe)	75	71	75	67	288	1350
	Jean VAN DE VELDE	(Fr)	74	72	75	67	288	1350
	David HIGGINS	(Ire)	76	68	74	70	288	1350
	Stephen ALLAN	(Aus)	74	73	73	68	288	1350
54	Raphaël JACQUELIN	(Fr)	69	77	73	70	289	1170
	Raymond RUSSELL	(Scot)	72	72	72	73	289	1170
56	Thomas LEVET	(Fr)	74	73	71	72	290	1050
	Retief GOOSEN	(SA)	74	73	71	72	290	1050
58	Jarmo SANDELIN	(Swe)	71	75	75	70	291	930
	Mårten OLANDER	(Swe)	75	72	68	76	291	930
	Stephen SCAHILL	(NZ)	67	72	72	80	291	930
61	Patrik SJÖLAND	(Swe)	72	72	77	71	292	825
	Mats LANNER	(Swe)	72	72	70	78	292	825
	Matthias DEBOVE	(Fr)	74	72	74	72	292	825
	Warren BENNETT	(Eng)	78	69	73	72	292	825
65	Darren COLE	(Aus)	75	72	73	74	294	750
66	Mark DAVIS	(Eng)	72	73	75	75	295	450
67	Jon ROBSON	(Eng)	74	73	77	74	298	448
68	Miguel Angel MARTIN	(Sp)	71	73	78	77	299	446

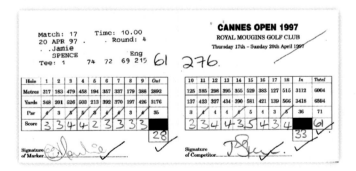

halfway cut. It's a miracle. I'm happy to be alive, let alone playing golf and finishing second.'

Broadhurst, who finished with a 68, moved up to fifth place in the Ryder Cup table with his tied second place, while Eales and Jamie Spence also had plenty to smile about.

Eales, like Cage, had suffered severe stomach trouble in South Africa and, for a time, was so weak he lost 30 yards on his drive. Yet he recovered so well in Cannes he finished joint fourth with Spence.

Spence had the most incredible rise in the field for he shot a ten under par 61 on the final day to move up from tied 32nd,

had nine birdies in his first 14 holes and had visions of a 59. But he had only one more birdie, at the 18th, and had to be content with the best score ever recorded over the Royal Mougins course.

Unfortunately for Spence his great round could not count as a new course record because preferred lies were in force after heavy overnight rain.

Three other golfers, Paul Affleck, Italian Massimo Florioli and Sweden's Joakim Haeggman, were in the news at Cannes but for very different reasons.

Affleck holed-in-one with a seven iron at the 213-yard fifth hole in the first round; Florioli became the first player in 1997 to be penalised one stroke and fined £500 for slow play in the second round; while Haeggman proved that hope should never die.

Haeggman shot 83 in the first round but, instead of withdrawing as many players might have done, shot a 63 in the second round to make the halfway cut.

John Oakley

Message from the Chairman

Mark James demonstrated that his role as Chairman of the European Tour Tournament Committee had not affected his desire to win

After 21 successful seasons on the European Tour, Mark James could be forgiven for deciding that his best years are behind him.

Newly installed as Chairman of the influential Tournament Committee which acts as the principal conduit between the players and the Executive, James had found tournament golf a struggle in 1996, sliding out of the top 100 in the Volvo Ranking for the first time, after failing to finish in the top ten on any of his 18 appearances. And that after he had played a crucial part in Europe's 1995 Ryder Cup victory at Oak Hill, by beating Jeff Maggert in the singles after qualifying for the match in seventh automatic place, aided by his 17th Tour win in the Moroccan Open.

That victory had been achieved with a long putter but it had subsequently become an untrustworthy ally, and when James arrived in Dubai for the 1997 Desert Classic he had discarded it in favour of an orthodox Ping club for which he paid £50 in the Emirates Club shop.

Seven weeks later the modest investment paid a handsome dividend when 'Jesse' gunned down the Great White Shark, Greg Norman, in a thrilling extra-time climax to the Peugeot Open de Espana at the La Moraleja II Club in Madrid. Six months short of his 44th birthday, James proved not only that his nerve was still strong 'coming down the stretch', but that his driving, iron play, and to his great surprise his putting, were still good enough to make him a match for the best.

Norman certainly represents that, for

since the Sony Ranking began in April 1986 he has never been out of the top ten, holding the record for the most weeks at number one (312) and the most in succession (97).

The flamboyant Australian might have been a Test cricketer or a fighter pilot. Instead, because of his ability to strike a little white ball with power and precision, he is a multi-millionaire who runs a vast business empire with interests from boats to restaurants, and golf courses construction to turf farms.

He owns an airliner and a helicopter, an ocean-going yacht and four boats. At his Florida mansion he has

Greg Norman (top) bowed out in the play-off. Top ten finishes for David Howell (above) and Jarmo Sandelin (right).

seven Ferraris, six Chevrolets, a Mercedes, and two Harley Davidsons.

If pushed, James with his nice line in self-deprecating humour, would cite the sweet peas and vegetables in his garden at Ilkley as his most cherished possessions, although with career earnings approaching £3 million he could also have afforded to indulge his materialistic fancies, albeit upon a slightly lesser scale.

Instead he has earned a reputation as one of the most determined and resilient opponents and it was not surprising that the first Tour honour gained by the former English champion and Amateur Championship

SHOT OF THE WEEK

Spaniards finished 1-2-3 in this category with José Antonio Rozadilla setting the standard with an ace from his six iron at the 17th to win a motor car. José Maria Olazábal followed him into the hole six hours later on the second day with a seven iron, but neither quite matched the timing or showmanship of Ryder Cup captain Seve Ballesteros. He staged a grandstand finish on Sunday by wedging into the 18th hole from 118 yards for an eagle two. That was real Madrid magic from Seve.

Mark James stayed ahead of Greg Norman before and after the play-off (top and above). David Carter (right) and caddie make a point .

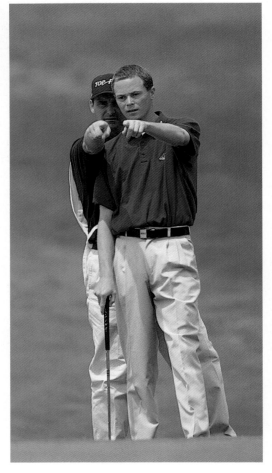

finalist, was the European Match-Play title.

James has always been at his best in head-to-head competition as Norman was reminded on that hot Sunday afternoon in the Spanish capital after the Englishman had shot a closing round of 69 to set the clubhouse target of 277, eleven under par.

Norman had moved to that mark when he holed from off the green for an eagle three at the 11th, and remained firm favourite when he was still level with three holes remaining. But he missed the green at the short 17th to lose a shot and suddenly found himself needing a birdie at the dog-leg 18th to force a play off.

The Shark responded with a thrashing drive, towering pitch, and a putt from 20 feet that had the gallery chattering in anticipation of further excitement as the pair returned to the 18th tee.

Norman was bunkered on his second visit to the green, but holed from ten feet to match an orthodox four from James. Then it was the latter's turn to sweat, as Norman missed a birdie chance, and he had to get down from six feet to avoid defeat.

The third extra hole was the 17th, measuring only 177 yards, but slightly uphill with the flag awkwardly positioned on the right side of the sloping green.

Just as he had done almost an hour earlier, the Australian again failed to hit the putting surface and then left his recovery chip some 12 feet short of the hole, giving James the chance he was seeking.

Two putts from 40 feet, the second from inside a yard, and it was over. James was back on the path towards another possible Ryder Cup appearance, and Norman en route to the Far East, his next stop in his round-the-world dash.

'I keep myself pretty fit and I feel my nerve is still intact,' said James. 'My only worry these days is my technique, for as you get older you no longer have the inclination to work your butt off on the practice ground.'

For Norman whose desire to keep playing, despite his many business interests, remains intense, it was a question of the ball 'not going where I wanted it to.'

Mike Britten

GOLF LA MORALEJA II, MADRID, APRIL 24-27, 1997 · YARDAGE 7054 · PAR 72

Pos	Name	Country	Rnd 1	Rnd 2	Rnd 3	Rnd 4	Total	Prize Money £
1	Mark JAMES	(Eng)	67	68	73	69	277	84843
2	Greg NORMAN	(Aus)	69	70	68	70	277	56506
3	Jarmo SANDELIN	(Swe)	72	71	69	66	278	28677
	Eduardo ROMERO	(Arg)	68	70	71	69	278	28677
5	David HOWELL	(Eng)	70	71	67	71	279	18213
	Jean Louis GUEPY	(Fr)	71	68	70	70	279	18213
	José COCERES	(Arg)	72	69	70	68	279	18213
8	Roger CHAPMAN	(Eng)	70	67	74	69	280	11425
	Howard CLARK	(Eng)	74	70	69	67	280	11425
	Fredrik JACOBSON	(Swe)	73	71	69	67	280	11425
11	Stephen AMES	(T&T)	68	75	70	68	281	8590
	Peter MITCHELL	(Eng)	70	69	69	73	281	8590
	José Maria OLAZABAL	(Sp)	69	71	74	67	281	8590
	Thomas BJORN	(Den)	68	69	72	72	281	8590
15	Costantino ROCCA	(It)	70	70	71	71	282	7466
16	Gary CLARK	(Eng)	72	69	72	70	283	6472
	Adam HUNTER	(Scot)	70	71	73	69	283	6472
	Jamie SPENCE	(Eng)	73	70	70	70	283	6472
	Miguel Angel JIMÉNEZ	(Sp)	68	74	71	70	283	6472
	Lee WESTWOOD	(Eng)	69	68	73	73	283	6472
	Gary EMERSON	(Eng)	67	72	70	74	283	6472
	Ian GARBUTT	(Eng)	69	70	70	74	283	6472
23	Clinton WHITELAW	(SA)	69	70	71	74	284	5599
	Andrew SHERBORNE	(Eng)	72	71	71	70	284	5599
	David CARTER	(Eng)	70	72	67	75	284	5599
26	Greg TURNER	(NZ)	72	71	71	71	285	4496
	Ross DRUMMOND	(Scot)	73	69	70	73	285	4496
	Andrew COLTART	(Scot)	72	71	73	69	285	4496
	Rolf MUNTZ	(Hol)	70	68	70	77	285	4496
	Mark ROE	(Eng)	70	71	73	71	285	4496
	Ignacio GARRIDO	(Sp)	68	74	71	72	285	4496
	Stuart CAGE	(Eng)	71	73	70	71	285	4496
	Seve BALLESTEROS	(Sp)	70	73	73	69	285	4496
	Dennis EDLUND	(Swe)	73	68	75	69	285	4496
	Silvio GRAPPASONNI	(It)	71	72	70	72	285	4496
36	Iain PYMAN	(Eng)	68	70	76	72	286	3224
	Ignacio FELIU	(Sp)	73	70	71	72	286	3224
	Niclas FASTH	(Swe)	69	74	72	71	286	3224
	Sam TORRANCE	(Scot)	70	70	74	72	286	3224
	Padraig HARRINGTON	(Ire)	66	76	74	70	286	3224
	Bernhard LANGER	(Ger)	72	72	74	68	286	3224
	Jay TOWNSEND	(USA)	73	68	75	70	286	3224
	Paul EALES	(Eng)	70	74	69	73	286	3224
	Gary ORR	(Scot)	72	69	72	73	286	3224
	Pierre FULKE	(Swe)	74	70	74	68	286	3224
	Carl WATTS	(Eng)	71	69	74	72	286	3224
47	Per HAUGSRUD	(Nor)	73	69	73	72	287	2502
	Patrik SJÖLAND	(Swe)	73	70	74	70	287	2502
	Barry LANE	(Eng)	68	75	76	68	287	2502
	Klas ERIKSSON	(Swe)	73	69	75	70	287	2502
	Francisco CEA	(Sp)	70	74	71	72	287	2502
	David HIGGINS	(Ire)	70	70	75	72	287	2502
	Sergio GARCIA (AM)	(Sp)	71	73	70	73	287	
53	Rodger DAVIS	(Aus)	70	71	77	70	288	2078
	Paul MCGINLEY	(Ire)	72	72	71	73	288	2078
	Carl SUNESON	(Sp)	74	69	75	70	288	2078
	Andrew OLDCORN	(Scot)	72	71	70	75	288	2078
57	Carl MASON	(Eng)	73	71	72	73	289	1654
	Paul LAWRIE	(Scot)	72	69	76	72	289	1654
	Santiago LUNA	(Sp)	71	71	70	77	289	1654
	Jean VAN DE VELDE	(Fr)	72	71	74	72	289	1654
	Peter BAKER	(Eng)	73	68	77	71	289	1654
	Francisco VALERA	(Sp)	69	72	75	73	289	1654
63	Per-Ulrik JOHANSSON	(Swe)	74	70	74	72	290	1315
	David GILFORD	(Eng)	70	74	69	77	290	1315
65	Emanuele CANONICA	(It)	72	67	73	79	291	975
	Miguel Angel MARTIN	(Sp)	72	72	72	75	291	975
67	Gordon BRAND JNR.	(Scot)	73	71	75	73	292	759
	Ivo GINER	(Sp)	76	66	74	76	292	759
	Mark MCNULTY	(Zim)	76	68	74	74	292	759
	Ross MCFARLANE	(Eng)	73	71	75	73	292	759
71	Alex CEJKA	(Ger)	66	73	75	79	293	754
72	Pedro LINHART	(Sp)	71	70	78	75	294	752
73	José GARCIA	(Sp)	72	72	69	82	295	749

THE COURSE

La Moraleja II, designed by the Jack Nicklaus organisation, is part of the 36 holes complex created in one of Madrid's most exclusive residential areas, just north of the Spanish capital. Venue for the 1992 World Cup won by Fred Couples and Davis Love III for the USA, it has a strong American flavour, in particular its feature hole, the 533-yard 16th where the green is within reach of a wood or long iron struck with authority over the lake.

Langer sets cheerful tone

After a winless 1996 in Europe,

Bernhard Langer was back

in familiar territory

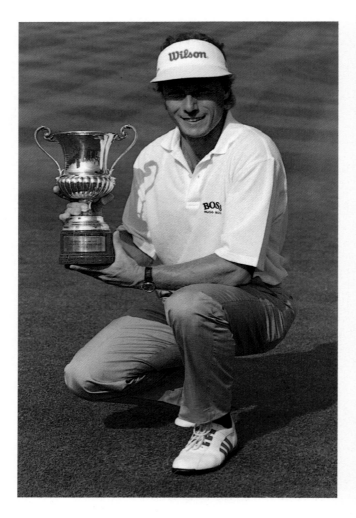

*B*ernhard Langer in the winner's enclosure after 19 months away, a spectacular course record to put the finishing touches to his Italian Job: Reasons to be cheerful part one.

José Maria Olazábal continuing his amazing comeback, only thwarted from securing his second European Tour success by Langer's irresistible putting display over the closing holes at Gardagolf: Reasons to be cheerful part two.

Langer, runner-up Olazábal and third-placed Darren Clarke, one of Ryder Cup captain Severiano Ballesteros's forecasts for a Valderrama debut, holding automatic places on the Cup points table after an exhilarating finish in Italy: Reasons to be cheerful part three. And there was an abundance of cheer all week from the setting, a glorious Alps backdrop and glimpses of Lake Garda. Then there were the stunning signorinas. What more could anyone want?

Well, in the opening round of the Conte of Florence Italian Open, Retief Goosen would have settled for a dry nose.

The South African coughed and sneezed to a six under par 66 to lead the way, warning 'beware of the sick golfer' as he used up several boxes of tissues on his way round.

Ian Woosnam's bogey-free 67 was not to be sniffed at either. The Welshman had reverted to his old wooden driver because his game left a lot to be desired off the tee

when using metal. His faithful wooden driver made him happy again, reversing Lee Trevino's philosophy. You could talk to a hook, felt Woosnam, but a slice don't listen. However, a couple of hooks finishing off his second round didn't take much notice either and three bogeys to close, ended his bid for the week. And when the aspirin-gorgeing Goosen ran up a quadru-ple-bogey on the eighth, a hole which proved a bitter pill to many during the week, he fell away too.

Fourteen had been Eduardo Romero's unlucky number. The affable Argentinian was dismayed to discover he had accidentally grounded his putter during a practice swish on the 14th green in round one, denying himself a share of the lead through two penalty strokes. He shrugged it off to capture the second round lead. His seven under par was one better than Gordon J. Brand and Brian Davis from England and Sweden's Patrik Sjöland.

It was a fine effort by Sjöland who ran up a triple-bogey on the eighth when his ball plopped down out of a bush while the Swede and his playing companion

SHOT OF THE WEEK

Paolo Qurici's seven iron ace at the 168-yard second on Saturday put the Swiss on a roll and Costantino Rocca's 12-inch approach at the death to make the cut in front of his adoring fans, were memorable, but Langer's left-to-right putt from 15 feet from the fringe on the last was the shot which won the tournament and showed he is among the world's top putters once again.

combed the foliage. Because it could not be deduced who had disturbed the ball, Sjöland had to accept a penalty – and a further stroke because the ball had scuttled into an unplayable lie.

For 22-year-old Davis and 41-year-old Brand it was truly spring and autumn in May. Rookie Davis underlined his potential first shown at the European Tour Qualifying School and then with a sixth place in Morocco. Another sixth place went on his record but there was only a fleeting hint of former glory from Brand, who had regained his card at the School.

The Yorkshireman who finished second to Greg Norman in the 1986 Open at Turnberry, startling many with his stall at the top of his swing, pausing only briefly on the leaderboard before, like his distinctive delays at the top now eradicated by a swing-change, slipping into obscurity.

Lurking, though, was Olazábal, just two shots off the lead. By Saturday night he had claimed it, despite a spectacular performance from his playing companion Paolo Quirici.

The week before, Olazábal had hit a hole-in-one in Madrid. This time his Swiss partner played the ace, holing out at the second before Romero had even started. Quirici, on a medical extension after a year dogged by diabetes problems, refused to rest on his laurels. Only at the last hole did Olazábal get the better of Quirici, a birdie taking the Spaniard one ahead of Quirici, who bogeyed, finding lucky seven was not his favourite number after all. He made his ace with a seven iron – and then

missed the green with it on the 18th.

On ten under par, Olazábal was also two in front of a pack of British young bloods, Steve Webster, Raymond Russell and Dean Robertson, along with Romero and Sjöland. It developed into a two-horse race on the final day – although Clarke could have come up on the rails had he found better form on the par fives – and then the two horses turned into a cat and a mouse.

Langer found the birdies to become Olazábal's only serious challenger but the Spaniard kept the German at bay, always picking up a shot if his arch-rival got too close for comfort. That was until Langer birded the 16th to draw level for the first

time and survived a risky shot to the flag at the treacherous short 17th.

When Langer homed in a nerve-jangling putt from the fringe of the green on the last, he was in front for the first time. It was all Olazábal could do to make par at all the closing holes and victory was snatched from under his nose by a stroke.

Victory, though, was not lost but won

Costantino Rocca (left) crosses flower-laden bridge. Darren Clarke (above) came close again.

THE COURSE

Breathtaking is the only way to describe the parkland lay-out watched over by the Alps, with spectacular Lake Guarda glistening nearby. But the undulating course, abutted by olive groves and vineyards, near Brescia, can be a beast as well as a beauty. Its hazard-fringed eighth and 17th holes provide timely reminders that course management is paramount.

105

GARDAGOLF BRESCIA, MAY 1-4, 1997 • YARDAGE 7111 • PAR 72

Pos	Name	Country	Rnd 1	Rnd 2	Rnd 3	Rnd 4	Total	Prize Money £
1	Bernhard LANGER	(Ger)	71	69	69	64	273	77897
2	José Maria OLAZABAL	(Sp)	68	71	67	68	274	51924
3	Darren CLARKE	(N.Ire)	70	69	71	67	277	29259
4	Philip WALTON	(Ire)	71	70	70	67	278	21583
	Steve WEBSTER	(Eng)	68	75	65	70	278	21583
6	Lee WESTWOOD	(Eng)	69	74	69	67	279	11741
	Costantino ROCCA	(It)	71	73	69	66	279	11741
	Daren LEE	(Eng)	71	69	70	69	279	11741
	Raymond RUSSELL	(Scot)	72	70	66	71	279	11741
	Brian DAVIS	(Eng)	68	70	75	66	279	11741
	Dean ROBERTSON	(Scot)	71	69	68	71	279	11741
12	Roger WESSELS	(SA)	74	69	66	71	280	7231
	Patrik SJÖLAND	(Swe)	68	70	70	72	280	7231
	Stephen SCAHILL	(NZ)	70	72	70	68	280	7231
	Eduardo ROMERO	(Arg)	68	69	71	72	280	7231
	Jarmo SANDELIN	(Swe)	69	73	70	68	280	7231
17	Jonathan LOMAS	(Eng)	72	70	71	68	281	5756
	Manuel PIÑERO	(Sp)	70	73	70	68	281	5756
	Stephen ALLAN	(Aus)	70	74	69	68	281	5756
	Retief GOOSEN	(SA)	66	75	69	71	281	5756
	Raymond BURNS	(N.Ire)	70	71	70	70	281	5756
	Paolo QUIRICI	(Swi)	69	70	68	74	281	5756
23	José COCERES	(Arg)	68	73	73	68	282	4627
	Massimo FLORIOLI	(It)	75	69	68	70	282	4627
	Santiago LUNA	(Sp)	72	67	73	70	282	4627
	Martin GATES	(Eng)	70	73	70	69	282	4627
	Thomas GÖGELE	(Ger)	70	71	73	68	282	4627
	Mark JAMES	(Eng)	69	73	71	69	282	4627
	Ian WOOSNAM	(Wal)	67	73	73	69	282	4627
	Michel BESANCENEY	(Fr)	69	72	69	72	282	4627
	Wayne WESTNER	(SA)	69	74	68	71	282	4627
32	Van PHILLIPS	(Eng)	74	68	76	65	283	3645
	Ian GARBUTT	(Eng)	73	70	71	69	283	3645
	Robert KARLSSON	(Swe)	70	70	74	69	283	3645
	Padraig HARRINGTON	(Ire)	70	70	71	72	283	3645
	Anders GILLNER	(Swe)	71	71	70	71	283	3645
	Daniel WESTERMARK	(Swe)	71	73	67	72	283	3645
	John BICKERTON	(Eng)	71	70	71	71	283	3645
39	David HOWELL	(Eng)	72	70	69	73	284	3178
	Ariel CAÑETE	(Arg)	73	67	73	71	284	3178
	John MELLOR	(Eng)	72	70	72	70	284	3178
42	Emanuele CANONICA	(It)	72	71	73	69	285	2710
	Silvio GRAPPASONNI	(It)	71	71	71	72	285	2710
	Marco GORTANA	(It)	72	70	71	72	285	2710
	Ricky WILLISON	(Eng)	72	72	69	72	285	2710
	Thomas BJORN	(Den)	69	70	73	73	285	2710
	Greg TURNER	(NZ)	72	70	72	71	285	2710
	Mark MOULAND	(Wal)	70	71	70	74	285	2710
49	Robert COLES	(Eng)	71	72	74	69	286	2243
	Niclas FASTH	(Swe)	68	73	73	72	286	2243
	Wayne RILEY	(Aus)	70	72	73	71	286	2243
52	Steven BOTTOMLEY	(Eng)	71	72	73	71	287	2056
53	Peter BAKER	(Eng)	72	71	77	68	288	1776
	Ben TINNING	(Den)	73	71	71	73	288	1776
	David HIGGINS	(Ire)	71	72	71	74	288	1776
	Mathias GRÖNBERG	(Swe)	72	69	70	77	288	1776
	John WADE	(Aus)	72	72	75	69	288	1776
58	André BOSSERT	(Swi)	73	70	72	74	289	1448
	Marco DURANTE	(It)	73	70	75	71	289	1448
	Robert LEE	(Eng)	76	65	73	75	289	1448
61	Raphaël JACQUELIN	(Fr)	72	67	74	77	290	1332
	Stephen GALLACHER	(Scot)	71	73	74	72	290	1332
63	Christy O'CONNOR JNR	(Ire)	73	71	73	74	291	1215
	Gordon J BRAND	(Eng)	68	70	77	76	291	1215
	Carlos DURAN	(Swi)	69	74	71	77	291	1215
66	Richard GREEN	(Aus)	73	71	74	74	292	702
67	Alan TAIT	(Scot)	73	71	73	76	293	700
68	Stuart CAGE	(Eng)	72	71	74	77	294	698

Bernhard Langer's record-breaking final round.

Match: 30   Time: 11.54
04 MAY 97 .   Round: 4
. .Bernhard
LANGER   Ger
Tee: 1   71 69 69 209   64

273

54
Conte di Florence
ITALIAN OPEN

Buca	1	2	3	4	5	6	7	8	9	Out	10	11	12	13	14	15	16	17	18	In	Total
Metri	410	145	480	405	520	365	315	425	170	3235	400	470	385	410	225	365	495	175	345	3270	6505
Par	4	3	5	4	5	4	4	4	3	36	4	5	4	4	3	4	5	3	4	36	72
Score	3	3	4	4	4	4	3	3		32	5	4	4	4	2	3	4	3	3	32	64

Signature of Marker

Signature of Competitor

by Langer on 15-under-par with a 64 his arch-opponent called 'unbelievable', breaking by one the record shared by Webster, Robert Lee and Van Phillips. The German birded four of the last five holes and single-putted all five. It was a triumph for the long-handled putter to which he turned the year before and, like Woosnam, a wooden driver, to which he returned, having lost his way with metal.

'To win again after nearly two years is fantastic,' said Langer, collecting £77,897. 'To shoot a record doing it is marvellous. I'd thought I'd need a 65 or 66 to go past José Maria, so it just shows what you have to do to get the better of him now. I always knew he would be the man to beat and he's going to be a great world champion again.'

Reasons to be cheerful part four.

Norman Dabell

Clear Leaders on the Fairway.

"We have used Ransomes equipment to prepare the courses for many years during which time the company and its machines have established a sound track record. The move to go exclusively Ransomes has received the backing of all our head greenkeepers and their maintenance crews."

Jimmy Kidd, Director of Turfgrass Management at Gleneagles Golf Developments.

Ransomes®

Fairway Mowers.

First class turf demands a first class cut. That's why many of the great golf courses of the world specify Ransomes mowers. They know that Ransomes has no equals when it comes to producing the finest finish on fine turf.
Take the Ransomes "right-weight" family of fairway mowers. Each one is designed from the turf up to produce a precision cut, day in, day out, come rain or shine. From the light-treading Fairway 250 to the rugged Fairway 305, and the versatile Commander 3500DX to the 7-unit Fairway 405 which offers genuine <u>extra</u> productivity with a big 4 metre cut, there is a Ransomes fairway mower to suit every golf course, everywhere.
To stay ahead of the game in comfort and style, you won't do better than Ransomes. Ask for a no obligation demonstration and see the difference Ransomes can make to your Fairways in quality of cut, manoeuvrability and productivity. Call us today on freephone 0500 026208 for full details.

RANSOMES is an Official Supplier to the PGA European Tour.

RANSOMES CUSHMAN RYAN
For The Best Results

Ransomes, Ransomes Way, Ipswich, England IP3 9QG. Tel: 01473 270000. Fax: 01473 276300.
© Ransomes 1996. All rights reserved.

Langer defies the elements

Bernhard Langer remained imperturbable

in tempestuous conditions

at The Oxfordshire

The more you throw at Bernhard Langer the more he seems to relish the challenge. Certainly, the gods at The Oxfordshire hurled everything from gale force winds to torrential rain at the 39-year-old, and he took it all in his stride and came back for more.

The Benson and Hedges International Open, dogged as it has been in recent years by inclement weather, once again demanded enormous reserves of stamina and resilience from its winner. No one on the European Tour has more of both these elements in his make-up than Bernhard Langer, and so it was entirely appropriate that the Bavarian picked up the 49th victory of his career.

Langer, a devout Christian, was up early on Sunday to go to church, and was then transplanted from the peace and tranquillity of a morning service into an almighty storm. Clouds raced across the sky, staying just long enough to drop their load. He holed a long, snaky putt at the first and from then on never looked like letting anyone in the field or anything in the sky distract him.

However, halfway through his final round in the afternoon, the hail became so violent that play was suspended for an hour and a half. As darkness loomed, it looked a very real possibility that they might all have to come back on Monday. Langer remained imperturbable. His final round of 69 was the only round in the sixties all day and his two-stroke victory underlined how he has become one of the most dependable and indomitable players over the last two decades.

The key to his success was his putting, his Achilles heel on so many previous occasions. Wielding his long putter (supposedly so difficult to control in high winds) he was always solid on the greens and at times no less than sensational. On Friday morning, for instance, he holed putts of 10, 60, 12 and six feet on the first four holes, to start with four consecutive birdies on his way to a six under par 66.

It was a week when the

SHOT OF THE WEEK

The easy-swinging Ian Woosnam produced the week's biggest crowd-pleaser with the penultimate shot of his third round 70. On the difficult uphill 18th, he unleashed a wonderful two iron which kept low beneath the wind, almost went in, and finished six inches from the hole.

Colin Montgomerie looks for a sign.

cream, with one or two exceptions, really did come to the top. Several other Ryder Cup hopefuls dominated the leaderboard, most notably, the youngster from Worksop, Lee Westwood. The 24-year-old proved his potential once again, and was right in contention until finding water at the notorious 17th on Sunday.

Westwood received glowing tributes during the week from, among others, Ian Woosnam, who slipped in front of him into second place right at the death. They played together in the first two rounds, and the Welshman, who is anything but short off the tee, found himself being outdriven by some 40 yards. Woosnam compared his playing partner with Tiger Woods, and while that may be stretching it a little and while there have been many false dawns, Westwood really now does have the potential to be the standard bearer for a new generation in Europe.

While Europe's number one, Colin Montgomerie,

THE COURSE

Finished in 1994 and designed by Rees Jones, son of the grand master of architects, Robert Trent Jones, The Oxfordshire lies in rolling countryside, five miles from Thame. The feature hole, the par five 17th, lived up to its billing and as usual shattered as many dreams as it made.

was disappointingly blown away in the vicious winds, by contrast, the diminutive Ian Woosnam buckled down the hatches, kept his feet firmly on the ground, and finished with five birdies in the final eight holes.

And there was a pleasing return to form for Severiano Ballesteros, who had only made one cut in his previous eight tournaments and yet played 18 holes without a bogey on Friday. The Spaniard always seems to play better when he is in relaxed form off the course as well as on it, and he

Lee Westwood (above) led the new generation. Eduardo Romero's second round 65 (below) was lowest of the week.

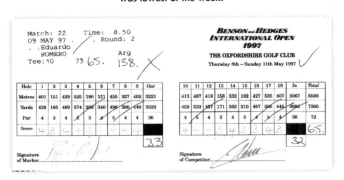

was insisting to a boisterous press room that he could still play his way into his own Ryder Cup team. 'Why you laugh?'

he asked the press corps when they obviously didn't believe him. 'I can win this week and next week. Why not? I can win the British Open.'

Despite the weather, the week was one to remember, not least because of the remarkably cosmopolitan leaderboard. With ten different nationalities in the first 12 places, a German was followed home by a Welshman, an Englishman, and Irishman, a Swede, and a Finn.

Jock Howard   III

The Oxfordshire GC, May 8-11, 1997 • Yardage 7205 • Par 72

Pos	Name	Country	Rnd 1	Rnd 2	Rnd 3	Rnd 4	Total	Prize Money £
1	Bernhard LANGER	(Ger)	70	66	71	69	276	116660
2	Ian WOOSNAM	(Wal)	70	68	70	70	278	77770
3	Lee WESTWOOD	(Eng)	69	69	70	72	280	43820
4	Padraig HARRINGTON	(Ire)	73	67	71	71	282	35000
5	Kalle VAINOLA	(Fin)	70	69	71	73	283	27070
	Robert KARLSSON	(Swe)	71	71	70	71	283	27070
7	Fabrice TARNAUD	(Fr)	75	69	67	73	284	16198
	Darren CLARKE	(N.Ire)	69	68	72	75	284	16198
	Eduardo ROMERO	(Arg)	73	65	71	75	284	16198
	Patrik SJÖLAND	(Swe)	69	69	74	72	284	16198
	Bob MAY	(USA)	69	72	71	72	284	16198
12	Thomas BJORN	(Den)	71	70	70	74	285	12040
13	Christy O'CONNOR JNR	(Ire)	68	74	70	74	286	10535
	David GILFORD	(Eng)	71	72	70	73	286	10535
	Greg TURNER	(NZ)	67	68	77	74	286	10535
	Jamie SPENCE	(Eng)	71	73	68	74	286	10535
17	Retief GOOSEN	(SA)	69	67	76	76	288	9240
	Niclas FASTH	(Swe)	70	72	72	74	288	9240
19	Andrew OLDCORN	(Scot)	75	69	74	71	289	8540
	Mark MOULAND	(Wal)	74	67	74	74	289	8540
21	Wayne WESTNER	(SA)	73	70	72	75	290	8085
	Mark JAMES	(Eng)	73	70	71	76	290	8085
23	Carl SUNESON	(Sp)	70	71	74	76	291	7245
	Paul MCGINLEY	(Ire)	72	71	72	76	291	7245
	Miguel Angel JIMÉNEZ	(Sp)	72	69	75	75	291	7245
	Peter HEDBLOM	(Swe)	71	73	73	74	291	7245
	Santiago LUNA	(Sp)	70	70	75	76	291	7245
	Iain PYMAN	(Eng)	72	69	75	75	291	7245
29	Paul LAWRIE	(Scot)	70	73	75	74	292	6020
	Ignacio GARRIDO	(Sp)	71	70	74	77	292	6020
	Sven STRÜVER	(Ger)	73	70	74	75	292	6020
	Seve BALLESTEROS	(Sp)	72	69	76	75	292	6020
	Peter MITCHELL	(Eng)	69	71	76	76	292	6020
	Ross MCFARLANE	(Eng)	70	66	78	78	292	6020
35	Steve WEBSTER	(Eng)	72	72	76	73	293	5180
	Stephen AMES	(T&T)	74	70	77	72	293	5180
	Richard GREEN	(Aus)	75	69	74	75	293	5180
	Derrick COOPER	(Eng)	71	73	73	76	293	5180
	Stephen FIELD	(Eng)	75	69	73	76	293	5180
40	Ricky WILLISON	(Eng)	73	71	71	79	294	4410
	John MURRAY	(Ire)	73	69	72	80	294	4410
	Emanuele CANONICA	(It)	73	71	79	71	294	4410
	Ignacio FELIU	(Sp)	72	71	72	79	294	4410
	Gordon BRAND JNR.	(Scot)	75	69	73	77	294	4410
	Gary ORR	(Scot)	70	74	73	77	294	4410
46	Paolo QUIRICI	(Swi)	71	71	75	78	295	3570
	David TAPPING	(Eng)	74	69	74	78	295	3570
	Philip WALTON	(Ire)	73	71	72	79	295	3570
	Andrew COLTART	(Scot)	69	75	75	76	295	3570
	Olle KARLSSON	(Swe)	75	67	80	73	295	3570
	Paul EALES	(Eng)	71	71	77	76	295	3570
52	Thomas GÖGELE	(Ger)	76	67	75	78	296	2800
	Jonathan LOMAS	(Eng)	69	72	75	80	296	2800
	Ian GARBUTT	(Eng)	74	67	77	78	296	2800
	Sam TORRANCE	(Scot)	74	70	77	75	296	2800
	Rodger DAVIS	(Aus)	73	71	76	76	296	2800
57	Paul BROADHURST	(Eng)	70	73	78	76	297	2310
	Stuart CAGE	(Eng)	74	70	74	79	297	2310
59	José COCERES	(Arg)	71	69	77	81	298	2030
	David HOWELL	(Eng)	70	71	77	80	298	2030
	Colin MONTGOMERIE	(Scot)	70	71	76	81	298	2030
	Jim PAYNE	(Eng)	72	71	78	77	298	2030
	Joakim HAEGGMAN	(Swe)	72	70	76	80	298	2030
64	Michael JONZON	(Swe)	74	70	76	79	299	1785
	Stephen ALLAN	(Aus)	72	72	76	79	299	1785
66	Gary EMERSON	(Eng)	71	71	79	80	301	1050
67	Daren LEE	(Eng)	73	71	78	80	302	1048
68	Ian MOSEY	(Eng)	73	70	80	80	303	1046

Seve Ballesteros sparkled in the second round.

SMOKING WHEN PREGNANT
HARMS YOUR BABY

Chief Medical Officers' Warning
12 mg Tar   0.9 mg Nicotine

Johansson's eagle clinches it

A spectacular eagle three at the 12th
in the final round sent him on his way
to his fourth European Tour victory

Serious students of the great game could have been on a nice little earner if they had backed the 30-year-old Swede, Per-Ulrik Johansson to win the £650,000 Alamo English Open. He was certainly a form horse having finished fifth in the tournament in1991, second in 1992, sixth in 1993 and fourth last year.

(The Editor, a stickler for accuracy, points out, however, that Johansson also finished 68th in the 1995 English Open but that doesn't count as he probably had bad biorythms that week or had eaten something that hadn't agreed with him).

'Looking at my previous results, it has been a very good tournament for me,' said Johansson, winner by two strokes after his last round of 67 had given him a 19 under par total of 269. Johansson's previous success had been in the 1996 Smurfit European Open but that had surprised him as he hadn't played particularly well.

'This week, however, I felt really good with my game and I have to thank my coach David Whelan for that. He has worked very hard with me this week. My swing is now more compact, shorter and wider and when I'm playing into the wind I grip it a bit lower for more control and greater clubhead speed,' he explained.

SHOT OF THE WEEK

In the second round Roger Chapman holed his second shot at the 410-yard tenth for an eagle two. He had hit a two iron off the tee and was left with 185 yards to the hole. He hit a five iron which covered the flag all the way but he didn't see the ball drop into the hole because the green is elevated.

Yet Johansson's presence for Media Centre interview had not been requested for the first two days. He was just another competitor in a bunch chasing Roger Chapman, the tall, lean, Kenya-born pro, who led the field after two 66s. Chapman has been one of the eternal bridesmaids since joining the Tour back in 1981 – 11 runners-up spots but nary a win. But his bank manager hasn't moaned too much down the years for Chapman's proficiency with the clubs has won him over a million pounds, titles or not.

Chapman, who was playing in the 393rd event of his career, had switched from glasses to contact lenses in a bid to break his duck and had also taken on board a sports psychologist and martial arts expert, Chris Linstead, to teach him

Third round leader Gary Emerson saw it slip away.

Room 119 wants a break from golf at Hanbury Manor.

What could be more relaxing for Colin Montgomerie than a golf break? If playing golf is your profession, quite a lot actually.

At the Marriott Hanbury Manor Hotel & Country Club, as well as a superb golf course, you'll find a whole range of leisure

 facilities. If you're looking for a golf break, or even a break from golf, there are 23 Marriott Hotels throughout

the UK, 7 of which are hotel & country clubs offering golf breaks for players at any level. For reservations

call 0800 221 222 or for our best ever value Golf Breaks brochure call 0800 444 878. | ITV Teletext p387 |

When you're comfortable you can do anything.  **Marriott**
HOTELS · RESORTS · SUITES

ABERDEEN, BIRMINGHAM, BRADFORD, BRISTOL, CARDIFF, CHEPSTOW, CHESHUNT, CHICHESTER, DERBY, EDINBURGH, GLASGOW, HEATHROW, LEEDS, LONDON, MAIDSTONE, MANCHESTER (1998), NEWCASTLE, PORTSMOUTH, PRESTON, SOUTHAMPTON (1998), SWANSEA, SWINDON, WARE.

to channel his aggression better. Horse-racing fan Roger looked back on two satisfactory days at the office and said with a smile: 'Two more 66s would be nice. I'm over Becher's Brook, now I have to get over Valentine's and then it's the Chair.'

Easier said than done, Chapman's put-ter turned cold on him – there was no truth in the rumour that someone had swopped it for a jockey's whip – and the lead on Saturday night was held by Gary Emerson, the Salisbury and South Wilts club professional, who returned a 65.

Warm sunshine and a cooling breeze promised low scores on the final day and most of the names on the leaderboard were seeking first-ever Tour victories. But Johansson had already been there, done that, got the tee shirt, and his expe-

Runner-up Dennis Edlund (below) in twirling finish. Halfway leader Roger Chapman (right).

rience of three previous Tour victories, plus a 1995 Ryder Cup appearance, was to prove invaluable.

His fellow countryman, Dennis Edlund hit the front fleetingly when he birdied three of the first four holes but Johansson then rapped back with a birdie at the tenth where he chipped in from an awkward lie followed by a spectacular eagle at the 12th where he hit his five iron approach shot 208 yards to within a foot of the stick.

'Those two holes were the big turn around,' he said. Edlund finished in second place, picking up more than £72,000, which wasn't a bad pay day for a player who was so disillusioned he was set to quit the Tour in 1995.

Johansson is a wine connoisseur and the first slice of his £108,330 winnings that evening went on an expensive bottle of Chateau Margaux. Now here's a thought. Maybe it's the good wines they sell at places like The Belfry, the Forest of Arden and Hanbury Manor, that help him play so well in the English Open.

Frank Clough

THE COURSE

Hanbury Manor is a parkland course just outside Ware, about 25 miles North of London. Originally it comprised only nine holes designed by former Open Champion Harry Vardon but in recent years it has been extended to 18 holes and championship length by Jack Nicklaus Junior and the Women's Tour held an event there in 1996. Its greens are reputed to be among the best in Britain.

MARRIOTT HANBURY MANOR HOTEL, MAY 15-18, 1997 · YARDAGE 7016 · PAR 72

Pos	Name	Country	Rnd 1	Rnd 2	Rnd 3	Rnd 4	Total	Prize Money £
1	Per-Ulrik JOHANSSON	(Swe)	70	68	64	67	269	108330
2	Dennis EDLUND	(Swe)	68	65	69	69	271	72210
3	Jay TOWNSEND	(USA)	72	63	70	67	272	36595
	Steve WEBSTER	(Eng)	68	66	70	68	272	36595
5	David HOWELL	(Eng)	70	70	66	67	273	25140
	Roger CHAPMAN	(Eng)	66	66	71	70	273	25140
7	Sam TORRANCE	(Scot)	73	67	67	67	274	17875
	Russell CLAYDON	(Eng)	69	69	66	70	274	17875
9	Mark JAMES	(Eng)	72	67	69	67	275	14510
10	Gary EMERSON	(Eng)	68	68	65	75	276	12480
	Gary ORR	(Scot)	71	70	71	64	276	12480
12	Ian GARBUTT	(Eng)	75	66	67	69	277	9091
	Phillip PRICE	(Wal)	73	68	67	69	277	9091
	Colin MONTGOMERIE	(Scot)	72	68	70	67	277	9091
	Darren CLARKE	(N.Ire)	72	64	70	71	277	9091
	Miguel Angel MARTIN	(Sp)	73	68	66	70	277	9091
	Silvio GRAPPASONNI	(It)	72	66	71	68	277	9091
	Stephen MCALLISTER	(Scot)	71	69	67	70	277	9091
	Clinton WHITELAW	(SA)	73	67	68	69	277	9091
	Stephen AMES	(T&T)	68	72	69	68	277	9091
	Niclas FASTH	(Swe)	70	70	68	69	277	9091
22	Paul LAWRIE	(Scot)	68	73	66	71	278	7117
	José Maria OLAZABAL	(Sp)	69	72	69	68	278	7117
	Lee WESTWOOD	(Eng)	72	64	69	73	278	7117
	Robert KARLSSON	(Swe)	71	67	73	67	278	7117
26	Carl SUNESON	(Sp)	68	74	69	68	279	6045
	Daniel CHOPRA	(Swe)	70	70	68	71	279	6045
	Peter BAKER	(Eng)	71	69	67	72	279	6045
	Miguel Angel JIMÉNEZ	(Sp)	68	72	69	70	279	6045
	Eduardo ROMERO	(Arg)	73	68	65	73	279	6045
	Rodger DAVIS	(Aus)	72	68	70	69	279	6045
	David CARTER	(Eng)	73	67	71	68	279	6045
33	Thomas GÖGELE	(Ger)	67	70	68	75	280	4875
	Tony JOHNSTONE	(Zim)	73	66	70	71	280	4875
	Andrew COLTART	(Scot)	73	67	70	70	280	4875
	Katsuyoshi TOMORI	(Jap)	71	70	68	71	280	4875
	Peter LONARD	(Aus)	71	70	70	69	280	4875
	Wayne RILEY	(Aus)	69	71	70	70	280	4875
	Raymond BURNS	(N.Ire)	73	67	69	71	280	4875
	José COCERES	(Arg)	73	64	72	71	280	4875
41	Mark MCNULTY	(Zim)	70	69	70	72	281	4030
	Paul AFFLECK	(Wal)	72	69	70	70	281	4030
	Stuart CAGE	(Eng)	71	70	67	73	281	4030
	Per HAUGSRUD	(Nor)	70	69	73	69	281	4030
	Massimo FLORIOLI	(It)	75	66	69	71	281	4030
46	Ross DRUMMOND	(Scot)	70	71	72	69	282	3185
	Fredrik JACOBSON	(Swe)	72	70	72	68	282	3185
	Paolo QUIRICI	(Swi)	71	71	68	72	282	3185
	John MELLOR	(Eng)	69	73	70	70	282	3185
	Brian DAVIS	(Eng)	68	73	69	72	282	3185
	Francisco VALERA	(Sp)	72	68	71	71	282	3185
	Anders FORSBRAND	(Swe)	70	72	69	71	282	3185
	Pedro LINHART	(Sp)	71	71	71	69	282	3185
54	Peter MITCHELL	(Eng)	72	70	68	73	283	2600
55	Iain PYMAN	(Eng)	73	67	75	69	284	2275
	Carl WATTS	(Eng)	71	69	72	72	284	2275
	Joakim HAEGGMAN	(Swe)	73	69	69	73	284	2275
	Mats HALLBERG	(Swe)	68	71	73	72	284	2275
59	Jim PAYNE	(Eng)	70	72	67	76	285	1885
	Steven BOTTOMLEY	(Eng)	69	73	70	73	285	1885
	Robert LEE	(Eng)	69	72	69	75	285	1885
	Jarmo SANDELIN	(Swe)	72	70	69	74	285	1885
	Santiago LUNA	(Sp)	73	69	69	74	285	1885
64	Jean VAN DE VELDE	(Fr)	74	68	73	71	286	1657
	Gary CLARK	(Eng)	71	68	75	72	286	1657
66	Wayne WESTNER	(SA)	71	71	73	72	287	975
67	Jamie SPENCE	(Eng)	70	72	70	77	289	973
68	David HIGGINS	(Ire)	71	70	73	76	290	971

Jay Townsend's (above) second round set the course record.

Match: 27 Time: 12.15
16 MAY 97 Round: 2
.Jay TOWNSEND USA
Tee: 1 72 63. 135.

Alamo English Open ✓

Hanbury Manor Golf and Country Club, Hertfordshire
Thursday 15th – Sunday 18th May 1997

Hole	1	2	3	4	5	6	7	8	9	Out	10	11	12	13	14	15	16	17	18	In	Total
Metres	317	512	405	171	424	173	330	425	503	3260	377	193	494	378	361	371	169	453	357	3153	6413
Yards	347	560	443	187	464	189	361	465	550	3566	412	211	540	414	395	406	185	496	391	3450	7016
Par										36	4									36	72
Score	3	4	4	3	4	3	3	4	4	32	4	2	4	3	4	4	2	4	4	31	63

Signature of Marker...........

Signature of Competitor...........

Your Nº1 Driver

For a 24 hour a day chauffeur service, simply call 0345 886688

OFFICIAL SPONSORS OF THE 1997 ENGLISH OPEN

 Alamo Chauffeur Service features Vauxhall cars

Alamo

Chauffeur Service

Montgomerie the magnificent

Colin Montgomerie swept all before him
at The Buckinghamshire

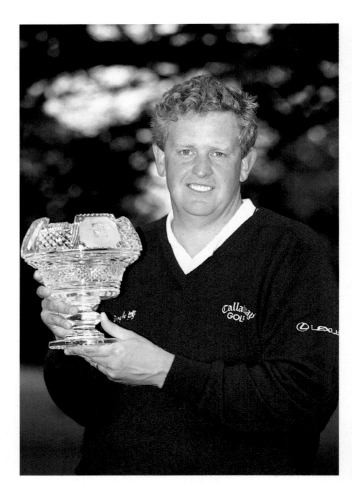

There are times when Colin Montgomerie is invincible. Ample evidence of that came in the Andersen Consulting European Championship, and the witnesses and victims at The Buckinghamshire Club were José Maria Olazábal, Sam Torrance and Costantino Rocca. Montgomerie moved past them one by one to put himself forward as a strong candidate for the Andersen Consulting World Championship of Golf in Arizona in January where his reward, if successful, will be $1 million.

At The Buckinghamshire Club he earned $200,000 (£121,689), and he was worth every penny. Montgomerie, quite simply, was magnificent. In the first round against Olazábal, the Scot sparkled from tee to green, albeit that his putting touch was by his own admission less than satisfactory. However, Montgomerie virtually dispensed with the need to use his putter when he struck a six iron to three feet at the 14th and a five iron to four feet at the 16th. So Olazábal, who beat Montgomerie

5 and 4 in the final of the 1984 Amateur Championship, went out as did Ian Woosnam, who lost to Sam Torrance 4 and 3, Bernhard Langer, beaten 2 and 1 by Darren Clarke, and Jesper Parnevik, who went down at the 20th to Costantino Rocca.

Torrance, who represented Europe in the previous season's Andersen Consulting World Championship of Golf, was six under when he beat Woosnam. He needed to improve on that to contend with Montgomerie. It was not to be. Montgomerie, out in 31, turned four up and he was seven under when he won 6 and 4. What is more he had his putting touch back. He had arranged for Callaway to deliver three new putters the previous evening, but it was his diligence that was rewarded. From 6.00am to 7.30, as the greenstaff went to work on the course, he worked alone on the practice putting green. In all he holed 200 putts from two feet. 'I don't think I've ever worked so hard on any aspect of my game,' he said.

Rocca joined Montgomerie in the final by beating Clarke at the 19th. Three up after four holes, Clarke seemed assured of victory but the fascination of match-play is that once a lead begins to disappear then the pressure mounts. Rocca got onto a

THE COURSE

The Buckinghamshire Club, set in 226 acres of magnificent English parkland eighteen miles west of London in Denham, was opened for play in September 1992. Designed by John Jacobs, the course has been highly praised and the variety of holes lend themselves well to match-play. With the fairway dissected by two streams, and a lake to the right of the green, a watery grave awaits anything other than an accurate shot at the seventh, while the 17th plays every inch of its 470 yards as it plays uphill, often into the prevailing wind, and dog-legs left around a majestic circle of mature oaks.

Colin Montgomerie (right) was centre stage at the prize-giving. Costantino Rocca (opposite) found little joy against Montgomerie.

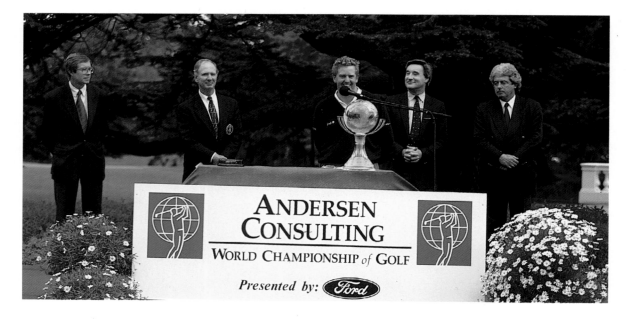

SHOT OF THE WEEK

In match-play there is only one sure way to win – shut the door when you have the chance. Colin Montgomerie did exactly this in the first round against José Maria Olazábal. Montgomerie had not dropped a shot, but he was still only one ahead playing the 16th – having watched Olazábal hole from 30 feet on the previous green. But the Scot struck a five iron approach at the 16th with such authority that the putt was just a formality – the door had been shut.

roll, took the match to extra time then at the first extra hole got down in two from the water's edge to win.

The prospect of a close encounter in the final dawned when Rocca won the opening hole, but it disappeared the moment that Montgomerie began to wave that putter like the proverbial magic wand again. He holed from 30 feet at the second, from 15 feet to go one up at the third, notched six birdies in all to turn in 30 and by the 11th was five up.

To Rocca's credit he countered by winning the 13th, but Montgomerie brought the curtain down at the next. In two matches in one day, he had collected 13 birdies and an eagle without playing the last four holes. 'My game has rarely felt as good as then,' he said. 'Whatever happens this year, I can now look forward to spending New Year in Arizona and emulating the European Tour's Barry Lane, who won the first Andersen Consulting World Championship of Golf.'

Mitchell Platts   125

Woosnam's happy anniversary

Nine years after his first

Volvo **PGA** Championship victory

Ian Woosnam was celebrating again

*I*n 1988 Volvo took over the sponsorship of the PGA Championship, injected a healthy prize fund and set about making the event the showpiece of the European Tour. The winner on that occasion was a 30-year-old Welshman by the name of Ian Woosnam whose total of 274 gave him the winner's cheque for £50,000 by two strokes from Severiano Ballesteros and Mark James. Bernhard Langer finished seventh and Nick Faldo tenth.

Plus ça change plus ça même chose. The Championship is now established as *the* event on the Tour, a Bank Holiday gathering which, this year, attracted record crowds, prize-money stood at a record £1.1 million with £183,340 going to the winner. And whose name headed the leaderboard at the end of 72-holes? None other than that same Welshman, this time with an aggregate of 275 to win by two shots from Darren Clarke, Ernie Els and his old adversary, Nick Faldo.

A week in politics may be a long time but nine years in golf must seem incalculable. Yet there was very little difference between Ian Woosnam, circa 1988, and Ian Woosnam, circa 1997. The same uncomplicated swing sent the ball down the fairway, the step was as jaunty as ever and even the putter, often a source of mistrust in the past, was behaving itself.

Those observers with the retentive capacity of a herd of elephants may have

SHOT OF THE WEEK

Scotland's Dean Robertson made a perfect start to the Championship when he holed his second shot to the 471-yard first hole in his opening round. He struck a five iron into the hole from 181 yards to record the first eagle there anyone could remember in top-class competition.

noted the significance of Woosnam's opening round of 67, the same as his start in 1988, but their attention was probably diverted by the attention given to Clarke and Eamonn Darcy. Both were round in 66 to give Ireland a lock on top.

Clarke was five under par on the par fives but stated that the key was his improved temperament: 'I keep my head on better than I used to,' he said. Darcy's day was saved by a visit to the Tour's 3M physiotherapy unit. A stiff back could have caused him to withdraw but the magic was applied, appropriately in this Year of the Tiger, by a potion called Tiger Balm, a mix of menthol and camphor which is made in Singapore. Now able to

Colin Montgomerie in full bloom.

Nick Faldo in the rough, putting ice on a nose bleed, and under the watchful gaze of Fanny.

swing freely, Darcy picked up four birdies in the first six holes and thoroughly earned his stripes for the day. Joining Woosnam on 67 were Robert Karlsson, David Gilford, Andrew Sherborne and Langer with Colin Montgomerie and Els lurking on 69 and Faldo tucked in handily on 70.

A swirling wind fortified Wentworth's defences on the second day but it did not prevent Woosnam from breezing in at lunchtime with a 68 to set a halfway target of 135. Faldo, with an outward 31, made light of the conditions and moved to within two of Woosnam with a 67 and was joined by Gilford on the same mark.

Montgomerie, aided by two chip-ins, produced another 69 but Clarke fell back with a 74 and was joined by Els on 140. The cut fell at 147 and the most notable casualty was Ballesteros who withdrew before the second round with severe back pains.

The third day saw over 17,000 people pour through the gates, most of them it appeared, intent on following the penultimate pairing of Faldo and Montgomerie. Neither of them were in peak form. Montgomerie suffered a double bogey on the third, then three-putted the short fifth and the heart seemed to go out of his game and he eventually laboured in with 76. Faldo also struggled. He suffered a nose-bleed on the 11th, 'the excitement was too much for me', missed a short putt on

3M is Proud to be an Official Sponsor of the European Tour

3M is delighted to be providing a state of the art physiotherapy for the golfers in what is an ideal partnership for the company. 3M has extensive experience in the development of innovative, high-quality, health care products, available on demand in the 3M European Tour Physio Unit.

The European Tour features the world's best players in high profile, positive association with 3M. But sponsorship goes far beyond showcasing 3M products across Europe. The European Tour is a way to attract people's participation in a healthy, outdoor sport that can be played by all ages.

3M's Physio Unit, a fully-equipped, mobile physical therapy unit, supports European Tour Events. Within the unit minor injuries can be immediately treated by one of the three permanent standby physiotherapists. The Physio Unit is a travelling showpiece for the 3M brand and a wide variety of innovative 3M products.

3M *Innovation*

THE COURSE

Once again, Course Super-intendent Chris Kennedy presented the West Course in immaculate condition for the Championship. The only threat to his handiwork came from a fire on Chobham Common three days before the start. At one point the fire crossed the railway line to the left of the ninth fairway and some trees were lost. 'I wasn't worried about the players burning up the course, but the real thing,' said Kennedy.

the 17th and then took two shots to escape from a fairway bunker on the 18th. A putt from fully 50 feet on the 18th green for his par put him round in 70 and the damage had been limited.

Woosnam had moved two clear with birdies at the third and fourth but a flyer to the ninth green put him among the silver birches and he took six. This put him back into a share of the lead with Els who had just eagled the 12th. Birdies at the

Out of the trees from Ernie Els (above), and out of the sand from Angel Cabrera (opposite).

12th and 17th put Woosnam in the driver's seat again but his closest challenger emerged in the shape of Clarke who was round in 66. Stephen Ames would have been within two strokes of Woosnam but for a rules infringement on the 12th green when his ball moved while he was addressing it. He failed to replace the ball back in its original spot so the two-stroke penalty he incurred turned a 68 into a 70.

Patience was a virtue that Woosnam had to possess in large quantities at the start of the final round. While Clarke birdied the fourth and the eighth, the Welshman churned out nine successive pars to the turn to trail the Ulsterman by one. Faldo had also moved up with Woosnam after an outward 33.

In the space of three holes, the

danger from Clarke was removed when he bunkered his tee shot and barely made it over the ditch with his second. Woosnam took his par quietly and the title was his.

Clarke, Els and Faldo made a formidable trio in the runners-up spot and Montgomerie made amends for his third round lapse with a sparkling 64, a 12 stroke disparity which was out of

Sandmen at work. Darren Clarke (left), Lian-Wei Zhang (above) and Berhard Langer (below).

Championship took on a different complexion. Woosnam birdied the 12th and 14th while Clarke dropped a shot at the 13th. Faldo also dropped a stroke at the 14th and from then on neither he nor Els could find the bottom of the cup.

Woosnam missed a short putt on the 15th for par but Clarke three-putted there so the margin between them was two. Clark hit the 17th in two but Woosnam had to lay up after his drive finished in the rough. He then pitched up dead and the margin was preserved. Woosnam hooked into the rough off the 18th tee but any

character from the Tour's most consistent performer.

'It gives your confidence a boost to win against one of our strongest fields,' said Woosnam afterwards. 'It was difficult today with the wind swirling around. Wentworth does fetch the best out of players. You need experience here.'

Nine years ago, Woosnam had enjoyed the experience of a victory in the Volvo PGA Championship. The only surprising thing was that it took him so long to repeat it.

Chris Plumridge   135

WENTWORTH CLUB, MAY 23-26, 1997 · YARDAGE 6957 · PAR 72

Pos	Name	Country	Rnd 1	Rnd 2	Rnd 3	Rnd 4	Total	Prize Money £
1	Ian WOOSNAM	(Wal)	67	68	70	70	275	183340
2	Darren CLARKE	(N.Ire)	66	74	66	71	277	82023
	Nick FALDO	(Eng)	70	67	70	70	277	82023
	Ernie ELS	(SA)	69	71	67	70	277	82023
5	Colin MONTGOMERIE	(Scot)	69	69	76	64	278	46640
6	David GILFORD	(Eng)	67	70	72	70	279	35750
	Angel CABRERA	(Arg)	73	67	70	69	279	35750
8	Dennis EDLUND	(Swe)	70	72	68	70	280	27500
9	Lee WESTWOOD	(Eng)	70	72	70	69	281	24530
10	Barry LANE	(Eng)	69	72	69	72	282	22000
11	Eamonn DARCY	(Ire)	66	75	76	67	284	18930
	Eduardo ROMERO	(Arg)	71	70	70	73	284	18930
	Frank NOBILO	(NZ)	68	71	77	68	284	18930
14	Philip WALTON	(Ire)	69	72	70	74	285	15510
	Raymond BURNS	(N.Ire)	72	71	72	70	285	15510
	Carl MASON	(Eng)	73	71	69	72	285	15510
	David CARTER	(Eng)	68	74	70	73	285	15510
	Stephen AMES	(T&T)	70	69	70	76	285	15510
19	Peter HEDBLOM	(Swe)	73	71	75	67	286	12388
	José Maria OLAZABAL	(Sp)	72	71	73	70	286	12388
	Miguel Angel MARTIN	(Sp)	70	75	67	74	286	12388
	Thomas BJORN	(Den)	68	74	75	69	286	12388
	Iain PYMAN	(Eng)	71	73	73	69	286	12388
	Ronan RAFFERTY	(N.Ire)	74	72	72	68	286	12388
	Jon ROBSON	(Eng)	71	71	71	73	286	12388
	Paul CURRY	(Eng)	71	74	71	70	286	12388
27	Mark DAVIS	(Eng)	70	73	73	71	287	10230
	José COCERES	(Arg)	74	72	72	69	287	10230
	André BOSSERT	(Swi)	73	70	75	69	287	10230
	Peter O'MALLEY	(Aus)	73	71	72	71	287	10230
	Carl SUNESON	(Sp)	73	72	69	73	287	10230
32	Andrew OLDCORN	(Scot)	72	71	74	71	288	8800
	Retief GOOSEN	(SA)	73	74	69	72	288	8800
	Bernhard LANGER	(Ger)	67	75	76	70	288	8800
	Vijay SINGH	(Fij)	70	73	73	72	288	8800
	Gary EMERSON	(Eng)	71	70	75	72	288	8800
37	Sam TORRANCE	(Scot)	71	75	71	72	289	7370
	Marc FARRY	(Fr)	68	78	72	71	289	7370
	Paul BROADHURST	(Eng)	72	75	73	69	289	7370
	Mark ROE	(Eng)	72	73	71	73	289	7370
	Dean ROBERTSON	(Scot)	72	74	73	70	289	7370
	Per-Ulrik JOHANSSON	(Swe)	70	75	74	70	289	7370
	Diego BORREGO	(Sp)	70	75	74	70	289	7370
	Roger CHAPMAN	(Eng)	71	75	69	74	289	7370
45	Emanuele CANONICA	(It)	74	73	69	74	290	5940
	Ian GARBUTT	(Eng)	71	73	72	74	290	5940
	Wayne WESTNER	(SA)	74	70	71	75	290	5940
	Gary EVANS	(Eng)	71	75	74	70	290	5940
	Joakim HAEGGMAN	(Swe)	69	76	72	73	290	5940
50	Clinton WHITELAW	(SA)	69	78	71	73	291	4950
	Gary ORR	(Scot)	67	78	73	73	291	4950
	Ignacio GARRIDO	(Sp)	74	73	73	71	291	4950
	Peter TERAVAINEN	(USA)	74	73	71	73	291	4950
54	Klas ERIKSSON	(Swe)	70	71	78	73	292	3868
	Stuart CAGE	(Eng)	71	75	73	73	292	3868
	Miguel Angel JIMÉNEZ	(Sp)	75	71	70	76	292	3868
	Jarmo SANDELIN	(Swe)	72	71	70	79	292	3868
	Robert ALLENBY	(Aus)	73	72	76	71	292	3868
	Manuel PIÑERO	(Sp)	73	74	75	70	292	3868
60	Jay TOWNSEND	(USA)	74	71	73	75	293	3080
	Ross MCFARLANE	(Eng)	74	71	70	78	293	3080
	Padraig HARRINGTON	(Ire)	74	73	73	73	293	3080
	Niclas FASTH	(Swe)	72	75	71	75	293	3080
	Anders FORSBRAND	(Swe)	75	70	75	73	293	3080
65	Robert KARLSSON	(Swe)	67	76	80	71	294	1867
	Des SMYTH	(Ire)	71	72	78	73	294	1867
	Gordon BRAND JNR.	(Scot)	76	71	73	74	294	1867
	Alex CEJKA	(Ger)	74	72	74	74	294	1867
	Costantino ROCCA	(It)	70	76	71	77	294	1867
70	Mathias GRÖNBERG	(Swe)	73	72	70	80	295	1641
	Fernando ROCA	(Sp)	76	71	76	72	295	1641
72	David HIGGINS	(Ire)	72	75	76	73	296	1637
	Juan Carlos PIÑERO	(Sp)	71	71	80	74	296	1637
74	Greg TURNER	(NZ)	74	73	79	71	297	1634
75	Kevin DICKENS	(Eng)	73	74	78	73	298	1632
76	Bradley HUGHES	(Aus)	72	75	77	75	299	1630
77	Wayne RILEY	(Aus)	72	74	78	77	301	1628
78	Jonathan LOMAS	(Eng)	73	74	78	80	305	1625
	Tony CHARNLEY	(Eng)	76	71	82	76	305	1625

Unisys and The PGA

European Tour

Unisys is dedicated to delivering the benefits of information management. We are one of a select group of companies who combine our technical and business expertise to help our clients improve their business.

Unisys has worked with the European Tour to develop systems which provide the information they need; where they need it and when they need it.

We have gone beyond supplying computerised results to providing complete information services from consultancy to implementation and full internet services.

As part of our sports marketing programme Unisys is proud to have been associated with the PGA European Tour, and The Open Championship since 1980.

http://www.unisys.com

When information is everything.

McFarlane's moment to savour

Years of patience and effort were rewarded
when Ross McFarlane broke through
for his maiden European Tour victory

Many are the men who trundle the barrow of goods and chattels that forms their golf game around the tournament venues of Europe. Journeymen, they call them, wandering tinkers who are prepared to roam far and wide in their efforts to turn an honest bob. They know the best for which they can reasonably hope is the occasional top ten finish, the even rarer top five. Winning is a dream so distant that it can really only be imagined as an abstract concept. Ross McFarlane, if he will forgive the liberty, is just such a man.

McFarlane is a player whose talent has never been matched by achievement. For years he has struck the ball as well as anybody around, but there has always seemed to be somebody who, on any given week, was striking just that little bit better. As recently as 1993 he had had to go back to the European Tour Qualifying School to get his playing rights back.

And then, suddenly and quite without warning, it all came right. It happened in a breezy corner of northern Germany in early June, and it obviously surprised McFarlane as much as anybody else. If ever the old saw about tournaments not being won until the last nine holes on Sunday was bang on the button, this was it. McFarlane left his bid to win the Deutsche Bank Open-Tournament Players' Championship of Europe so late it was almost too late. But not quite.

With eight holes to go he was out of it. And then this cheery, slightly round-shouldered son of Manchester suddenly produced the golf of a champion as he rampaged through the field to take the title, £125,000 and a precious five-year exemption for being the Tournament Players' Champion with a total of 282, six under par. His ever-distinctive walk, which makes him look as if he is constantly trying to keep up with a hurrying nose, suddenly had a hint of a swagger about it. He was entitled to it.

He was nowhere to be seen on the first day, after which Paul Broadhurst led with a 68 that contained a parsimonious

THE COURSE

The Gut Kaden course was for a number of years a layout of vivid contrasts, with its long-established front nine and an inward half that was very much newer. It is a tribute to the team that runs the course that the difference is becoming less obvious as the years go on. In a tournament that was bedevilled by a cruel wind, it retained its ability to reward good golf. Ross McFarlane would attest to that.

27 putts. He was one of an elite band of only 26 players to beat par on a cold and windy day in Schleswig-Holstein.

There were any number of small sub-plots as much of the field seemed caught in a state of suspended animation. Sam Torrance had to give best to a neck injury and was replaced by Warren Bennett, who played nine holes before dropping out himself with, would you believe it, a neck injury. Two withdrawals in the same group on the same day – Miguel Angel Jimenez and Jamie Spence, the other two in the three-ball, must have thought it was something they had said.

McFarlane was similarly out of the picture on day two, when the pace was taken up by Van Phillips, he of the goatee beard and nattty line in neckwear. If anybody had been looking for a winner as the cut was

made on Friday night, it would surely not have been McFarlane. He played much

better on the third day with a 66, but was still by no means the favourite as the final day dawned as chilly and blustery as the previous three. That unsolicited tag would probably have been awarded to Howard Clark, 12 times a European winner, Gordon Brand Junior, who has eight victories to his name or Anders Forsbrand, who has won six times. Forsbrand, Clark and Thomas Bjorn shared the lead on six under par, McFarlane? Not present on the leaderboard for the third day.

Brand went into the lead on seven under par when he sank his second birdie putt of the day on the sixth, and held that advantage to the moment he missed a short putt for par on the 13th. Up to then the Bristol-based Scot had looked the likely

Gordon Brand Junior was in the running for the title.

Anders Forsbrand shared second place.

winner. Surely he would hold on; he had trodden the victory path before. He knew how to win, and if he forgot, there was always Forsbrand, the enigmatic Swede, to take up the baton.

Few would have given McFarlane a second thought as the tournament moved towards its closing stages. If he was a contender at all, the double-bogey six he ran up after driving into a ditch on the tenth seemed certain to eliminate him from the contest. But this was a man on a mission, and if it looked an impossible one as he trudged off that tenth green it became possible, then probable, then highly likely as he birdied the next three holes with putts of ten, 15 and 25 feet, overtaking Brand as he did so. He was never again headed as he finished with a 71 to give himself a belated birthday

present – he passed 36 the week before.

'I'm not quite sure how I'm supposed to feel,' he said as he lifted a beer bottle to his lips afterwards with a hand that was still shaking slightly with the emotion of it all. 'It's fantastic. I'm sure it will begin to sink in sooner or later, but all I feel right now is excited.'

Brand was eventually to finish joint second with Forsbrand, a shot behind McFarlane, while the most significant move came from Darren Clarke, who had a 69, the best score of the day, to finish fourth.

All of these men had reason to be pleased with themselves. They had achieved much in this windswept corner of northern Germany and had gone away happy. After they had all disappeared, McFarlane was still savouring his big moment. His 15 minutes of fame had stretched into hours; he was not willing to let it go just yet.

Mel Webb

SHOT OF THE WEEK

Ross McFarlane, fourth round, 11th hole. McFarlane had just had a double-bogey six on the tenth and was desperately in need of something to lift him back into contention. He got it with a beautifully crisp four iron that drew the ball in to ten feet against a powerful left-to-right wind. He was back on track. It was the defining moment of his round, his tournament, his career, even.

GUT KADEN, HAMBURG, MAY 29 - JUNE 1, 1997 · YARDAGE 7029 · PAR 72

Pos	Name	Country	Rnd 1	Rnd 2	Rnd 3	Rnd 4	Total	Prize Money £
1	Ross MCFARLANE	(Eng)	70	73	68	71	282	125000
2	Anders FORSBRAND	(Swe)	73	68	69	73	283	65130
	Gordon BRAND JNR.	(Scot)	72	72	67	72	283	65130
4	Darren CLARKE	(N.Ire)	74	72	68	70	284	37500
5	Roger WESSELS	(SA)	70	75	70	70	285	24817
	Paul MCGINLEY	(Ire)	72	73	66	74	285	24817
	Raymond RUSSELL	(Scot)	72	72	70	71	285	24817
	Miguel Angel MARTIN	(Sp)	69	71	76	69	285	24817
9	Adam HUNTER	(Scot)	73	72	68	73	286	12632
	Scott HENDERSON	(Scot)	73	70	71	72	286	12632
	Peter MITCHELL	(Eng)	71	72	69	74	286	12632
	Thomas BJORN	(Den)	72	72	66	76	286	12632
	Robert ALLENBY	(Aus)	76	70	70	70	286	12632
	Howard CLARK	(Eng)	73	69	68	76	286	12632
	David CARTER	(Eng)	70	75	70	71	286	12632
	Ben TINNING	(Den)	72	70	71	73	286	12632
	Katsuyoshi TOMORI	(Jap)	73	70	72	71	286	12632
18	Andrew SANDYWELL	(Eng)	76	70	69	72	287	8937
	Paul BROADHURST	(Eng)	68	76	71	72	287	8937
	Retief GOOSEN	(SA)	70	71	72	74	287	8937
	Van PHILLIPS	(Eng)	71	68	74	74	287	8937
	Santiago LUNA	(Sp)	72	72	68	75	287	8937
	Michael JONZON	(Swe)	72	73	69	73	287	8937
24	Emanuele CANONICA	(It)	70	70	74	74	288	7200
	Angel CABRERA	(Arg)	73	70	75	70	288	7200
	Jamie SPENCE	(Eng)	73	73	70	72	288	7200
	Tony JOHNSTONE	(Zim)	70	73	73	72	288	7200
	Rodger DAVIS	(Aus)	72	72	72	72	288	7200
	Jon ROBSON	(Eng)	70	71	73	74	288	7200
	Paul AFFLECK	(Wal)	73	73	71	71	288	7200
	Mats HALLBERG	(Swe)	71	72	75	70	288	7200
	Darren COLE	(Aus)	72	74	69	73	288	7200
33	Mark MOULAND	(Wal)	72	73	73	71	289	6000
	Malcolm MACKENZIE	(Eng)	72	72	70	75	289	6000
	Alex CEJKA	(Ger)	73	73	70	73	289	6000
36	Niclas FASTH	(Swe)	71	75	73	71	290	4950
	Simon HURLEY	(Eng)	70	76	69	75	290	4950
	Michel BESANCENEY	(Fr)	72	72	71	75	290	4950
	Silvio GRAPPASONNI	(It)	72	71	74	73	290	4950
	Ross DRUMMOND	(Scot)	72	73	70	75	290	4950
	Roger CHAPMAN	(Eng)	70	73	71	76	290	4950
	Alberto BINAGHI	(It)	69	73	70	78	290	4950
	Barry LANE	(Eng)	69	72	74	75	290	4950
	Ronan RAFFERTY	(N.Ire)	73	71	70	76	290	4950
	Pedro LINHART	(Sp)	73	71	71	75	290	4950
	Bob MAY	(USA)	74	72	71	73	290	4950
47	Diego BORREGO	(Sp)	75	70	69	77	291	3825
	Phillip PRICE	(Wal)	75	70	71	75	291	3825
	Robert LEE	(Eng)	74	72	71	74	291	3825
	Thomas GÖGELE	(Ger)	79	67	70	75	291	3825
51	John WADE	(Aus)	73	73	75	71	292	3375
	Dean ROBERTSON	(Scot)	70	73	74	75	292	3375
53	Francisco VALERA	(Sp)	75	71	70	77	293	2850
	Carl SUNESON	(Sp)	71	73	78	71	293	2850
	Gary EMERSON	(Eng)	73	73	76	71	293	2850
	Paul EALES	(Eng)	74	72	74	73	293	2850
	Ignacio GARRIDO	(Sp)	71	73	74	75	293	2850
58	Mats LANNER	(Swe)	74	72	71	77	294	2250
	Mike MCLEAN	(Eng)	73	73	72	76	294	2250
	Michael CAMPBELL	(NZ)	75	67	74	78	294	2250
	David GILFORD	(Eng)	73	72	73	76	294	2250
	Mathias GRÖNBERG	(Swe)	70	71	71	82	294	2250
63	Gary CLARK	(Eng)	72	73	75	75	295	1743
	Mark DAVIS	(Eng)	73	72	71	79	295	1743
	Jarmo SANDELIN	(Swe)	72	74	72	77	295	1743
	Daren LEE	(Eng)	75	71	69	80	295	1743
67	Jeff HAWKES	(SA)	74	72	75	80	301	1123

Ben Tinning
was tied on
cloud nine.

One Market. One Bank.

Deutsche Bank

Montgomerie aims for number five

Victory at Slaley Hall put Colin Montgomerie

back into contention for a record-breaking

fifth consecutive Volvo Ranking title

Colin Montgomerie's decision to alter his schedule and play in the Compaq European Grand Prix at Slaley Hall instead of taking the week off to prepare for the US Open was the best news the tournament organisers could have had.

It got even better when he won with a record-equalling final round of 65 and the crowds flocked to watch Europe's number one finish five shots ahead of South African Retief Goosen who made an impressive fist of defending his title.

Montgomerie was more than impressed with the numbers who turned out

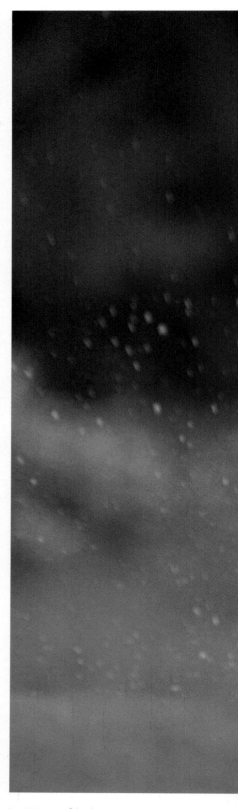

Lee Westwood (top)
continued to impress.
Peter Hedblom (left)
didn't bloom. Australia's
Matthew Goggin (above)
gets out from down under.

to watch the action over the beautiful but demanding Dave Thomas-designed course and he had his own version of the 'Toon-Army' on the last day. They weren't disappointed with him rattling in seven birdies in the last 11 holes, covering the back nine in 30 for his closing 65. 'This tournament has proved that there is golfing life 'North of Watford,' said Montgomerie after being presented with the impressive trophy by Joe McNally, the managing director of Compaq UK. 'We need tournaments like this, sponsors like Compaq and venues like Slaley Hall. It's a great, great venue and the week was everything I thought it would be – I'll be back to defend this title.'

Montgomerie opened with 69 to be

147

THE COURSE

Work has started on a second course at Slaley Hall. Designed by Neil Coles, the new course is reputed to match and even surpass some of the spectacular views of the original and is due to open in 1998. It's not difficult to believe given the stunning setting of the Tyne Valley which Dave Thomas enthused over when he first saw the 1,000 acre Slaley Hall estate. Thomas's 7,053-yard design has become the flagship course in the north-east alongside the five star hotel. During the year several changes were made to the original lay-out in order to prepare for the Compaq European Grand Prix. On the advice of the European Tour, the sloping par five 11th green was made less severe and a couple of tee changes were also made.

SHOT OF THE WEEK

Colin Montgomerie's final round of 65 contained so many wonderful strokes that several would have qualified for the shot of the week. His approach to the 18th which left him a putt of ten feet to equal the Slaley Hall course record would have been a popular choice but undoubtedly it was his wedge at the raised tenth which covered a pin, pitched beyond. spun back and lipped out for what would have been a spectacular eagle.

three shots adrift of Steve Webster but a second round 68 put him right in contention.

At the ninth, Slaley's signature hole, Montgomerie's tee shot hit the railway sleepers in the creek which runs across the fairway and his ball bounced clear and into the rough from where he was able to make a par four on a hole which has wrecked many a card. Another 68 in the third round took Montgomerie to 11 under par and close to his prediction that four 68s would probably be enough to take the first prize of £108,330.

It put him one ahead of the impressive Lee Westwood and Goosen and three clear of Scott Henderson and Jamie Spence. Westwood caught him at the fourth with a birdie and Goosen was hanging in there as Montgomerie went to the turn in 35 with a birdie putt at the eighth.

Montgomerie really cut loose on the back nine with birdies at the tenth and 12th and showed the rest of the field the way home with further birdie putts at the 14th, 16th and 17th and, at the last, his ball toppled into the hole to equal the record and bring a smile as wide as the Tyne Bridge to his face.

Westwood almost holed from around 35 feet on the last to tie with Goosen and he said: 'No one can live with Monty when he's in that sort of form although I felt fairly confident when we started out. To shoot 65 on the last day was unbelievable.'

In fact, Montgomerie only had two bogeys in four rounds and his game was on a plateau that the rest of us can only dream about. As Mel Webb wrote in The Times: This was not the final round of golf tournament, it was more like a royal procession. Colin Montgomerie produced a performance that was majestic even by his own exalted standards.

Alan Hedley

SLALEY HALL, NORTHUMBERLAND, JUNE 5-8, 1997 • YARDAGE 7053 • PAR 72

Pos	Name	Country	Rnd 1	Rnd 2	Rnd 3	Rnd 4	Total	Prize Money £
1	Colin MONTGOMERIE	(Scot)	69	68	68	65	270	108330.00
2	Retief GOOSEN	(SA)	69	69	68	69	275	72210.00
3	Lee WESTWOOD	(Eng)	70	70	66	70	276	40690.00
4	David GILFORD	(Eng)	71	69	69	69	278	30015.00
	Scott HENDERSON	(Scot)	69	71	68	70	278	30015.00
6	Roger WESSELS	(SA)	71	69	73	67	280	17202.00
	Jon ROBSON	(Eng)	72	68	70	70	280	17202.00
	David CARTER	(Eng)	69	70	70	71	280	17202.00
	John MELLOR	(Eng)	71	72	67	70	280	17202.00
	Jamie SPENCE	(Eng)	69	72	67	72	280	17202.00
11	Stephen ALLAN	(Aus)	72	71	69	69	281	11200.00
	Paul MCGINLEY	(Ire)	73	71	67	70	281	11200.00
	Sam TORRANCE	(Scot)	72	71	67	71	281	11200.00
14	Jean Louis GUEPY	(Fr)	73	71	70	68	282	9550.00
	Ross MCFARLANE	(Eng)	72	69	68	73	282	9550.00
	Neal BRIGGS	(Eng)	70	70	70	72	282	9550.00
17	Gordon SHERRY	(Scot)	73	72	69	69	283	8580.00
	Paul LAWRIE	(Scot)	70	69	72	72	283	8580.00
19	Robert COLES	(Eng)	70	70	72	72	284	7419.29
	Barry LANE	(Eng)	70	68	76	70	284	7419.29
	Peter HEDBLOM	(Swe)	71	72	71	70	284	7419.29
	Gary EVANS	(Eng)	72	68	71	73	284	7419.29
	Phil GOLDING	(Eng)	73	68	71	72	284	7419.29
	Jonathan LOMAS	(Eng)	74	70	68	72	284	7419.29
	Emanuele CANONICA	(It)	68	73	72	71	284	7419.29
26	Ignacio FELIU	(Sp)	71	68	71	75	285	5871.67
	John WADE	(Aus)	71	72	71	71	285	5871.67
	Mathew GOGGIN	(Aus)	72	71	72	70	285	5871.67
	Padraig HARRINGTON	(Ire)	67	74	72	72	285	5871.67
	Derrick COOPER	(Eng)	72	72	71	70	285	5871.67
	Fredrik ANDERSSON	(Swe)	67	73	74	71	285	5871.67
	Michael LONG	(NZ)	71	73	71	70	285	5871.67
	Miles TUNNICLIFF	(Eng)	73	69	69	74	285	5871.67
	Fredrik JACOBSON	(Swe)	70	70	72	73	285	5871.67
35	Steven BOTTOMLEY	(Eng)	68	71	74	73	286	4810.00
	Andrew OLDCORN	(Scot)	69	75	70	72	286	4810.00
	Andrew COLTART	(Scot)	72	72	70	72	286	4810.00
	Dean ROBERTSON	(Scot)	72	71	73	70	286	4810.00
	Anders HANSEN	(Den)	71	73	71	71	286	4810.00
40	Bob MAY	(USA)	72	70	73	72	287	4095.00
	Gordon J BRAND	(Eng)	69	72	72	74	287	4095.00
	Massimo FLORIOLI	(It)	73	72	70	72	287	4095.00
	Greg TURNER	(NZ)	70	72	70	75	287	4095.00
	Russell CLAYDON	(Eng)	71	74	69	73	287	4095.00
	Paul AFFLECK	(Wal)	70	72	74	71	287	4095.00
46	Jay TOWNSEND	(USA)	71	72	73	72	288	3510.00
	Wayne WESTNER	(SA)	71	69	72	76	288	3510.00
	Steve WEBSTER	(Eng)	66	76	72	74	288	3510.00
49	Paolo QUIRICI	(Swi)	72	73	68	76	289	2860.00
	Van PHILLIPS	(Eng)	74	70	71	74	289	2860.00
	Carl MASON	(Eng)	71	73	72	73	289	2860.00
	Patrik SJÖLAND	(Swe)	70	73	75	71	289	2860.00
	Paul BROADHURST	(Eng)	69	76	71	73	289	2860.00
	Gordon BRAND JNR.	(Scot)	74	71	72	72	289	2860.00
	Mathias GRÖNBERG	(Swe)	73	71	72	73	289	2860.00
56	Per HAUGSRUD	(Nor)	69	73	74	74	290	2119.00
	Andrew BEAL	(Eng)	69	73	74	74	290	2119.00
	Andrew SANDYWELL	(Eng)	75	69	74	72	290	2119.00
	Ross DRUMMOND	(Scot)	71	71	75	73	290	2119.00
	Carl SUNESON	(Sp)	70	73	71	76	290	2119.00
61	Juan Carlos PIÑERO	(Sp)	68	74	76	73	291	1787.50
	Stephen GALLACHER	(Scot)	72	72	74	73	291	1787.50
	Mats HALLBERG	(Swe)	68	76	75	72	291	1787.50
	Wayne RILEY	(Aus)	70	73	71	77	291	1787.50
65	Peter O'MALLEY	(Aus)	71	72	73	76	292	1300.00
	Pedro LINHART	(Sp)	72	73	73	74	292	1300.00
67	Daniel WESTERMARK	(Swe)	75	70	73	75	293	970.00
	Alan TAIT	(Scot)	69	76	73	75	293	970.00
	Daren LEE	(Eng)	75	69	72	77	293	970.00
	Tony JOHNSTONE	(Zim)	72	72	74	75	293	970.00
71	Christian CÉVAER	(Fr)	73	72	72	77	294	965.00
72	David HIGGINS	(Ire)	73	72	75	77	297	962.00
	Ben TINNING	(Den)	73	72	72	80	297	962.00
74	Brian DAVIS	(Eng)	72	73	76	77	298	959.00
75	Mark MOULAND	(Wal)	73	70	80	77	300	957.00
76	Raymond BURNS	(N.Ire)	70	75	76	80	301	955.00

Retief Goosen finishing at the double.

In his father's footsteps

It was a case of like father, like son,

when Ignacio Garrido won

his first European Tour title

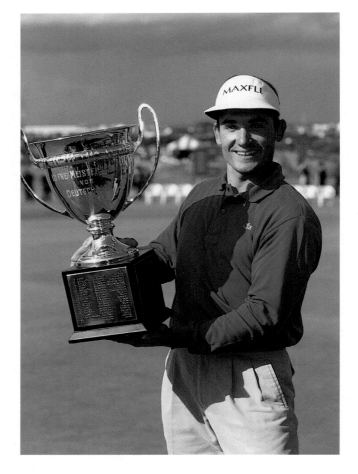

Learning good habits at an early age is important for any youngster who wants to succeed in sport. When the instructors have played with distinction at the highest level and temper their wisdom with shrewd psychology, then the pupil enjoys a priceless advantage over the rest.

So it was with Ignacio Garrido, son of former Ryder Cup player Antonio and nephew of club professional German, whose grounding in professional tournament golf began in his early teens, as a caddie for his father during school holidays. From the very start of his golf career young Ignacio was surrounded by experts. Watching his father, who played with Severiano Ballesteros in the first European Ryder Cup team in 1979, and contemporaries like Jose Maria Canizares and Manuel Pinero at close hand, proved invaluable when he began to play. Ignacio quickly showed his aptitude for golf, and with his father and uncle always on hand to pass on the finer points of the game, progress was rapid.

By the time he was called up for national service in the Spanish army, the young Garrido had a plus four handicap. He proved he possessed a remarkable talent when, while on leave, he was a runaway winner of the Brabazon Trophy at Hollinwell, beating all the leading Walker Cup hopefuls. Ignacio went on to play for Spain in the Eisenhower Trophy later that year.

It was only a matter of time before he graduated to the European Tour, where his father, now a champion on the burgeoning Seniors tour, had achieved five victories between 1972 and 1986. Ignacio's victory in the 1993 Spanish PGA Championship, the last Challenge Tour event of the season, provided the passport a few months after his 21st birthday.

The 1997 Volvo German Open at Schloss Nippenburg provided the stepping stone to even greater achievement, as the most able of the new generation of Spanish tournament professionals, swept to an impressive victory over a field that included Masters champions Bernhard Langer and Ian Woosnam, the newly-crowned Volvo PGA champion, and Mark James, who had won the Peugeot Spanish Open six weeks previously in Garrido's home city of Madrid. What is more, Garrido scored his maiden European Tour success by leading from start to finish for a 13 under par aggregate of 271 that left him four strokes ahead of runner-up Russell Claydon.

Ignacio had hinted he was on the brink of raising his game to a new level when he beat Nick Price, the former

Rough recovery from
Per Haugsrud (left).
Second place finish for
Russell Claydon (right).

Sweden's Anders Gillner holed in one with his six iron at the 187-yard fifth, but it was the first ace in 22 years of tournament golf by Mark James, chairman of the Tournament Players' Committee, that took the honour. James hit a five iron at the 194-yard eighth that pitched 12 feet short of the flag before disappearing. It was the penultimate hole of a second round 67 that helped him take home almost £44,000 prize-money.

world number one and Open Champion to win the Hassan Trophy at Royal Dar-es-Salem. Then the week before he arrived at Stuttgart he had won the Spanish PGA title for a second time, at the RACE, helped by two brush-up lessons from uncle German, the head professional at Club de Campo. So an opening 65 to share the lead with newcomer Mike Weir, Dutchman Rolf Muntz, and former Walker Cup player Van Phillips, was no more than he expected, although few suspected it would turn out to be so decisive.

Woosnam, as defending champion, was eager to put further distance between himself and European number one Colin Montgomerie in the Volvo Ranking, while Langer, who designed the course, was seeking his tenth European Tour win on home soil, having already won the Conte of Florence Italian Open and the Benson and Hedges International Open in successive weeks. Then there were Ryder Cup stalwarts Costantino Rocca and Sam Torrance also with eyes on the £116,000 top award, as well as a dozen other tournament winners.

Woosnam had been 20 under par in winning over 54 holes in 1996, but was unable to beat the card for the much-toughened course on the first day, while Langer, architect of the sterner test, did so only by one stroke.

Neither were able to make up the lost ground over the next two rounds. The weather might have been unsettled, with a series of heavy showers, but Garrido was

not, as he confidently moved to ten under after 36 holes, and 14 below after 54, to take a five stroke lead into the final stage. His nearest pursuers were James, who had scored the first ace of his career at the eighth in the course of a second round 67, and Brian Davis, a rookie from Hertfordshire, who had been runner-up at the 1996 European Tour Qualifying School. His 66 was the lowest third round score.

But no one had approached Garrido's strike rate of 18 birdies in the first 54 holes, and only Claydon found birdies plentiful in the blustery wind after overnight rain had caused a three-hour

delay. However, the Cambridge golfer was only four under on Sunday morning, and too far back to be a real threat, provided Garrido kept cool and maintained his concentration. Claydon had seven birdies in his first 16 holes but was unable to get closer than two shots, his outside chance disappearing when he found sand with his tee shot at the short 17th. Neither could Davis, despite the birdie at the short 12th which took him to ten under par after Garrido had dropped two strokes by going out in 38. The young Englishman met disaster at the 14th when he hit a metal wood second shot into a bush.

James was also unable to sink the

153

THE COURSE

Bernhard Langer designed the European Tour course of Schloss Nippenburg just outside Stuttgart, which was extensively toughened with new tees and bunkers for its third hosting of the Volvo German Open. Set on rolling downland, the feature hole is the 439-yard ninth where a lake which runs the entire length of the fairway to the green threatens any pulled or hooked tee shot. A visit to the water invariably means a double bogey unless like champion Ignacio Garrido you are prepared to take your courage in your hands. He drove into the lake to incur a penalty shot, but then hit a three wood from 225 yards to 12 feet, and sank the par putt to sign for a first day 65.

birdie putts, although the one he sank at the last took him to third place, one behind Claydon, whose 66 for 275 secured him more than £77,000.

With the winning post so clearly visible, Garrido wisely adopted a no-risks policy as he ground out eight successive pars from the turn to be three ahead on the final tee. Then he showed he was a worthy champion by holing from 20 feet

with the last stroke of his 72 to sign off with a flourish by marking a birdie four on his card.

Almost as impressive as his golf was his eloquent English as he described his pride at following in his father's footsteps, and his wish to celebrate this success with his family. But linguistic skill is part of the education of the new generation of global golfers, and father Antonio ensured his

son acquired it, although it hurt at the time. Ignacio explained: 'Every summer as a teenager I was sent to England for a month to stay with families in Hampshire. My father was very cruel because he would not let me take my golf clubs. He told me I had to study first. Now that I study psychology myself, I know why he did it.'

Mike Britten

SCHLOSS NIPPENBURG ETC, STUTTGART, JUNE 19-22, 1997 · YARDAGE 6850 · PAR 71

Pos	Name	Country	Rnd 1	Rnd 2	Rnd 3	Rnd 4	Total	Prize Money £
1	Ignacio GARRIDO	(Sp)	65	67	67	72	271	116660
2	Russell CLAYDON	(Eng)	68	69	72	66	275	77770
3	Mark JAMES	(Eng)	68	67	69	72	276	43820
4	Richard GREEN	(Aus)	71	66	71	69	277	25528
	Bernhard LANGER	(Ger)	70	69	69	69	277	25528
	Eduardo ROMERO	(Arg)	67	67	73	70	277	25528
	Per HAUGSRUD	(Nor)	70	68	68	71	277	25528
	Brian DAVIS	(Eng)	68	70	66	73	277	25528
9	Alex CEJKA	(Ger)	66	76	69	67	278	14163
	Sam TORRANCE	(Scot)	70	68	70	70	278	14163
	Barry LANE	(Eng)	68	70	68	72	278	14163
12	Max ANGLERT	(Swe)	70	70	71	68	279	12040
13	Robert KARLSSON	(Swe)	68	67	73	72	280	10990
	Ian WOOSNAM	(Wal)	71	69	68	72	280	10990
15	Jim PAYNE	(Eng)	66	71	75	69	281	10080
	Domingo HOSPITAL	(Sp)	70	71	69	71	281	10080
17	Johan SKOLD	(Swe)	68	71	74	69	282	9053
	Greg TURNER	(NZ)	70	72	70	70	282	9053
	Phillip PRICE	(Wal)	71	70	69	72	282	9053
20	Mike WEIR	(Can)	65	75	72	71	283	7980
	Mark MOULAND	(Wal)	72	67	72	72	283	7980
	Daniel CHOPRA	(Swe)	71	72	68	72	283	7980
	Van PHILLIPS	(Eng)	65	70	74	74	283	7980
	Bob MAY	(USA)	67	70	72	74	283	7980
25	Ross MCFARLANE	(Eng)	71	71	71	71	284	7035
	Heinz P THÜL	(Ger)	70	70	74	70	284	7035
	Richard BOXALL	(Eng)	71	72	72	69	284	7035
	Derrick COOPER	(Eng)	72	68	69	75	284	7035
29	Padraig HARRINGTON	(Ire)	71	71	71	72	285	5940
	Philip WALTON	(Ire)	72	70	72	71	285	5940
	Anders FORSBRAND	(Swe)	68	73	73	71	285	5940
	Stephen FIELD	(Eng)	73	68	75	69	285	5940
	Per-Ulrik JOHANSSON	(Swe)	72	71	69	73	285	5940
	David HOWELL	(Eng)	72	71	69	73	285	5940
	Lian-Wei ZHANG	(Chi)	72	71	67	75	285	5940
36	Miguel Angel JIMÉNEZ	(Sp)	70	71	72	73	286	5040
	Jeff REMESY	(Fr)	68	73	74	71	286	5040
	Joakim RASK	(Swe)	73	70	70	73	286	5040
	Andrew SHERBORNE	(Eng)	69	68	75	74	286	5040
	Thomas GÖGELE	(Ger)	69	71	71	75	286	5040
41	Massimo FLORIOLI	(It)	70	72	71	74	287	4340
	Stephen ALLAN	(Aus)	68	71	74	74	287	4340
	Andrew OLDCORN	(Scot)	72	71	71	73	287	4340
	Carl SUNESON	(Sp)	69	72	73	73	287	4340
	Stephen LEANEY	(Aus)	68	71	73	75	287	4340
46	Mark ROE	(Eng)	69	71	73	75	288	3640
	Paul EALES	(Eng)	68	74	74	72	288	3640
	Daren LEE	(Eng)	70	71	75	72	288	3640
	Stuart CAGE	(Eng)	66	72	73	77	288	3640
	Klas ERIKSSON	(Swe)	73	70	68	77	288	3640
51	Paul AFFLECK	(Wal)	67	76	73	73	289	3010
	Angel CABRERA	(Arg)	69	71	76	73	289	3010
	Jeff HAWKES	(SA)	73	70	70	76	289	3010
	Rolf MUNTZ	(Hol)	65	74	72	78	289	3010
55	Anders HANSEN	(Den)	70	71	72	77	290	2520
	Patrik SJÖLAND	(Swe)	73	68	74	75	290	2520
	Darren COLE	(Aus)	69	72	78	71	290	2520
58	Katsuyoshi TOMORI	(Jap)	71	71	73	76	291	2170
	Silvio GRAPPASONNI	(It)	70	71	74	76	291	2170
	Santiago LUNA	(Sp)	71	71	77	72	291	2170
61	Jarmo SANDELIN	(Swe)	74	68	72	79	293	1925
	Patrick PLATZ	(Ger)	70	73	73	77	293	1925
	Miles TUNNICLIFF	(Eng)	71	72	73	77	293	1925
	John MELLOR	(Eng)	71	71	75	76	293	1925
65	Gordon J BRAND	(Eng)	71	71	78	74	294	1400
	Paolo QUIRICI	(Swi)	71	71	78	74	294	1400
67	Niclas FASTH	(Swe)	69	74	71	82	296	1048
68	Marc FARRY	(Fr)	70	73	76	78	297	1046

Bernhard Langer.

Goosen earns his lie-in

A series of early starts due to bad weather

did not prevent **Retief Goosen** from capturing

his second European Tour title

*V*ictories come in all shapes and sizes. But few start with an eagle two and end with a double bogey seven.

That is how it was, though, for South African Retief Goosen as he followed up second place in the Compaq European Grand Prix at Slaley Hall with success at the Peugeot Open de France, staged for the seventh year in succession at Le Golf National near Versailles.

Prize money was £600,000 and Colin Montgomerie had chosen the championship as his first appearance after the US Open, where he made another monumental effort for his first major title. As in 1994, however, Ernie Els denied him and Montgomerie, who bogeyed the 71st hole to lose by one, could not hide his disappointment.

An opening 66 in France perfectly

demonstrated his determination to carry on regardless. But it was good enough only for second place again after first round which stretched long into the second day because of rain delays.

Only 3½ hours' play was possible on the Thursday, but during that time 28-year-old Goosen kicked off his challenge by holing a 126-yard wedge shot for a two on the 377-yard 10th (his first),

THE COURSE

Few finishes on the European Tour are as spectacular as Le Golf National. Water comes into play on three of the last four holes and the other is a bruising 470-yards par four. The amphitheatre surroundings only add to the drama and if ever the Ryder Cup comes to France then this course looks a natural to stage it. The designer was Hubert Chesneau and it took 400 lorries three years to bring sufficient earth to mould the humps and hollows on what was previously flat land. Historic Versailles is nearby and with a hotel on site it is one of the most popular stops on Tour.

went to the turn in 31 and birdied the first as well before being forced in.

Early the next morning he finished off the round by collecting two more birdies for an eight under par 64. It was only one outside the course record, but because of the sodden fairways preferred lies were in operation all week and so all record bids were off.

By the time Montgomerie, who had beaten him by five at Slaley Hall, came in later with his 66 Goosen was into his second round. That had to be halted too, but

not before he had completed 14 more holes in four under. At 12 under he led by five from Sweden's Jarmo Sandelin.

The downpours brought back memories for Goosen of the most dramatic day in his life ten years earlier. Back home in Pietersburg he was walking past a tree which was suddenly struck by lightning and he was left with injuries so bad – a burst eardrum, burns and a heart irregularity – that he spent the next two months in hospital.

He recovered to become the South

African amateur champion in 1990 and after turning professional later the same year he won in his first season on the Sunshine Tour, then three times in 1992. That season ended with him winning the European Tour Qualifying School and in his first Tour outing he finished second – behind compatriot Wayne Westner – in the Dubai Desert Classic.

That it took him until the 1996 Slaley Hall Northumberland Challenge to grab his first victory on the Tour surprised many, but he said: 'Good amateurs seem

SHOT OF THE WEEK

Albatrosses are rare things. There was only one in the entire 1996 European Tour, by Anders Forsbrand in the Catalan Open. So far in 1997 there had been only one as well — remarkably by Forsbrand again at the Benson and Hedges International Open. But this week he found some company. The third hole on the appropriately-named Albatros course at Le Golf National is 530 yards long and after his drive Diego Borrego still had 261 of them to cover. Out came his driver again and into the hole the ball went. 'I couldn't see it,' he said, 'but I could see the people around the green knew.' The same hole also witnessed a two by Norwegian Per Haugsrud during the 1995 Peugeot Open de France.

Marc Farry and Martin Gates find themselves marking time.

to play well at first, then fade away and come back again. I still have a lot to learn, but watching Ernie (Els) play and seeing him do so well encouraged me.'

By Saturday morning in Paris, Goosen was becoming accustomed to setting his alarm clock early. Good weather allows golfers at least one lie-in and if they are doing well they get three because of late tee-off times, but bad weather causes havoc and he found himself getting up at 6am every day.

On this occasion he had four holes to complete and by playing them in one under he set a challenging halfway target of 131, 13 under. Nobody could get close. Montgomerie was only two behind after a charge which included a remarkable birdie off the wooden bridge at the back of the 514-yard 18th – he chipped to nine feet off it and made the putt – but at the 197-yard eighth he flew over the green into deep rough, almost missed the ball with his first chip and walked to the next tee with a

double bogey five on his card. He was never go get as close again and eventually finished joint 11th.

By this time the Scot was in a two-ball with Lee Westwood, defending champion Robert Allenby having been disqualified after failing to spot that Montgomerie had put him down for a three at the short 11th in the first round when he actually took four. And Westwood feared he might be disqualified as well after television commentator Ken Brown, the former Ryder Cup player, trod on his ball in joining a search. Westwood played on without asking for a ruling – the ball should be replaced – but after being contacted at his hotel he was cleared when he said he did not know until later that Brown did stand on it.

The delays meant 36 holes on the final day. Goosen, up early again, led throughout. Four clear of Martin Gates and Marc Farry at the start, his morning

70, which included four successive birdies after the turn, left him three in front and another 70 after the briefest of lunches made three the winning margin too.

That does not tell the whole story, though. Gates played brilliantly to cut the gap to one with four to play, but then bogeyed the 15th, went in the water for a double bogey five at the 16th and dropped shots on the last two as well. It allowed Jamie Spence to leap almost from nowhere into second place and Gates had to settle for joint third with Darren Clarke, Raymond Russell and Van Phillips.

Goosen stood on the final tee five ahead. His winner's speech was forming in his head as he carelessly hit a 66-yard wedge into the lake. He could have done it again and still won, but he was safely on next time and the title was his. A not-so-magnificent seven, but a win is a win – and next morning he could lie in.

Mark Garrod   159

NATIONAL GOLF CLUB, PARIS, JUNE 26-29, 1997 · YARDAGE 7122 · PAR 72

Pos	Name	Country	Rnd 1	Rnd 2	Rnd 3	Rnd 4	Total	Prize Money £
1	Retief GOOSEN	(SA)	64	67	70	70	271	100000.00
2	Jamie SPENCE	(Eng)	68	71	67	68	274	66660.00
3	Raymond RUSSELL	(Scot)	75	68	66	66	275	28490.00
	Darren CLARKE	(N.Ire)	70	69	67	69	275	28490.00
	Van PHILLIPS	(Eng)	70	68	71	66	275	28490.00
	Martin GATES	(Eng)	68	67	69	71	275	28490.00
7	Steve WEBSTER	(Eng)	67	71	69	69	276	18000.00
8	Ross MCFARLANE	(Eng)	70	70	69	68	277	13480.00
	Robert COLES	(Eng)	72	66	69	70	277	13480.00
	Eduardo ROMERO	(Arg)	68	70	71	68	277	13480.00
11	Robert KARLSSON	(Swe)	72	67	67	72	278	10320.00
	Peter LONARD	(Aus)	68	71	72	67	278	10320.00
	Colin MONTGOMERIE	(Scot)	66	70	73	69	278	10320.00
14	Jarmo SANDELIN	(Swe)	68	68	73	70	279	9180.00
15	Des SMYTH	(Ire)	73	70	69	68	280	8460.00
	Dean ROBERTSON	(Scot)	71	68	72	69	280	8460.00
	José COCERES	(Arg)	68	68	70	74	280	8460.00
18	Costantino ROCCA	(It)	70	71	71	69	281	7248.00
	Jeff REMESY	(Fr)	70	72	68	71	281	7248.00
	Thomas BJORN	(Den)	70	69	71	71	281	7248.00
	Carl SUNESON	(Sp)	70	68	72	71	281	7248.00
	Lee WESTWOOD	(Eng)	67	70	73	71	281	7248.00
23	Michael JONZON	(Swe)	69	72	70	71	282	6390.00
	Peter MITCHELL	(Eng)	73	70	69	70	282	6390.00
	Stephen FIELD	(Eng)	70	69	70	73	282	6390.00
	David HOWELL	(Eng)	70	68	71	73	282	6390.00
27	Santiago LUNA	(Sp)	68	73	72	70	283	5580.00
	Katsuyoshi TOMORI	(Jap)	71	71	71	70	283	5580.00
	Raphaël JACQUELIN	(Fr)	73	67	72	71	283	5580.00
	Anders FORSBRAND	(Swe)	68	71	73	71	283	5580.00
	Roger CHAPMAN	(Eng)	69	69	72	73	283	5580.00
32	Stuart CAGE	(Eng)	68	73	70	73	284	4320.00
	Stephen AMES	(T&T)	71	70	71	72	284	4320.00
	Tony JOHNSTONE	(Zim)	72	69	70	73	284	4320.00
	Derrick COOPER	(Eng)	71	71	69	73	284	4320.00
	Alex CEJKA	(Ger)	73	69	70	72	284	4320.00
	Mark JAMES	(Eng)	70	72	67	75	284	4320.00
	Steven RICHARDSON	(Eng)	74	68	70	72	284	4320.00
	Daniel CHOPRA	(Swe)	73	70	69	72	284	4320.00
	Thomas GÖGELE	(Ger)	75	66	72	71	284	4320.00
	Paul AFFLECK	(Wal)	71	69	72	72	284	4320.00
	Bob MAY	(USA)	70	69	75	70	284	4320.00
	Diego BORREGO	(Sp)	69	69	71	75	284	4320.00
	John WADE	(Aus)	68	68	73	75	284	4320.00
45	Raymond BURNS	(N.Ire)	72	68	71	74	285	3420.00
	Sandy LYLE	(Scot)	68	71	70	76	285	3420.00
47	Philip WALTON	(Ire)	73	69	73	71	286	2940.00
	Paul EALES	(Eng)	73	69	70	74	286	2940.00
	Jean VAN DE VELDE	(Fr)	70	73	72	71	286	2940.00
	Paolo QUIRICI	(Swi)	72	71	73	70	286	2940.00
	Paul BROADHURST	(Eng)	70	71	72	73	286	2940.00
	Jim PAYNE	(Eng)	69	71	74	72	286	2940.00
53	Olivier EDMOND	(Fr)	71	71	71	74	287	2460.00
	Marc FARRY	(Fr)	67	68	75	77	287	2460.00
55	Antoine LEBOUC	(Fr)	68	73	76	71	288	2160.00
	Gordon BRAND JNR.	(Scot)	70	72	76	70	288	2160.00
	Gary EVANS	(Eng)	72	71	74	71	288	2160.00
58	Niclas JOAKIMIDES	(Fr)	69	72	79	69	289	1860.00
	Gary ORR	(Scot)	70	73	74	72	289	1860.00
	Robert LEE	(Eng)	71	72	72	74	289	1860.00
61	Massimo FLORIOLI	(It)	67	74	76	73	290	1680.00
	Silvio GRAPPASONNI	(It)	71	71	73	75	290	1680.00
	Brian DAVIS	(Eng)	68	72	75	75	290	1680.00
64	Richard GREEN	(Aus)	76	67	73	75	291	1560.00
65	Mats HALLBERG	(Swe)	71	71	75	75	292	1500.00
66	Steven BOTTOMLEY	(Eng)	70	73	74	76	293	900.00
67	Ignacio GARRIDO	(Sp)	70	69	80	75	294	898.00
68	Adam HUNTER	(Scot)	68	74	75	78	295	896.00

Colin Montgomerie enjoys a joke during the second round.

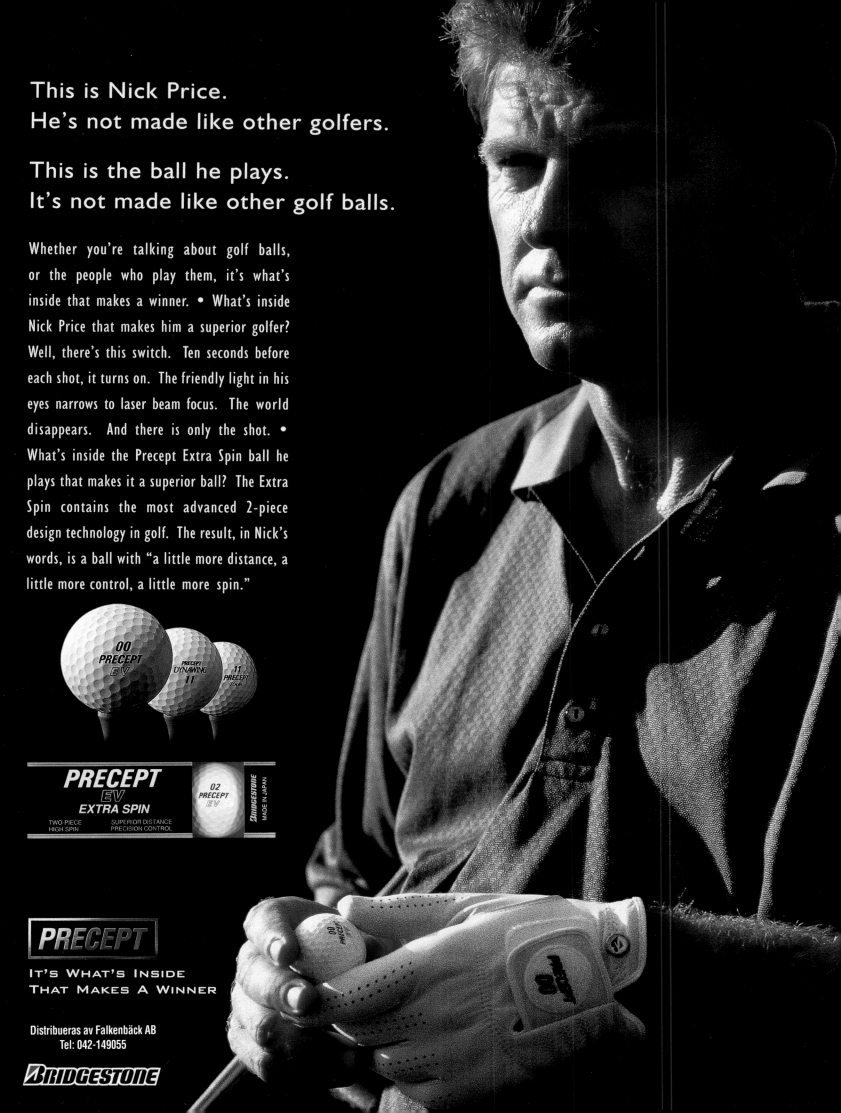

This is Nick Price.
He's not made like other golfers.

This is the ball he plays.
It's not made like other golf balls.

Whether you're talking about golf balls, or the people who play them, it's what's inside that makes a winner. • What's inside Nick Price that makes him a superior golfer? Well, there's this switch. Ten seconds before each shot, it turns on. The friendly light in his eyes narrows to laser beam focus. The world disappears. And there is only the shot. • What's inside the Precept Extra Spin ball he plays that makes it a superior ball? The Extra Spin contains the most advanced 2-piece design technology in golf. The result, in Nick's words, is a ball with "a little more distance, a little more control, a little more spin."

PRECEPT
EV
EXTRA SPIN

TWO-PIECE
HIGH SPIN
SUPERIOR DISTANCE
PRECISION CONTROL

BRIDGESTONE
MADE IN JAPAN

PRECEPT

IT'S WHAT'S INSIDE
THAT MAKES A WINNER

Distribueras av Falkenbäck AB
Tel: 042-149055

BRIDGESTONE

Montgomerie defends in record style

With a course record 62 in the final round,
Colin Montgomerie made it
many happy returns at Druids Glen

Colin Montgomerie did not believe it was possible to score 62 on a course as tough as Druids Glen. 'But,' he added after his successful defence of the Murphy's Irish Open title, 'I did not believe it was possible to shoot 65 at Congressional in the US Open, either. Druids Glen is not as tough as Congressional but the way it was set up for the tournament, I would have to rate the round among the best of my career.'

It was a performance of excellence in the midst of a high quality field that included Nick Faldo, Ian Woosnam, José Maria Olazábal and Costantino Rocca among the established stars and men of the future like Lee Westwood, Darren Clarke, Thomas Bjorn. It was Westwood who set the pace from the start with a record 65 on the first day and although that score was beaten by a shot by Sweden's Michael Jonzon, he retained the halfway lead and, indeed, stretched it to three shots by the end of the third round.

Paired with Montgomerie in the final

group on Sunday, the young pretender to the throne of Europe, had every reason to fancy his chances. He is unflappable and apparently fearless in such exalted company and when asked on Saturday evening who he feared most in the field he said: 'No one. You must fancy your chances with a three-shot lead.' But he could only

watch in awe as the great Scot, plundered the par of 71 with eight birdies and an eagle to bring about a ten-shot swing and add to an already impressive six tournament trip.

Starting with the Alamo English Open and including the US Open at Congressional, he had finished 12th, fifth, first, second, 11th and first. 'It is a great feeling to come back and defend your title. I am very proud to be the Irish National Champion for the second time. It is such a great championship and such a good course,' he told an appreciative crowd. 'You know, it is almost a major in its own right. The crowd were phenomenal. It is just great that there were 35,000 of them out there and they are golf educated. They know the game.'

It may have been a great piece of public relations but you got the feeling he meant every word of it. The pain of finishing second in the US Open may not have been totally eradicated but it was

certainly lessened by this remarkable performance and if he has not yet graduated from tournament winner to major championship winner, that final step into the legend league cannot be far away.

Young Westwood was well aware of the strength of the talent all around him. Before he came to the county known as The Garden of Ireland, he had lost from a position of authority on the last day to Olazábal in the Canaries, Bernhard Langer in the Benson and Hedges International Open and Montgomerie in the Compaq European Grand Prix.

If he needed confirmation that things would not come easily in this kind of company he got it as early as the first hole which he three-putted and Montgomerie birdied. They were level by the third which the champion birdied but Westwood regained the lead, albeit briefly, at the next where the Scot made his only bogey of the day.

From there on it was akin to watching Tiger Woods at the Masters in Augusta. The only questions to be answered were who would be second and by what margin? All hope of catching the leader vanished for Westwood when he bogeyed the tenth off a poor tee shot and made only par instead of an expected birdie at the par five 11th where he was forced to take a penalty drop from heather.

It was time to turn his attention to the men behind, particularly Olazábal and Faldo who were breathing down his neck. The Spaniard went into self-destruct mode with double bogeys at the 13th and 15th while Faldo, having looked at the scoreboard, realised that best he could finish was third and declared after his 68: 'I'm pleased with that. It's a few more Ryder Cup points for Seve.'

Three times an Irish champion, Faldo

SHOT OF THE WEEK

The 11th hole measures 522 yards with a dog-leg to the right but Lee Westwood reduced it to a drive, a brilliant four iron of 228 yards to a well-protected green and one putt for an eagle three. It came in the midst of a superb run of birdie, eagle, birdie, par, birdie from the tenth to lay the foundation for his record opening round of 65.

related how his caddie Fanny Sunesson was momentarily stunned when she hit her head on a sponsor's board. 'Some guy came out of the crowd and carried the bag for me. I asked him was it expensive or cheap and then he gave me the wrong club. Luckily Fanny came back and I thought of getting a five minute medical break but she was ok.'

Montgomerie first, Westwood sec-

Nick Faldo and Fanny Sunesson confer over a putt.

165

THE COURSE

The course is named after an ancient Druid altar which still stands to the right of the 12th green, one of two short holes, in a spectacular glen. The terrain is parkland with a fair share of water, none more dangerous than that which cascades through a series of falls in front of the 18th green. It was opened only in 1993 and each year the flora and fauna has made it more attractive.

ond, Faldo third, Woosnam in a share of fourth and Olazábal sixth, Ballesteros, who missed the cut, must have been pleased for his Ryder Cup prospects, but the home gallery was once again disappointed with no serious challenge from one of theirs, the best of them being Padraig Harrington and Philip Walton in a share of seventh place.

The new champion was among the first to praise the decision of the sponsors to bring the tournament back to Druids

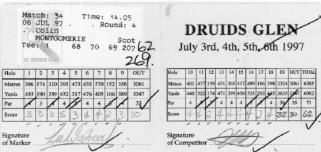

Glen next season when it will be one year older and more mature. The weather this time was a lot kinder than the previous year but the course took a dreadful pounding from torrential rain through

Wednesday night, so much so that Tournament Director Andy McFee thought about preferred lies but decided that the course had held up well enough.

There were complaints about spike marks on the greens but Montgomerie was obviously very happy. He holed a birdie putt of 30 feet on the short 17th and admitted: 'It was the only putt that I hit and just wanted to get close but it dropped in. That was nice.'

Colm Smith

DRUIDS GLEN, DUBLIN, JULY 3-6, 1997 • YARDAGE 6982 • PAR 71

Pos	Name	Country	Rnd 1	Rnd 2	Rnd 3	Rnd 4	Total	Prize Money £
1	Colin MONTGOMERIE	(Scot)	68	70	69	62	269	113636
2	Lee WESTWOOD	(Eng)	65	69	70	72	276	75745
3	Nick FALDO	(Eng)	69	73	68	68	278	42672
4	Ian WOOSNAM	(Wal)	71	70	70	69	280	31486
	Michael JONZON	(Swe)	72	64	75	69	280	31486
6	José Maria OLAZABAL	(Sp)	74	71	65	71	281	23863
7	Daniel CHOPRA	(Swe)	71	69	71	72	283	14003
	David TAPPING	(Eng)	72	68	69	74	283	14003
	Wayne WESTNER	(SA)	70	70	70	73	283	14003
	Padraig HARRINGTON	(Ire)	71	72	71	69	283	14003
	Paul LAWRIE	(Scot)	72	72	72	67	283	14003
	Thomas BJORN	(Den)	66	70	74	73	283	14003
	Philip WALTON	(Ire)	76	69	70	68	283	14003
	Peter HEDBLOM	(Swe)	72	73	68	70	283	14003
15	David CARTER	(Eng)	71	71	74	68	284	8751
	Ronan RAFFERTY	(N.Ire)	72	72	72	68	284	8751
	Van PHILLIPS	(Eng)	72	73	71	68	284	8751
	Darren CLARKE	(N.Ire)	72	73	71	68	284	8751
	Eduardo ROMERO	(Arg)	72	67	76	69	284	8751
	Katsuyoshi TOMORI	(Jap)	72	69	73	70	284	8751
	Carl WATTS	(Eng)	74	69	73	68	284	8751
	Klas ERIKSSON	(Swe)	71	71	72	70	284	8751
23	Barry LANE	(Eng)	73	71	66	75	285	7363
	Eamonn DARCY	(Ire)	70	71	69	75	285	7363
	Rolf MUNTZ	(Hol)	70	73	71	71	285	7363
26	John WADE	(Aus)	73	71	73	69	286	6545
	Roger CHAPMAN	(Eng)	69	73	70	74	286	6545
	Joakim RASK	(Swe)	76	70	72	68	286	6545
	Miguel Angel MARTIN	(Sp)	74	71	73	68	286	6545
	Carl MASON	(Eng)	75	70	71	70	286	6545
31	Daren LEE	(Eng)	71	73	69	74	287	5534
	Peter O'MALLEY	(Aus)	73	71	72	71	287	5534
	Gordon BRAND JNR.	(Scot)	73	70	70	74	287	5534
	Niclas FASTH	(Swe)	72	74	71	70	287	5534
	Diego BORREGO	(Sp)	72	73	73	69	287	5534
	Michael LONG	(NZ)	76	70	72	69	287	5534
37	Phillip PRICE	(Wal)	70	73	69	76	288	4909
	Richard GREEN	(Aus)	72	70	75	71	288	4909
	Mathias GRÖNBERG	(Swe)	71	71	75	71	288	4909
40	Tony JOHNSTONE	(Zim)	73	70	70	76	289	4363
	David GILFORD	(Eng)	68	75	72	74	289	4363
	Paul MCGINLEY	(Ire)	72	73	75	69	289	4363
	Anders FORSBRAND	(Swe)	71	70	76	72	289	4363
	David HOWELL	(Eng)	71	73	73	72	289	4363
45	Gary MURPHY	(Ire)	74	72	72	72	290	3613
	Sam TORRANCE	(Scot)	71	73	70	76	290	3613
	Rodger DAVIS	(Aus)	68	75	74	73	290	3613
	Mark ROE	(Eng)	71	73	69	77	290	3613
	Steven RICHARDSON	(Eng)	67	75	72	76	290	3613
	Miles TUNNICLIFF	(Eng)	73	67	75	75	290	3613
51	José COCERES	(Arg)	72	72	75	72	291	2931
	Costantino ROCCA	(It)	69	74	74	74	291	2931
	Robert ALLENBY	(Aus)	68	72	73	78	291	2931
	Alberto BINAGHI	(It)	70	76	73	72	291	2931
55	Eoghan O'CONNELL	(Ire)	71	72	75	74	292	2159
	Neal BRIGGS	(Eng)	77	69	74	72	292	2159
	Darren COLE	(Aus)	72	74	75	71	292	2159
	Damian MCGRANE	(Ire)	73	72	76	71	292	2159
	Robert LEE	(Eng)	70	72	73	77	292	2159
	Wayne RILEY	(Aus)	74	70	75	73	292	2159
	Jim PAYNE	(Eng)	72	73	72	75	292	2159
	Jonathan LOMAS	(Eng)	72	70	76	74	292	2159
	Andrew SHERBORNE	(Eng)	71	73	75	73	292	2159
64	Ross DRUMMOND	(Scot)	73	71	76	73	293	1772
65	Per HAUGSRUD	(Nor)	73	73	74	75	295	1363
	Ross MCFARLANE	(Eng)	67	76	77	75	295	1363
67	Malcolm MACKENZIE	(Eng)	73	72	78	76	299	1020
68	Emanuele CANONICA	(It)	75	70	75	80	300	1019

Montgomerie's remarkable last round scorecard (opposite). Thomas Bjorn (right)

Lehman flies high

With only two dropped shots in 72 holes,

Tom Lehman left the field in his

slipstream at Loch Lomond

*I*t was written in the stars – and in huge shimmering neon letters – that Tom Lehman would most probably capture the Gulfstream World Invitational at hauntingly beautiful Loch Lomond. Even a novice clairvoyant armed with the basic astrological charts and a persuasive line in mumbo-jumbo could have read the signs accurately. Here was a golfer, not just any golfer but the reigning Open champion and the PGA Tour's Player of 1996, on a

mission to right a few wrongs.

It had been the same story twelve months earlier when the 38-year-old Minnesota-born, Arizona-based American flew to Britain nursing a grievous sense of injustice and plotting his next career move. Lehman, by his own admission, had just 'blown' the US Open at Oakland Hills. The British version was the perfect platform for Lehman to exact his revenge, or as he called it, to fulfill his destiny by

winning the original Open at Royal Lytham and St. Annes.

So it was that Lehman arrived in Scotland, one year on, nursing an even more passionate sense of outrage after allowing yet another US Open to evade his grasp.

Sure enough, the combination of Lehman's awesome, physical power game and mental motivation proved a potent and irresistible mix. The Open champion,

169

THE COURSE

Opinion was undivided during the tournament. Loch Lomond is, quite simply, paradise on earth. The combination of the towering mountains, dense forests and the gentle lapping of the waves on the lochside created a golfing idyll. Greg Norman and Tom Lehman were among those captivated by the breathtaking beauty and immaculate conditioning. Ten out of ten.

A good week for Pierre Fulke.

in the final few days of his reign, delivered as regal a performance as anyone could wish to see on the Bonnie, Bonnie Banks. Ever tactful and unfailingly modest, even Lehman was moved to admit: 'I am not sure I can do a whole lot better.' He added 'It was a very fulfilling week of golf. To play that well for four days is not something you do very often. Any time you win is special. To come over and win in Scotland and to shoot 19 under par on this golf course makes you ecstatic.'

Lehman had every reason to feel euphoric as he received his trophy from the Duke of York, even poking fun at Prince Andrew's choice of jacket bearing the European Ryder Cup logo.

On that week in July, Lehman felled all his challengers with a swaggering flourish. With only two bogeys in four days, his scores of 65, 66, 67 and 67 left Ernie Els - the beneficiary of Lehman's late slip at Congressional - a distant second, five strokes adrift. Another South African, Retief Goosen, filled third place with the round of the week, a record breaking nine under par 62.

That quite brilliant score was the third time in four days that the Loch Lomond standard had been lowered. The first round lead had been shared by Swede Joakim Haeggman and Paul Curry from Essex. Haeggman posted his score of 63 early, surpassing the 65 set by Jean van de Velde the previous year. Curry, the last man to tee off, left it late by emerging from the gathering gloom with his record-equalling card.

Then Lehman, just two off the pace with a solid 65, engaged gear and slipped into overdrive. His second round was a marathon which lasted more than nine hours, including a five-hour delay for an electric storm. Lehman controlled the game admirably, stayed patient, and con-

SHOT OF THE WEEK

One classic shot sealed Tom Lehman's victory. It came at the 440-yard par four seventh hole on the final day. Sharing the lead with Pierre Fulke at the time, the American pulled his drive into a wiry clump of rough. Bogey territory. Undaunted, Lehman crouched behind his ball, face contorted in concentration. He then punched a six iron under one tree and over another to 25 feet. He holed for birdie, Fulke bogeyed – the title was Tom's.

jured up a 66 to lead at halfway by three from his close friend, Steve Jones (65) and Swede Pierre Fulke, who went round in 64. The final putt on the longest day was holed at 10.31pm, the latest finish in the history of the European Tour. Lehman arrived for his press conference just before 10pm and prefaced his remarks by joking: 'I've just come to tuck you guys into bed. The milk and cookies will be along shortly.'

His good humour was to last right through the remainder of the tournament. Fulke's third round 65 to Lehman's 67 trimmed the American's lead to two shots going into the final round. But when it mattered, Lehman's class overpowered the highest quality field assembled in Europe prior to

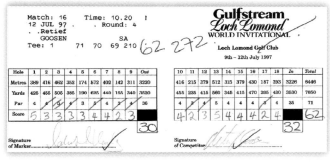

Payne in the Stewart tartan (above left)?
Retief Goosen's course record 62 (above).
Opening 63 from Paul Curry (below).

the Open. After a bogey at the third, he birdied three in a row from the seventh to turn in 34. Fulke faltered, Jones jolted to a halt – and Lehman powered home to victory. Els, with a closing 66 for 278, earned the runner-up position ahead of Goosen while Greg Norman finished strongly for a share of fourth with Fulke.

Colin Montgomerie's bonus for a share of tenth place was to overtake Bernhard Langer as the European Tour's richest career winner.

However, the battle for the leading membership card in the Millionaires' Club was incidental to the real drama being fought out. And in that respect, there was only one winner. Tom Lehman was a genuine class act, on and off the golf course.

Gordon Simpson   171

Loch Lomond, Glasgow, July 9-12, 1997 · Yardage 7050 · Par 71

Pos	Name	Country	Rnd 1	Rnd 2	Rnd 3	Rnd 4	Total	Prize Money £
1	Tom LEHMAN	(USA)	65	66	67	67	265	133330
2	Ernie ELS	(SA)	70	69	65	66	270	88880
3	Retief GOOSEN	(SA)	71	70	69	62	272	50070
4	Greg NORMAN	(Aus)	68	68	69	68	273	36940
	Pierre FULKE	(Swe)	70	64	66	73	273	36940
6	Payne STEWART	(USA)	73	67	66	68	274	24000
	Mats HALLBERG	(Swe)	67	71	71	65	274	24000
	Paul BROADHURST	(Eng)	68	70	68	68	274	24000
9	Steve JONES	(USA)	69	65	68	73	275	17840
10	Colin MONTGOMERIE	(Scot)	69	70	70	67	276	15360
	Peter O'MALLEY	(Aus)	71	68	68	69	276	15360
12	Joakim HAEGGMAN	(Swe)	63	72	71	71	277	13760
13	Robert ALLENBY	(Aus)	68	72	70	68	278	12293
	Thomas BJORN	(Den)	72	67	70	69	278	12293
	Tom PURTZER	(USA)	68	69	70	71	278	12293
16	Jesper PARNEVIK	(Swe)	70	71	68	70	279	10384
	Mark JAMES	(Eng)	72	71	65	71	279	10384
	Joakim RASK	(Swe)	70	70	68	71	279	10384
	Angel CABRERA	(Arg)	67	72	67	73	279	10384
	Glen DAY	(USA)	66	72	68	73	279	10384
21	Nick FALDO	(Eng)	67	73	72	68	280	9360
22	Lee WESTWOOD	(Eng)	70	73	66	72	281	8880
	Larry MIZE	(USA)	70	69	70	72	281	8880
	Stephen MCALLISTER	(Scot)	69	68	77	67	281	8880
25	Patrik SJÖLAND	(Swe)	75	67	72	68	282	7800
	Costantino ROCCA	(It)	70	71	66	75	282	7800
	Robert LEE	(Eng)	70	71	73	68	282	7800
	Darren CLARKE	(N.Ire)	72	68	72	70	282	7800
	Mathias GRÖNBERG	(Swe)	68	69	69	76	282	7800
	Paul CURRY	(Eng)	63	72	70	77	282	7800
31	Andrew COLTART	(Scot)	73	69	68	73	283	6330
	Paul EALES	(Eng)	68	74	71	70	283	6330
	Miguel Angel JIMÉNEZ	(Sp)	69	73	70	71	283	6330
	Per-Ulrik JOHANSSON	(Swe)	72	71	68	72	283	6330
	Rolf MUNTZ	(Hol)	69	74	73	67	283	6330
	Derrick COOPER	(Eng)	71	70	69	73	283	6330
	Raymond RUSSELL	(Scot)	70	70	72	71	283	6330
	David TAPPING	(Eng)	71	67	72	73	283	6330
39	Peter HEDBLOM	(Swe)	73	70	66	75	284	5360
	Dean ROBERTSON	(Scot)	71	72	67	74	284	5360
	Ian WOOSNAM	(Wal)	72	71	74	67	284	5360
	Ronan RAFFERTY	(N.Ire)	69	68	74	73	284	5360
43	Paul MCGINLEY	(Ire)	72	69	70	74	285	4560
	David HOWELL	(Eng)	67	75	72	71	285	4560
	Richard BOXALL	(Eng)	71	72	70	72	285	4560
	Robert KARLSSON	(Swe)	70	71	73	71	285	4560
	Peter MITCHELL	(Eng)	69	72	70	74	285	4560
	Carl SUNESON	(Sp)	70	70	72	73	285	4560
49	Wayne WESTNER	(SA)	72	70	70	74	286	3440
	Emanuele CANONICA	(It)	72	70	71	73	286	3440
	Stephen AMES	(T&T)	70	72	71	73	286	3440
	Silvio GRAPPASONNI	(It)	70	73	75	68	286	3440
	Klas ERIKSSON	(Swe)	68	75	71	72	286	3440
	Ian GARBUTT	(Eng)	69	71	75	71	286	3440
	Robert DAMRON	(USA)	70	69	75	72	286	3440
	Jarmo SANDELIN	(Swe)	67	72	71	76	286	3440
57	Jeff HAWKES	(SA)	72	70	70	75	287	2540
	Peter BAKER	(Eng)	70	72	76	69	287	2540
	Padraig HARRINGTON	(Ire)	71	72	71	73	287	2540
	Stephen FIELD	(Eng)	68	68	73	78	287	2540
61	David CARTER	(Eng)	70	73	75	70	288	2280
	Russell CLAYDON	(Eng)	72	71	75	70	288	2280
63	Mark ROE	(Eng)	73	70	73	73	289	2120
	Ricky WILLISON	(Eng)	73	70	72	74	289	2120
65	Gary NICKLAUS	(USA)	70	73	75	72	290	1600
	Howard TWITTY	(USA)	72	68	75	75	290	1600
67	Paolo QUIRICI	(Swi)	69	74	74	74	291	1198
68	Gary CLARK	(Eng)	68	74	77	73	292	1196
69	Howard CLARK	(Eng)	72	70	71	80	293	1192
	Martin GATES	(Eng)	69	73	77	74	293	1192
	David GILFORD	(Eng)	71	72	79	71	293	1192
72	Miles TUNNICLIFF	(Eng)	68	75	78	75	296	1188
73	Jamie SPENCE	(Eng)	73	70	79	76	298	1186

Joakim Haeggman (above) shared the first round lead.

BRUT IMPÉRIAL
MOËT & CHANDON
CHAMPAGNE
Official Suppliers to the
PGA European Tour

Justin's time

With a scintillating final round
Justin Leonard grabbed the
glory at Royal Troon

This was the Open Championship when the heavyweights of world golf were coming to Royal Troon with their reputations and form at the highest level. Take Tom Lehman for example. The week before he had cruised to a comfortable victory at Loch Lomond and was in a buoyant mood to defend the Championship he had won so handsomely at Royal Lytham the year before. Then there was Tiger Woods. The wunderkind of the game had collected his fourth US Tour title of the year ten days previously and was the hottest favourite since Young Tom Morris went for his fourth consecutive title in 1872. You couldn't ignore Greg Norman either, fresh from a US Tour victory at the end of June, and you certainly wouldn't discount Ernie Els, the latest US Open champion and a man who can make the game look ridiculously easy. Finally, there was Colin Montgomerie, the home-town boy returning to his roots on a course where even the seagulls give him a passing nod of acquaintance.

If you added Nick Faldo, Ian Woosnam, Nick Price, Phil Mickelson and Bernhard Langer you would be entitled to think that you had just about covered every potential winner.

However, recent form is no indicator when it comes to Open Championships, when a capricious wind and firm, bouncy fairways can play havoc with the smoothest of swings, and on the first day,

shone even brighter. Four more putts of a similar distance found the bottom of the cup and it all added up to a 66 and nine under par for the Championship. Two behind came Leonard, also with a 66 which contained two eagles, and one behind him was Parnevik (66) while completing a quartet of 66s was the relatively unknown David Tapping who found him-

Tiger Woods conducts the applause from his followers (left and above). Siesta time for Ross McFarlane (above).

self tied for fourth place with Couples.

The rest of the highly-touted contenders were struggling. Norman was nine shots off the pace, Faldo and Els 11 behind, Montgomerie 12 and Woods and Lehman 13. Woods had an altercation with a bush behind the 10th green to run up an eight and Lehman fell foul of the rule book when, on the second green, he failed to replace his ball in the right spot after marking it and turned a five into a seven.

Three years ago just down the road at Turnberry, Parnevik came within a whisker of winning, losing narrowly to Price. In the third round he set out to make amends. Out in 33 he still trailed Clarke by four after the Ulsterman had turned in 32 but as Clarke faltered coming home, Parnevik birdied the tenth, dropped a shot at the 11th (where his

playing companion, Couples, lobbed a five iron into the hole for a two), and then staged a grandstand finish with birdies at the 16th and 17th. It added up to another 66 and with Clarke falling back with a 71, Parnevik had established a two-shot lead. Couples and Leonard lay five shots off the pace so the outcome looked to be between these four, even though Woods had shown his mettle with a round of 64 to move within eight shots of

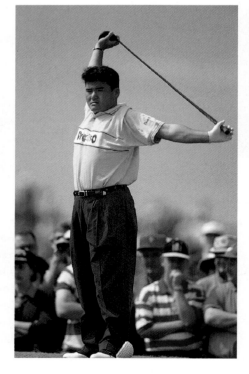

An uphill struggle for Jim Furyk (top). The scoreboard tells the story of Ian Baker-Finch's battle (far left), Shigeki Maruyama (near left), stretched into tenth place. Nick Price and Nick Faldo (above) silhouetted under a glorious Ayrshire sunset.

the lead.

If Woods was going to make any impression on the leaders in the final round it was vital that he made some early birdies but he opened with three mundane pars and although two birdies followed, a triple bogey six at the Postage Stamp (eighth) left him licking his wounds.

Clarke and Parnevik were the last pairing, preceded by Couples and Leonard.

Clarke was the only one of the quartet to birdie the first but he was also the only one to hit a full-blooded shank off the second tee to go out-of-bounds on the beach and run up a six. From then on the round was a struggle for him and he spent a lot of time in the right rough and only a deft short game kept him anywhere near the leader.

That man was Parnevik but he too was under the cosh. A birdie at the third

was offset by a dropped shot at the long sixth where his second shot caught the lip of a bunker and he took four more to get down. This halted his momentum considerably and although he reached the turn in 35, one under par, there was no doubt who was on a roll.

A dead ringer for the Duke of York, Leonard was making regal progress through the first nine with six birdies followed by one dropped shot at the tenth

but when the Swede birdied the 11th to go two ahead he appeared to have regained the initiative. Leonard kept churning out the pars as though he was waiting for his rival to falter, and he did when he dropped a shot at the 13th.

Now the margin was one and the first crucial moment came at the long 16th. Here Leonard lined up a putt of 12 feet for a birdie and ran it home. Then on the short 17th (the word short is relative as the hole measures 223 yards) the American holed from fully 30 feet. As the roar for this deafened most of Ayrshire, Parnevik was lining up a putt of four feet on the 16th for his birdie. He stepped away, walked around a little and then missed. Leonard had moved to 12 under par and Parnevik was 11 under. The situation worsened for Parnevik when he dropped a stroke at the 17th and Leonard did him no favours by coolly making a solid par on the last to complete an outstanding round of 65.

Parnevik now needed a two at the last

A dejected Jesper Parnevik on the 18th (above) tied with Darren Clarke (below) in second place.

to tie. He drove into the rough and as he hit his second shot the idiotic cry of 'Get in the hole' rose from the gallery. The ball did just that. Unfortunately, it was rather a large hole with sand in the bottom and

Parnevik could do no better than five. Clarke staged a mini-revival with a birdie at the 16th and a grand finale three at the last to tie for second place.

Although none of the top six players in the world finished any higher than tenth, there was no doubting the worthiness of the winner. While the more fancied men arrived with an entourage of managers, coaches and physiotherapists, Leonard landed with just his caddie for company. The man from Dallas, whose career prospects had been overshadowed by the impact of Woods, put together the second lowest final round by a winner in the history of the event and showed that a fundamentally sound, if a little ungainly, swing coupled with a putting stroke of Crenshaw-like smoothness is capable of coping with today's howitzer hitters.

There is no logical explanation why the world's leading players all fumbled their lines but when they did, Leonard seized the moment. It was Justin's time.

Chris Plumridge

THE COURSE

Measuring 7,079 yards, Royal Troon is one of the longest courses on the Championship rota with a second nine that is rated the toughest of all. The absence of any wind over the last three days meant that some of its teeth were drawn but holes such as the 11th, 13th and 17th still exacted retribution and if the wind had continued to blow as it did on the first day, then the firm fairways and quickening greens would have played havoc with par.

SHOT OF THE WEEK

The par five 16th is 542 yards long and intersecting the fairway at around the 270-yard mark is a small stream. This means even the longest hitters have to lay up with the tee shot and play for position with the second. That is unless your name is Tiger Woods. In his third round 64, Woods had 281 yards to the green after his drive and in order to maintain the momentum of a great round, smashed a driver from the fairway onto the green. The ball finished 15 feet away and the putt was dispatched for the rarest of eagles.

Royal Troon, July 17-20, 1997 • Par 71 • Yards 7079

Pos	Name	Country	Rnd 1	Rnd 2	Rnd 3	Rnd 4	Total	Prize Money £
1	Justin LEONARD	(USA)	69	66	72	65	272	250000
2	Darren CLARKE	(N.Ire)	67	66	71	71	275	150000
	Jesper PARNEVIK	(Swe)	70	66	66	73	275	150000
4	Jim FURYK	(USA)	67	72	70	70	279	90000
5	Stephen AMES	(T&T)	74	69	66	71	280	62500
	Padraig HARRINGTON	(Ire)	75	69	69	67	280	62500
7	Fred COUPLES	(USA)	69	68	70	74	281	40666
	Eduardo ROMERO	(Arg)	74	68	67	72	281	40666
	Peter O'MALLEY	(Aus)	73	70	70	68	281	40666
10	Retief GOOSEN	(SA)	75	69	70	68	282	24300
	Lee WESTWOOD	(Eng)	73	70	67	72	282	24300
	Tom WATSON	(USA)	71	70	70	71	282	24300
	Mark CALCAVECCHIA	(USA)	74	67	72	69	282	24300
	Robert ALLENBY	(Aus)	76	68	66	72	282	24300
	Shigeki MARUYAMA	(Jap)	74	69	70	69	282	24300
	Tom KITE	(USA)	72	67	74	69	282	24300
	Davis LOVE III	(USA)	70	71	74	67	282	24300
	Ernie ELS	(SA)	75	69	69	69	282	24300
	Frank NOBILO	(NZ)	74	72	68	68	282	24300
20	José Maria OLAZABAL	(Sp)	75	68	73	67	283	14500
	Mark JAMES	(Eng)	76	67	70	70	283	14500
	Brad FAXON	(USA)	77	67	72	67	283	14500
	Stuart APPLEBY	(Aus)	72	72	68	71	283	14500
24	Peter LONARD	(Aus)	72	70	69	73	284	10362
	Colin MONTGOMERIE	(Scot)	76	69	69	70	284	10362
	Ian WOOSNAM	(Wal)	71	73	69	71	284	10362
	David A RUSSELL	(Eng)	75	72	68	69	284	10362
	Tiger WOODS	(USA)	72	74	64	74	284	10362
	Tom LEHMAN	(USA)	74	72	72	66	284	10362
	Jay HAAS	(USA)	71	70	73	70	284	10362
	Phil MICKELSON	(USA)	76	68	69	71	284	10362
32	Mark MCNULTY	(Zim)	78	67	72	68	285	8750
33	Jonathan LOMAS	(Eng)	72	71	69	74	286	8283
	David DUVAL	(USA)	73	69	73	71	286	8283
	Rodger DAVIS	(Aus)	73	73	70	70	286	8283
36	Andrew MAGEE	(USA)	70	75	72	70	287	7950
	Greg NORMAN	(Aus)	69	73	70	75	287	7950
38	Raymond RUSSELL	(Scot)	72	72	74	70	288	7550
	Mark O'MEARA	(USA)	73	73	74	68	288	7550
	John KERNOHAN	(USA)	76	70	74	68	288	7550
	Mike BRADLEY	(USA)	72	73	73	70	288	7550
	Bernhard LANGER	(Ger)	72	74	69	73	288	7550
	Vijay SINGH	(Fij)	77	69	70	72	288	7550
44	José COCERES	(Arg)	76	70	71	72	289	7050
	David TAPPING	(Eng)	71	66	78	74	289	7050
	Curtis STRANGE	(USA)	71	71	70	77	289	7050
	Jerry KELLY	(USA)	76	68	72	73	289	7050
48	Steve JONES	(USA)	76	71	68	75	290	6700
	Jim PAYNE	(Eng)	74	71	74	71	290	6700
	Richard BOXALL	(Eng)	75	71	72	72	290	6700
51	Angel CABRERA	(Arg)	70	70	76	75	291	6156
	Jeff MAGGERT	(USA)	76	69	71	75	291	6156
	Wayne RILEY	(Aus)	74	71	75	71	291	6156
	Peter SENIOR	(Aus)	76	70	73	72	291	6156
	Corey PAVIN	(USA)	78	69	76	68	291	6156
	Peter MITCHELL	(Eng)	75	69	76	71	291	6156
	Nick FALDO	(Eng)	71	73	75	72	291	6156
	Greg TURNER	(NZ)	76	71	72	72	291	6156
59	Payne STEWART	(USA)	73	74	71	74	292	5800
60	Jack NICKLAUS	(USA)	73	74	71	75	293	5750
	Barclay HOWARD (AM)	(Scot)	70	74	76	73	293	
61	Tom PURTZER	(USA)	72	71	73	78	294	5625
	Jamie SPENCE	(Eng)	78	69	72	75	294	5625
	Steve STRICKER	(USA)	72	73	74	75	294	5625
	Peter TERAVAINEN	(USA)	74	72	73	75	294	5625
65	Paul MCGINLEY	(Ire)	76	71	77	71	295	5450
	Per-Ulrik JOHANSSON	(Swe)	72	75	73	75	295	5450
	Gary CLARK	(Eng)	74	72	72	77	295	5450
68	Tommy TOLLES	(USA)	77	68	75	76	296	5350
69	Billy ANDRADE	(USA)	72	72	78	76	298	5300

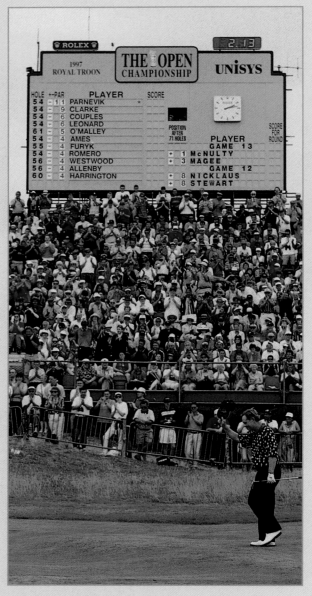

Jack Nicklaus: still a crowd-pleaser.

If your business trades abroad, we'll help ensure that nothing's overlooked.

Before you embark overseas, touch down at Barclays. Our international trade experts can help you reduce the risks of dealing abroad, by getting the details right. We design our products to suit the most complex demands. We can provide finance to support your trading and services that can help reduce the uncertainty of payment. What's more, we do all this through a single point of contact. If you want business to pick up abroad, pick up the telephone and contact your Corporate Manager. Or ring 0800 585 768.

Strüver ends bad spell

Sven Strüver ended
a depressing run of form
with victory in Holland

Whor asked if he would be
nervous being on top of the
leaderboard going into the final round at
Hilversumsche, Sven Strüver replied:
'Leading a tournament does not make me
nervous. Going home on Fridays makes
me nervous.'

The reason for the Hamburg-born
German's philosophy lay in his tournament record for the previous three

months or so: played nine, missed eight
cuts, missed the last six cuts; failed to
qualify for the Open Championship. And
he knew he had no trouble with winning.
Hadn't he shot a 63 in the final round of
the weather-affected South African PGA
Championship the year before, when he
left the new US Open Champion Ernie
Els far too much to do to catch him?

Also, the 30-year-old son and nephew

of professional golfing teachers, knew he was back with his trusty clubs which first saw him explode on the European Tour scene as an amateur who shot a 62 to impress the pros in the German Open in Frankfurt just before Tony Jacklin's 1989 Ryder Cup team was finalised. Finally, Strüver had a burning ambition. Ever since he had followed Alexander Cejka to the

winner's podium and become part of the new wave of German golfers coming through, he had wanted to prove he was no flash in the pan.

With Cejka's results deteriorating and his own leaving him bitterly disappointed after a bright start to the season, with a ninth in the South African Open and a steady defence of his Alfred Dunhill SA

PGA title to finish 12th, German pundits and fans were beginning to feel the young bloods aiming to follow in Bernhard Langer's footsteps had faded.

Knowing Langer's name was etched on the Dutch Open trophy twice, Strüver had extra-special reasons, therefore, to produce his second Tour success and pick up the £116,660 first prize, nearly three

THE COURSE

Another lengthy wet spell before the tournament made the par-71, 6,636-yard course play the longest yet, said the players, who also wondered if the trees and foliage had crept that much nearer the tight fairways. 'Miss a fairway and you're history' was the in-phrase, with the par four 470-yard 11th once more proving the scourge.

David Gilford (right) finds a place in the Sun. Wayne Westner (opposite) finds a place in the rough.

times the amount he had earned in Johannesburg the year before. He had a great desire to see his name on the trophy, too.

While Strüver sought the second victory to prove himself, his arch rival at the weekend was a player looking for a first success. Cambridgeshire professional Russell Claydon could turn to a record which included a runner-up place in the 1989 Australian Masters behind Greg Norman when still an amateur. Norman predicted great things for the man with the individual swing, designed to accommodate a not unsubstantial girth. And when he turned professional after helping Great Britain and Ireland to that memorable Walker Cup victory at Peachtree, Claydon was expected to be part of Britain's new wave which included another player with an individual swing, Steve Richardson.

But while Richardson notched up three titles, in eight years there were only second places for Claydon, including another runner-up slot when he came through the field in the Volvo German Open a few weeks before Hilversum. Almost exactly a year before, too, he had lost a play-off when Lee Westwood's raking putt from 50 feet pipped him and Paul Broadhurst in the Volvo Scandinavian Masters. So would the door he had been knocking on for eight years, finally open at Hilversum?

At first, neither Claydon nor Strüver had featured on top of the leaderboard.

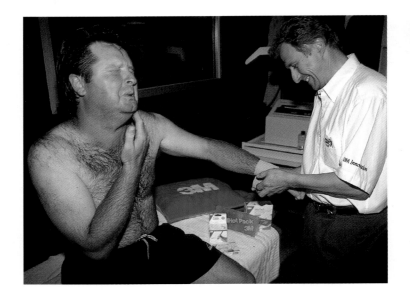

José Coceres' albatross on the 484-yard fourth on Sunday helped him to fifth place, the Argentinian homing in a four iron from 210 yards. On the same day Spain's Pedro Linhart holed out with an eight iron on the 144-yard lucky 13th – to win a bicycle made for one.

Wayne Riley (above) receives treatment in the 3M physio bus. Contenders Robert Coles (right) and Russell Claydon (below).

Young Essex professional Robert Coles, who had been taught golf by his market-trader father in return for helping out at Petticoat Lane, set out his stall in the first round by shooting a seven under par 64. That was only a stroke off the Hilversumsche record and it gave Coles, in his second year on Tour, a one-shot lead over Roger Chapman and David Gilford. Both second-placed men had outside Ryder Cup prospects and Chapman, twice as long a 'bridesmaid' without a victory as Claydon, kept in the hunt all week.

The next day, though, Strüver's 64 took him to the top, three strokes ahead of Coles, Gilford and Wayne Westner, at last finding confidence with his game. Strüver had returned to the type of club he had used in the heady days of Frankfurt 1989 after an ill-fated switch to a new club manufacturer earlier in the

season.

Claydon was a further stroke adrift but he signalled his intent for that elusive

first victory the next day when a 65 took him alongside Strüver, two strokes in front of the field. 'Of course I'll be nervous,' viewed Claydon, looking at his final round chances. By contrast with the German, he did have nerves about leading. 'Anybody who tells you he's not going to be nervous when he's never won before, is telling lies. It's how you handle it.' By his own admission, he did not handle it well. Only a deadly putter kept him in touch with Strüver on the last day.

The German was not to be denied. His second eagle of the afternoon, this one with a telling putt on the long 12th, took Strüver out of reach of the other bridesmaid Chapman and Argentinian Angel Cabrera. 'It was there for the taking,' observed a rueful Claydon, 'and I chose the day to hit the ball just about as badly as I can.'

A delighted Strüver only had eyes for the trophy. 'Bernhard Langer 1984; Bernhard Langer 1992,' he read. 'Now Sven Strüver 1997.'

Norman Dabell

HILVERSUMSCHE GC, HILVERSUM, JULY 24-27, 1997 • PAR 71 • YARDS 6636

Pos	Name	Country	Rnd 1	Rnd 2	Rnd 3	Rnd 4	Total	Prize Money £
1	Sven STRÜVER	(Ger)	67	64	69	66	266	116660
2	Russell CLAYDON	(Eng)	67	68	65	69	269	77770
3	Roger CHAPMAN	(Eng)	65	71	68	67	271	39410
	Angel CABRERA	(Arg)	71	66	67	67	271	39410
5	Richard BOXALL	(Eng)	68	70	67	67	272	27070
	José COCERES	(Arg)	69	70	69	64	272	27070
7	Raymond RUSSELL	(Scot)	70	70	68	65	273	19250
	Mark JAMES	(Eng)	69	69	70	65	273	19250
9	Gordon BRAND JNR.	(Scot)	67	70	69	68	274	13632
	Wayne WESTNER	(SA)	67	67	68	72	274	13632
	Michael LONG	(NZ)	69	71	65	69	274	13632
	David GILFORD	(Eng)	65	69	71	69	274	13632
13	Sam TORRANCE	(Scot)	74	68	65	68	275	11270
14	Daren LEE	(Eng)	67	69	68	72	276	10290
	Philip WALTON	(Ire)	72	70	65	69	276	10290
	Alex CEJKA	(Ger)	70	71	68	67	276	10290
17	Mark WIEBE	(USA)	69	69	69	70	277	8750
	Mark MOULAND	(Wal)	70	72	68	67	277	8750
	Roger WESSELS	(SA)	67	69	67	74	277	8750
	Robert KARLSSON	(Swe)	69	71	67	70	277	8750
	Miguel Angel JIMÉNEZ	(Sp)	67	68	71	71	277	8750
22	Stuart CAGE	(Eng)	70	70	68	70	278	7245
	David TAPPING	(Eng)	68	69	71	70	278	7245
	Pierre FULKE	(Swe)	71	68	71	68	278	7245
	Ian GARBUTT	(Eng)	69	70	69	70	278	7245
	Robert COLES	(Eng)	64	70	73	71	278	7245
	Pedro LINHART	(Sp)	70	71	68	69	278	7245
	Gary CLARK	(Eng)	72	70	66	70	278	7245
	Patrik SJÖLAND	(Swe)	69	72	72	65	278	7245
30	Costantino ROCCA	(It)	68	72	66	73	279	6090
	David A RUSSELL	(Eng)	76	67	69	67	279	6090
	Jarmo SANDELIN	(Swe)	70	69	70	70	279	6090
	Maarten LAFEBER (AM)	(Hol)	72	69	67	71	279	
33	Andrew SANDYWELL	(Eng)	72	71	68	69	280	5390
	Daniel CHOPRA	(Swe)	71	67	65	77	280	5390
	Van PHILLIPS	(Eng)	71	70	70	69	280	5390
	Mark ROE	(Eng)	70	71	66	73	280	5390
	Paul MCGINLEY	(Ire)	67	69	72	72	280	5390
	David CARTER	(Eng)	71	69	68	72	280	5390
39	Brian DAVIS	(Eng)	70	66	74	71	281	4760
	Paul WAY	(Eng)	70	72	72	67	281	4760
	Miles TUNNICLIFF	(Eng)	65	70	75	71	281	4760
42	Tony JOHNSTONE	(Zim)	69	72	71	70	282	4480
43	Scott HENDERSON	(Scot)	69	73	70	71	283	4060
	Max ANGLERT	(Swe)	72	65	74	72	283	4060
	Joakim HAEGGMAN	(Swe)	72	70	71	70	283	4060
	Ronan RAFFERTY	(N.Ire)	70	72	69	72	283	4060
	Paul CURRY	(Eng)	71	71	71	70	283	4060
	Maarten VAN DEN BERG (A	(Hol)	69	74	70	70	283	
48	José RIVERO	(Sp)	70	71	68	75	284	3500
	Rolf MUNTZ	(Hol)	69	71	73	71	284	3500
	Steve WEBSTER	(Eng)	70	67	74	73	284	3500
	Jack BOECKX (AM)	(Bel)	71	72	70	71	284	
51	Emanuele CANONICA	(It)	73	68	71	73	285	2940
	Gordon SHERRY	(Scot)	67	74	74	70	285	2940
	Klas ERIKSSON	(Swe)	67	70	69	79	285	2940
	Andrew COLTART	(Scot)	73	70	71	71	285	2940
	Ross DRUMMOND	(Scot)	71	70	72	72	285	2940
56	Howard CLARK	(Eng)	70	71	73	72	286	2380
	Fernando ROCA	(Sp)	69	72	72	73	286	2380
	Jeff HAWKES	(SA)	71	70	70	75	286	2380
59	Robert LEE	(Eng)	69	74	69	75	287	2030
	Marc FARRY	(Fr)	71	71	71	74	287	2030
	Darren COLE	(Aus)	69	74	74	70	287	2030
	Chris VAN DER VELDE	(Hol)	71	71	72	73	287	2030
	Raymond BURNS	(N.Ire)	72	71	69	75	287	2030
64	Thomas GÖGELE	(Ger)	70	70	79	69	288	1785
	Jamie SPENCE	(Eng)	69	68	73	78	288	1785
66	Ignacio FELIU	(Sp)	69	72	73	76	290	1050
67	Anders HANSEN	(Den)	68	74	72	77	291	1046
	Fredrik ANDERSSON	(Swe)	68	75	74	74	291	1046
	Massimo FLORIOLI	(It)	73	70	72	76	291	1046
70	Alan SADDINGTON	(Scot)	71	72	78	74	295	1042
71	Ariel CAÑETE	(Arg)	71	72	74	81	298	1039
	Malcolm MACKENZIE	(Eng)	69	72	79	78	298	1039

Solid finish from Angel Cabrera.

Haeggman makes it a Swedish double

Joakim Haeggman became the second Swedish player to win a European Tour event in his own country

There was all manner of scrapping for a variety of rewards among the ranks at Barseback. The name of the game was Ryder Cup Tag, and many were the sidelong glances directed at opponents during the week. And while they were all looking at each other, Joakim Haeggman sailed majestically past them like a four-master running before a force eight blow and beat them all into harbour.

Haeggman had become something of a forgotten man of European golf after he made history by becoming the first Swede to play in the Ryder Cup team in 1993. He finished 15th in the Volvo Ranking and tenth in the Johnnie Walker Ryder Cup qualification list that year and was one of Bernard Gallacher's wild-card selections for the team. He played well at The Belfry and beat John Cook in his singles, but in spite of decent finishes in the money list in 1994, 1995 and 1996 he was never truly a contender. He was not exactly anonymous – he's not that sort of a chap – but neither did he stamp himself on the European Tour scene, either.

A jovial young man off the course but occasionally hard on himself on it, Haeggman went into the tournament in 67th place on the Volvo Ranking; not many of the compatriots in front of whom he was playing would have given him a second glance in the list of runners and riders. It was not long before he changed all that.

He started well, continued in the same vein and by mid-afternoon on the Sunday he had completed his second Tour victory

with a total of 270, 18 under par, becoming in the process the only man to beat 70 in all four rounds. He was four strokes ahead of Ignacio Garrido, who seems destined to surpass the deeds of his famous father, Antonio, with Mats Hallberg and Peter Baker sharing third place a further shot behind. Mark Mouland stole almost unobserved into fifth place on 12 under.

There is something remarkable about attending golf tournaments in Sweden. The galleries are without a doubt the most knowledgeable spectators on the European mainland, but they are also probably the most partisan as well. They don't go as far as applauding the other man's missed putt, but they do let themselves whoop and holler. Whoever said that Swedes were reserved? Not when watching on the golf course, they're not.

It must be a little unnerving for those who are not Swedish, and heaven only knows what it might be like to have that huge outpouring of support for those who are. None of it, anyway, upset the equilibrium of Haeggman, who was calmness personified from first to last.

Haeggman's 67 left him two shots off a hot pace that was set by Costantino Rocca in a first round that was delayed for three and a half hours because of rain, thunder and lightning. Rocca, who had seven birdies, including five in his first nine holes, was celebrating a return to fit-

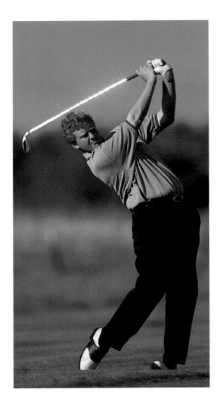

ness after injuring his shoulder then his ribs. The second injury came while trying to hack out of the rough at the Murphy's Irish Open a month earlier – 'The rough was stronger than I was,' he said, smiling his wide, sad, Pagliacci smile. Rocca, never the same after that birdie spectacular, eventually finished in joint 38th place.

By the same time the next day Haeggman had moved into the lead after a 69 but had to share it with seven others. José Maria Olazábal struggled to beat par and stayed in the tournament by the skin of his teeth while Ian Woosnam, a shot worse, missed the cut.

Came Saturday, and with it Haeggman's best golf of the week. He had eight birdies and only one dropped shot in his 65. He had a mere 27 putts and went into the last day four shots ahead of Stephen Allan, the young Australian who looks like a junior who has wandered into

THE COURSE

Barseback is the sort of layout that beguiles on first sight, and impresses with its toughness the more you look at it. It is a fascinating mixture of tree-lined parkland that becomes links-like when you cross the road and get near the sea. A big, raw-boned course, it rewards good golf and is unforgivingly hard on anything errant.

Colin Montgomerie (opposite) was boosted by final round 66. Darren Clarke (left) under swirling skies.

SHOT OF THE WEEK

Joakim Haeggman, third round, 18th hole: Haeggman's four-stroke lead had been whittled down to two by Peter Baker when he came to the 18th tee. He missed the fairway on the right, hit a tree with his club in his follow-through and put the ball through the back of the green. A bogey five was on the cards, and if Baker had parred his way in that would have left the Swede with a mere two-shot lead going into the last round. Instead, Baker bogeyed the 17th and from 25 yards Haeggman took out his lob-wedge and calmly chipped in – four in front again. He still had a round to play, but this might have been the shot that won the tournament.

the wrong tournament but unquestionably plays like an adult. The main threat seemed likely to come from Baker, who was in gung-ho mood after his 69. A former Scandinavian Masters champion – he took the title after a play-off in 1993 – he fancied his chances again this time.

Baker kept up the good work in the final round, and was good value for his two under par 70. Garrido, six shots adrift at the start of the day, maintained the pressure throughout, but the closest he got was three behind and Montgomerie, out of sorts with an uncontrolled hook off the tee earlier in the week, finally came out of his reverie with a 66 to move him into a share of eighth place.

They all strove mightily in front of 27,500 enthusiastic Swedes on the warmest day of the tournament. Led by the gallant Garrido, the pack swarmed all round Haeggman's heels, but he was in no mood to surrender. A 69 capped his best performance for four years. He was back. The way he took his victory, it seemed like he had never been away.

Mel Webb

Barsebäck G & CC, July 31–August 3, 1997 • Par 72 • Yards 7301

Pos	Name	Country	Rnd 1	Rnd 2	Rnd 3	Rnd 4	Total	Prize Money £
1	Joakim HAEGGMAN	(Swe)	67	69	65	69	270	125000
2	Ignacio GARRIDO	(Sp)	67	69	71	67	274	83320
3	Mats HALLBERG	(Swe)	72	68	67	68	275	42220
	Peter BAKER	(Eng)	70	66	69	70	275	42220
5	Mark MOULAND	(Wal)	68	72	67	69	276	31770
6	Padraig HARRINGTON	(Ire)	66	71	72	68	277	24375
	José RIVERO	(Sp)	66	70	70	71	277	24375
8	Miles TUNNICLIFF	(Eng)	68	68	74	68	278	16830
	Colin MONTGOMERIE	(Scot)	72	71	69	66	278	16830
	Roger CHAPMAN	(Eng)	72	69	71	66	278	16830
11	Miguel Angel JIMÉNEZ	(Sp)	71	71	69	68	279	12923
	David GILFORD	(Eng)	70	73	66	70	279	12923
	Stephen ALLAN	(Aus)	72	67	66	74	279	12923
14	Stephen FIELD	(Eng)	69	70	70	71	280	10360
	Steve WEBSTER	(Eng)	70	71	70	69	280	10360
	Lee WESTWOOD	(Eng)	72	69	71	68	280	10360
	Gordon J BRAND	(Eng)	70	73	70	67	280	10360
	Kalle VAINOLA	(Fin)	73	68	68	71	280	10360
	Daniel CHOPRA	(Swe)	71	71	72	66	280	10360
20	Darren CLARKE	(N.Ire)	69	71	69	72	281	8100
	Gary EVANS	(Eng)	68	68	73	72	281	8100
	Dennis EDLUND	(Swe)	70	70	70	71	281	8100
	Anders GILLNER	(Swe)	72	68	73	68	281	8100
	Iain PYMAN	(Eng)	70	70	68	73	281	8100
	David CARTER	(Eng)	70	71	70	70	281	8100
	Greg TURNER	(NZ)	71	70	70	70	281	8100
	Mark JAMES	(Eng)	70	69	72	70	281	8100
	Van PHILLIPS	(Eng)	70	67	71	73	281	8100
29	Eamonn DARCY	(Ire)	71	71	71	69	282	6540
	Jeff REMESY	(Fr)	69	74	70	69	282	6540
	Adam MEDNICK	(Swe)	71	72	66	73	282	6540
	Jesper PARNEVIK	(Swe)	70	68	71	73	282	6540
	Adam HUNTER	(Scot)	70	70	71	71	282	6540
34	Paul MCGINLEY	(Ire)	71	69	74	69	283	5775
	Carl SUNESON	(Sp)	68	74	71	70	283	5775
	Raymond RUSSELL	(Scot)	69	73	73	68	283	5775
	Derrick COOPER	(Eng)	75	66	72	70	283	5775
38	Domingo HOSPITAL	(Sp)	68	68	72	76	284	4950
	Robert KARLSSON	(Swe)	68	71	71	74	284	4950
	Costantino ROCCA	(It)	65	75	72	72	284	4950
	Silvio GRAPPASONNI	(It)	68	71	73	72	284	4950
	Des SMYTH	(Ire)	71	70	72	71	284	4950
	José Maria OLAZABAL	(Sp)	69	74	71	70	284	4950
	Phillip PRICE	(Wal)	72	70	71	71	284	4950
	Henrik STENSSON (AM)	(Swe)	69	72	73	70	284	
45	Steven BOTTOMLEY	(Eng)	68	74	72	71	285	3675
	Mark ROE	(Eng)	67	74	72	72	285	3675
	Alex CEJKA	(Ger)	73	69	71	72	285	3675
	Michael JONZON	(Swe)	69	67	74	75	285	3675
	Per HAUGSRUD	(Nor)	73	69	71	72	285	3675
	Marc FARRY	(Fr)	72	69	72	72	285	3675
	Roger WESSELS	(SA)	72	71	71	71	285	3675
	Paolo QUIRICI	(Swi)	69	70	78	68	285	3675
	Dean ROBERTSON	(Scot)	71	68	73	73	285	3675
	Per-Ulrik JOHANSSON	(Swe)	69	72	73	71	285	3675
55	Paul EALES	(Eng)	71	70	74	71	286	2464
	Andrew OLDCORN	(Scot)	73	70	71	72	286	2464
	Peter HEDBLOM	(Swe)	70	72	74	70	286	2464
	Santiago LUNA	(Sp)	71	72	73	70	286	2464
	Brian DAVIS	(Eng)	72	69	72	73	286	2464
	Jay TOWNSEND	(USA)	72	71	73	70	286	2464
	Ronan RAFFERTY	(N.Ire)	70	68	75	73	286	2464
62	Neal BRIGGS	(Eng)	74	68	72	73	287	1815
	Mårten OLANDER	(Swe)	70	69	77	71	287	1815
	Raymond BURNS	(N.Ire)	72	70	76	69	287	1815
	Bob MAY	(USA)	74	69	73	71	287	1815
	Alberto BINAGHI	(It)	70	73	71	73	287	1815
67	John MELLOR	(Eng)	69	73	73	73	288	1123
68	Sam TORRANCE	(Scot)	72	70	75	72	289	1119
	Fernando ROCA	(Sp)	71	71	73	74	289	1119
	Ben TINNING	(Den)	73	68	72	76	289	1119
71	Joakim RASK	(Swe)	72	70	72	78	292	1115
72	Klas ERIKSSON	(Swe)	74	67	76	76	293	1113

Australia's Stephen Allan.

BOSS

HUGO BOSS

Langer's weekend spree

Closing rounds of 64 and 63 gave

Bernhard Langer his third

European Tour title of the season

*B*ernhard Langer arrived in Prague fresh from a family holiday in Portugal and his native Germany. 'No golf for ten days,' he told reporters gleefully on the eve of the £800,000 Chemapol Trophy Czech Open at the spectacular Prague Karlstein GC course. 'But I did put in some practice towards the end of two weeks.'

His break from the game caused him to make an uncertain start to the tournament as the youngsters took command with a carefree scoring spree which was to last all four days. Langer's opening 70, which included a triple-bogey seven on the fifth hole, left him struggling in joint 55th place and he was still well adrift of the leaders after a second round 67, though a little nearer the front of the field in joint 30th position.

Those who have followed Langer's career since he first joined the European Tour in 1976 knew instinctively that he was still the man to beat, even though, at the halfway stage, he was six behind joint leaders Ignacio Garrido, who was about to secure his Ryder Cup place, fellow Spaniard Miguel Angel Jimeñez, still in the hunt for a Ryder Cup place but also earmarked by team captain Severiano Ballesteros to be his right-hand man at Valderrama, and Sweden's Patrik Sjöland, who matched Langer's first round score of 70 but then shattered the course record with a brilliant ten-birdie 61.

Scott Henderson, who had led on the first day with a 64, was still up with the leaders after a second round 68 and a host of players closed in at the top of the leaderboard, many of them looking for a maiden European Tour win. David Howell (68, 65) shared fifth spot with Daniel Chopra (70, 63) while four more players were within three shots of the lead — Clinton Whitelaw (68, 66), Paul Lawrie (70, 64), Stephen Gallacher (68, 66) and Stephen Field (68, 66). In all, 17 players were within four strokes of the lead going into the third round.

That was when Langer began to make his move with a superb weekend of golf which was to scatter the field in all directions. A 64 on day three eased him into joint fifth place but he was still four shots behind the now outright leader, Garrido, who was enjoying his pursuit of a first Ryder Cup cap, thus following in the footsteps of his father, Antonio. The younger Garrido supremely confident, was not only talking in terms of winning the tournament, but, with a knowing wink, of making it a double the following week in the US PGA Championship.

What he did not reckon with, how-

SHOT OF THE WEEK

In the final round, Bernhard Langer stood in the middle of the fairway at the 514 yards (470 metre) 17th hole facing a choice between a safe five iron layup for his second shot or a championship-winning, or possibly a championship-wrecking, three wood over a vast chasm filled with dense undergrowth. Langer never even considered the first option and hit his three wood into the heart of the green to collect his eighth birdie of the round on his way to victory.

Ignacio Garrido (left) and Lee Westwood (below) virtually secured their Ryder Cup places.

ever, was Bernhard Langer at his very best. 'I knew I had to do something special at the weekend, and I did,' said the popular German after striding to a last-round 63 to set a 20 under par target of 264, a target nobody could match. Garrido, whose worst score in the first three rounds was 66, needed a similar score to win. He did not watch the on-course leader boards at any stage and on the 16th tee he asked his caddie what he needed to do. 'Don't worry because Langer's already finished 20-under,' was the reply. Garrido was at that point four behind.

Although he birdied the 16th hole, Garrido dropped a shot at the long 17th and finished in a tie for second with Sweden's Niclas Fasth. But Garrido's £69,475 prize moved him into sixth place in the Johnnie Walker Ryder Cup points table, thus enabling him and his father to become only the second father-and-son pair to play in

the Ryder Cup, the others being, of course, Percy and Peter Alliss.

Jimenez, whose own Ryder Cup hopes were still alive, needed to win to boost his chances but, like Garrido, a level par 71 was the best he could manage on that last exciting afternoon and he improved his points position only slightly.

So the experience and exceptionally talented Langer came from four strokes behind to win his third European Tour title of the season and his 37th in all in an outstanding career spanning 21 years. He pushed aside his young challengers with a magnificent display of golf. 'I don't need any extra incentive to beat the younger guys just because I'm nearly 40,' said Langer in answer to a reporter's question. 'Lee Trevino always says the clubs and the ball don't know how old you are, and I'm the same.'

Richard Dodd

THE COURSE

Prague Karlstein GC, about 20 miles southwest of the Czech Republic's magnificent capital city, occupies a breathtaking setting with views of Karlstein Castle, built in the 14th century by King Charles VI. It is the only 18-hole golf course in the vicinity of Prague and lies within the boundaries of a vast nature reserve above the picturesque Berounka river.

PRAGUE KARLSTEIN GC, AUGUST 7-10, 1997 · PAR 71 · YARDS 6803

Pos	Name	Country	Rnd 1	Rnd 2	Rnd 3	Rnd 4	Total	Prize Money £
1	Bernhard LANGER	(Ger)	70	67	64	63	264	133330
2	Niclas FASTH	(Swe)	70	65	67	66	268	69475
	Ignacio GARRIDO	(Sp)	66	65	66	71	268	69475
4	Miguel Angel JIMÉNEZ	(Sp)	67	64	67	71	269	40000
5	Alex CEJKA	(Ger)	71	67	67	65	270	30940
	Patrik SJÖLAND	(Swe)	70	61	70	69	270	30940
7	Andrew COLTART	(Scot)	72	67	68	64	271	18512
	Peter HEDBLOM	(Swe)	67	71	66	67	271	18512
	Michael LONG	(NZ)	66	71	67	67	271	18512
	Lee WESTWOOD	(Eng)	67	68	68	68	271	18512
	Joakim HAEGGMAN	(Swe)	69	66	67	69	271	18512
12	Fredrik JACOBSON	(Swe)	68	68	69	67	272	12960
	Scott HENDERSON	(Scot)	64	68	71	69	272	12960
	Stephen ALLAN	(Aus)	69	66	65	72	272	12960
15	Jonathan LOMAS	(Eng)	69	70	66	68	273	10816
	Raymond RUSSELL	(Scot)	66	69	69	69	273	10816
	José RIVERO	(Sp)	68	68	68	69	273	10816
	Clinton WHITELAW	(SA)	68	66	67	72	273	10816
	David HOWELL	(Eng)	68	65	67	73	273	10816
20	Darren CLARKE	(N.Ire)	69	67	70	68	274	9000
	Paul LAWRIE	(Scot)	70	64	71	69	274	9000
	Klas ERIKSSON	(Swe)	69	67	69	69	274	9000
	Peter O'MALLEY	(Aus)	66	72	67	69	274	9000
	Stephen GALLACHER	(Scot)	68	66	70	70	274	9000
	Richard BOXALL	(Eng)	67	68	69	70	274	9000
26	Simon HURLEY	(Eng)	65	72	70	68	275	7560
	Rodger DAVIS	(Aus)	69	68	70	68	275	7560
	Martin GATES	(Eng)	70	67	69	69	275	7560
	Anders FORSBRAND	(Swe)	67	72	66	70	275	7560
	Daniel CHOPRA	(Swe)	70	63	70	72	275	7560
	Dennis EDLUND	(Swe)	70	65	68	72	275	7560
32	Padraig HARRINGTON	(Ire)	69	68	70	69	276	6480
	Stephen FIELD	(Eng)	68	66	70	72	276	6480
	Brian DAVIS	(Eng)	71	66	67	72	276	6480
	Santiago LUNA	(Sp)	68	71	65	72	276	6480
36	Stephen SCAHILL	(NZ)	72	67	68	70	277	5680
	Dean ROBERTSON	(Scot)	69	69	71	70	277	5680
	Andrew OLDCORN	(Scot)	67	69	71	70	277	5680
	Jean VAN DE VELDE	(Fr)	69	68	74	66	277	5680
	Juan Carlos PIÑERO	(Sp)	71	68	67	71	277	5680
	Gordon BRAND JNR.	(Scot)	69	69	67	72	277	5680
42	Domingo HOSPITAL	(Sp)	68	68	70	72	278	4720
	Phillip PRICE	(Wal)	68	67	71	72	278	4720
	Wayne RILEY	(Aus)	67	70	71	70	278	4720
	Sam TORRANCE	(Scot)	71	68	70	69	278	4720
	Van PHILLIPS	(Eng)	70	67	72	69	278	4720
	Massimo FLORIOLI	(It)	67	68	70	73	278	4720
48	Barry LANE	(Eng)	72	64	70	73	279	3520
	John MELLOR	(Eng)	70	68	69	72	279	3520
	Olle NORDBERG	(Swe)	69	69	69	72	279	3520
	Paul MCGINLEY	(Ire)	72	67	69	71	279	3520
	Roger CHAPMAN	(Eng)	69	68	72	70	279	3520
	Thomas GÖGELE	(Ger)	72	67	72	68	279	3520
	Gary ORR	(Scot)	73	66	73	67	279	3520
	Steven RICHARDSON	(Eng)	71	66	69	73	279	3520
	Adam HUNTER	(Scot)	71	66	69	73	279	3520
57	Sven STRÜVER	(Ger)	66	69	71	74	280	2586
	Robert LEE	(Eng)	73	66	70	71	280	2586
	Kalle VAINOLA	(Fin)	70	69	70	71	280	2586
60	Andrew SANDYWELL	(Eng)	70	67	70	74	281	2320
	Raymond BURNS	(N.Ire)	72	67	70	72	281	2320
	Philip WALTON	(Ire)	69	70	70	72	281	2320
63	Peter MITCHELL	(Eng)	70	69	68	75	282	1860
	Greg TURNER	(NZ)	68	71	70	73	282	1860
	Jamie SPENCE	(Eng)	68	71	74	69	282	1860
	Andrew SHERBORNE	(Eng)	70	69	67	76	282	1860
67	Ross MCFARLANE	(Eng)	72	67	69	75	283	1198
68	Paul EALES	(Eng)	69	67	73	77	286	1196
69	Tony JOHNSTONE	(Zim)	68	69	75	75	287	1194

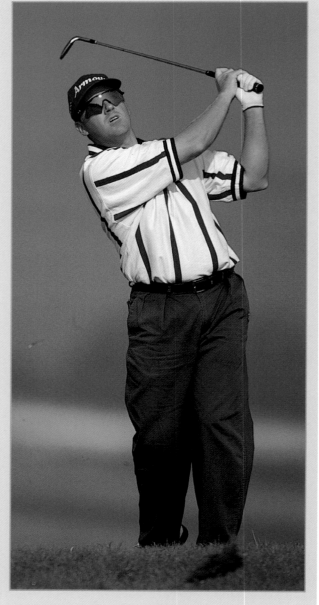

Adam Hunter plays through a glass darkly.

Distance
Spin
Balata

OH . . . MY . . . GOD.

Introducing **GOLF'S FIRST TITANIUM CORE BALL** for **BREAKTHROUGH FEEL** and **MAXIMUM DISTANCE.**

Two miracles in one game-improving ball. Let us all rejoice, and head to the tee.

As Per usual

It was the mixture as before as
Per-Ulrik Johansson cruised to a
second successive victory at The K Club

Per-Ulrik Johansson held nothing back when he was asked the secret to a stunning, six-stroke triumph. Home-made Irish soda-bread and freshly-squeezed orange juice: that, he explained, was the recipe for his successful defence of the £850,000 Smurfit European Open at The K Club.

It was clearly a powerful combination, judging from a 21 under par aggregate of 267 which equalled the lowest for a European Tour event in Ireland, set by Bernhard Langer in the 1984 Irish Open at Royal Dublin. And as a bonus on a thrilling weekend, there was the performance of José Maria Olazábal.

Entering the event in 12th position on the Ryder Cup table, Olazábal had words with the skipper, Severiano Ballesteros. 'Seve just told me to do my best,' said the younger half of the fearsome Spanish Armada. 'He said I was the only one (of three) who could play my way onto the team and he wished me well.'

That was on the Tuesday of European Open week. By the following Sunday

evening, Olazábal had delivered. With a wonderful, closing 65 – in fact he covered the last 36 holes in 132 strokes – he edged into a share of third place with Raymond Russell for 47,855 precious Ryder Cup points. The haul was sufficient to move him past Ireland's Padraig Harrington into 11th position in the points table. Not for the first time, he had responded to Seve's call.

Inevitably, there was much talk about the Ryder Cup at this, the penultimate qualifying tournament. Through the majesty of his play, however, Johansson ensured that due recognition was accorded his victory march.

Yet opening-day honours were unquestionably the preserve of Colin Montgomerie, who had travelled from Winged Foot to Straffan, via a Shell Wonderful World of Golf match against Phil Mickelson in Vale, Colorado. At a distance of only six weeks and 40 miles from the scene of his Murphy's Irish Open triumph, the Scot shot a course-record first round of 64. It meant he was a sparkling 17 under par for his last two competitive rounds on Irish soil, having surged to victory at Druids Glen with a course-record 62 on the final day. And his reaction at Straffan was like that of a schoolboy watching a thrilling movie. 'It was so good, I didn't want it to end... I wanted it to go on for 25 holes,' he said wistfully. 'That was almost as good as I can do – about three shots from being a

Seve Ballesteros (above) and Ian Woosnam (right) are one-handed wonders while Padraig Harrington (opposite) prefers two.

Costantino Rocca (left) Colin Montgomerie (centre) and Per-Ulrik Johansson (right).

perfect round. but we know there will never be the perfect round of golf.'

Twenty-four hours later, similar comments were being voiced by Johansson after he, too, had shot a 64 to lead by a stroke from Montgomerie at the halfway stage. 'Normally, when you have a good round like that, you would hit only about three really pure shots,' admitted the Swede. 'On this occasion, however, there were probably ten that came off exactly the way I visualised them. It was a great time to do it.'

Indeed the overall scoring was so good that the cut of two under was five strokes lower than the previous year and equalled the lowest cut for a Tour event in Ireland, set on that notable occasion at Royal Dublin in 1984. As it hap-

pened, Ireland's Ryder Cup challenger, Harrington, got through with a stroke to spare.

With persistent rain lashing the course, Saturday became moving day for Olazábal but a process of consolidation

for Johansson. The Spaniard created something of a stir, however, by suggesting he might not take up the Ryder Cup option. 'If I think my game is not good enough, I might say no,' he claimed.

But the mood seemed to brighten

205

Costantino Rocca (above) Mark James (below) in the driving seat.

SHOT OF THE WEEK

Faced with a birdie putt of 12 feet on the 72nd hole, José Maria Olazábal knew from the leaderboard what he had to do. 'For the top-five finish I needed, I had to hole it,' he said. When the putt went down, he punched the air with delight.

Seve Ballesteros (right) in full flight. Colin Montgomerie (below).

played rare exuberance by taking off his orange shirt and throwing it to a fan. Then he thought of matters close to his heart. 'Now that I can afford it, I'm looking for a baker who will send me fresh Irish bread wherever I travel,' he said.

Finally, with classic Swedish pragmatism, he reminded us of a notoriously fickle game. 'You know, it goes good only two per cent of the time,' he said. 'So you are not often happy.' With that, he permitted himself a quiet smile.

Dermot Gilleece

with Sunday's weather. At 198 (18 under), the Swede was four strokes clear of his closest challenger, Constantino Rocca, who happened to have been runner-up to him the previous year. And Johansson enhanced his position with a third successive bogey-free round. Behind him, the most significant moves came from Olazábal and from Peter Baker who, by improving to runner-up position from a share of fourth place overnight, produced his best performance of the season.

When it was all over, Johansson dis-

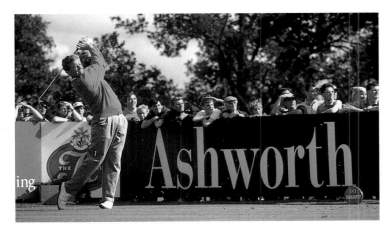

THE COURSE

With early drainage problems resolved, the course stood up admirably to relentless rain on the Saturday. Meanwhile, general satisfaction was expressed with the greens, reflecting the owner's commitment to making The K Club a truly world-class venue.

THE K CLUB, DUBLIN, AUGUST 21-24, 1997 · YARDAGE 7179 · PAR 72

Pos	Name	Country	Rnd 1	Rnd 2	Rnd 3	Rnd 4	Total	Prize Money £
1	Per-Ulrik JOHANSSON	(Swe)	68	64	66	69	267	141660
2	Peter BAKER	(Eng)	70	67	68	68	273	94440
3	Raymond RUSSELL	(Scot)	72	69	67	66	274	47855
	José Maria OLAZABAL	(Sp)	69	73	67	65	274	47855
5	Brian DAVIS	(Eng)	69	70	68	68	275	28125
	Costantino ROCCA	(It)	67	68	67	73	275	28125
	David CARTER	(Eng)	68	73	67	67	275	28125
	Mårten OLANDER	(Swe)	69	68	71	67	275	28125
9	Steven RICHARDSON	(Eng)	65	72	73	66	276	18970
10	Per HAUGSRUD	(Nor)	68	67	70	72	277	15235
	Eduardo ROMERO	(Arg)	70	66	70	71	277	15235
	Paul BROADHURST	(Eng)	70	71	69	67	277	15235
	Anders FORSBRAND	(Swe)	70	67	73	67	277	15235
14	Paul LAWRIE	(Scot)	69	71	69	69	278	11980
	Jon ROBSON	(Eng)	70	67	69	72	278	11980
	Ronan RAFFERTY	(N.Ire)	73	67	71	67	278	11980
	Daniel CHOPRA	(Swe)	66	69	75	68	278	11980
	Paul MCGINLEY	(Ire)	69	70	68	71	278	11980
19	Michael LONG	(NZ)	71	67	74	67	279	10228
	Andrew OLDCORN	(Scot)	71	68	72	68	279	10228
	Santiago LUNA	(Sp)	70	71	70	68	279	10228
22	Niclas FASTH	(Swe)	65	73	69	73	280	9180
	Jonathan LOMAS	(Eng)	67	74	66	73	280	9180
	Russell CLAYDON	(Eng)	67	70	71	72	280	9180
	Colin MONTGOMERIE	(Scot)	64	69	72	75	280	9180
	Derrick COOPER	(Eng)	68	69	73	70	280	9180
27	Patrik SJÖLAND	(Swe)	68	71	71	71	281	7662
	Jarmo SANDELIN	(Swe)	70	72	70	69	281	7662
	Andrew COLTART	(Scot)	68	73	69	71	281	7662
	Massimo FLORIOLI	(It)	70	68	75	68	281	7662
	Miguel Angel JIMÉNEZ	(Sp)	69	68	67	77	281	7662
	Ian WOOSNAM	(Wal)	71	71	70	69	281	7662
	Peter MITCHELL	(Eng)	70	67	73	71	281	7662
34	Joakim HAEGGMAN	(Swe)	71	69	76	66	282	6290
	Stephen FIELD	(Eng)	69	69	74	70	282	6290
	John MELLOR	(Eng)	70	69	71	72	282	6290
	Michael CAMPBELL	(NZ)	68	72	71	71	282	6290
	Ben TINNING	(Den)	70	68	72	72	282	6290
	Gary NICKLAUS	(USA)	72	69	71	70	282	6290
	Miles TUNNICLIFF	(Eng)	68	74	74	66	282	6290
41	Klas ERIKSSON	(Swe)	70	71	72	70	283	5185
	Wayne WESTNER	(SA)	72	70	72	69	283	5185
	Sven STRÜVER	(Ger)	73	67	72	71	283	5185
	David GILFORD	(Eng)	69	70	72	72	283	5185
	Greg TURNER	(NZ)	69	72	71	71	283	5185
	Daren LEE	(Eng)	69	72	70	72	283	5185
47	Peter HEDBLOM	(Swe)	70	72	69	73	284	4420
	Rodger DAVIS	(Aus)	71	71	74	68	284	4420
	Philip WALTON	(Ire)	68	68	79	69	284	4420
50	Domingo HOSPITAL	(Sp)	71	70	71	73	285	3825
	Padraig HARRINGTON	(Ire)	70	71	72	72	285	3825
	Paul AFFLECK	(Wal)	70	71	72	72	285	3825
	Dean ROBERTSON	(Scot)	69	67	78	71	285	3825
54	José COCERES	(Arg)	71	71	69	75	286	3145
	Clinton WHITELAW	(SA)	69	71	76	70	286	3145
	Mark ROE	(Eng)	71	71	70	74	286	3145
	Jay TOWNSEND	(USA)	71	66	75	74	286	3145
58	Andrew SHERBORNE	(Eng)	71	70	71	75	287	2635
	Mark JAMES	(Eng)	71	70	70	76	287	2635
	Stephen ALLAN	(Aus)	70	71	72	74	287	2635
61	Fredrik JACOBSON	(Swe)	75	64	78	71	288	2465
62	Paolo QUIRICI	(Swi)	75	67	75	73	290	2337
	Ross MCFARLANE	(Eng)	74	67	73	76	290	2337
64	Carl WATTS	(Eng)	70	71	73	78	292	2167
	Jeff HAWKES	(SA)	69	73	75	75	292	2167
66	David HIGGINS	(Ire)	76	66	77	76	295	1275

Stout finish from José Maria Olazábal.

A World Leader in Packaging

Workmanship from Waterford,
Ireland...

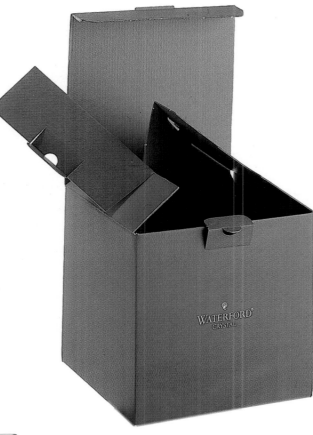

The development of global export markets has created sophisticated demands for packaging which will protect, present and promote a diverse range of products. Fruit and flowers are transported between continents, arriving as fresh as they were picked. Complex electronics need specialised protection for worldwide distribution. Delicate china and glassware must reach distant destinations in perfect condition.

Jefferson Smurfit Group plc has over sixty years' experience in meeting these demands innovatively and cost effectively. Together with its associates, Jefferson Smurfit Group has steadily grown to become the world's largest paper-based packaging organisation and largest recycler of paper, with 400 facilities in over 20 countries throughout Europe, Scandinavia, North and South America, and Asia Pacific.

Smurfit has total control of the packaging manufacturing process, starting with sourcing and sorting waste paper for its own recycling mills, or producing virgin pulp from its own forests, through to the manufacture of paper and board and the production of a broad range of packaging for diverse markets. Throughout its operations worldwide and across its product range, Smurfit applies its commitment to consistently reliable quality and to environmentally responsible production.

From corrugated board to newsprint; sturdy cases to colourful labels; intricate cartons to specialised sacks, Smurfit is skilled in answering the world's packaging needs.

Displayed in Denver,
USA!

JEFFERSON SMURFIT GROUP plc

Worldwide Headquarters:
Clonskeagh, Dublin 4, Ireland.
Phone: (+353 1) 2696622 Fax: (+353 1) 2694481
World Wide Web: htttp://www.smurfit.ie

Smurfit Ireland & UK • Smurfit Continental Europe • Smurfit Latin America • Jefferson Smurfit Corporation USA

Karlsson secures second success

As the battle for Ryder Cup points reached its climax, Robert Karlsson took the second European Tour victory of his career

At the Golfclub Munchen Nord-Eichenried in Munich, Padraig Harrington, Paul Broadhurst, Thomas Bjorn, Ignacio Garrido, Costantino Rocca, José Maria Olazábal all had something to prove. The race to be in Severiano Ballesteros's Europe team for the Ryder Cup by Johnnie Walker was finishing and though the course was flat it presented them with hills of one height or another to climb. Their goals in the BMW International Open were measured in terms of where they needed to finish in the tournament to remain in the top ten of the Ryder Cup points table (Rocca, Garrido, Bjorn) or what they needed to do to get into it (Broadhurst, Harrington, Olazábal, Chapman).

Harrington, who was 12th, was to be 26 on the Sunday. Whether he would celebrate it by getting into the Ryder Cup team would depend on his overtaking Olazábal who in turn wanted to overtake Miguel Angel Martin, out of action since missing the cut at the Open with a serious hand injury. There were so many possibilities anyone down to Miguel Angel Jimenez in 23rd position could play themselves onto the team.

The pressure was on from the start, though. 'It gets to you,' Roger Chapman, who was 15th in the Ryder Cup table, admitted. 'I shall be glad when the week is over and we can all play normal golf again.' Chapman's nerves were not calmed when he and his son had an accident in

Alexander Cejka's tee shot on the short eighth in the first round. The hole is 207 yards long and Cejka's ball, struck with a four iron, bounced twice before disappearing into the cup.

his car at the beginning of the week and after starting with a 66, Chapman faded from contention.

'I'm already in,' Bjorn, who lay eighth, said. 'They have to catch me and if they are good enough to do it there is nothing I can do about it. All I can do is try to play well and see what happens.' So saying, Bjorn did just that. A 65 in the second round and a 66 on Sunday earned him fifth place and a hug from Rocca, when they met outside the recorder's tent.

'Welcome to the team,' said Rocca, who had himself made certain of his place at Valderrama by courageously coming home in 31, five under par in his second round. Garrido missed the cut but his place was secure anyway. He and his father Antonio would definitely become only the second father and son to com-

pete in the Ryder Cup, following Percy and Peter Alliss.

Munich held good memories for Olazábal for it was there one year earlier that he had met Dr Hans-Wilhelm Muller-Wohlfahrt, the doctor whose diagnosis of his foot complaint set him back on the road to recovery. Olazábal and Muller-Wohlfahrt met up briefly and Olazábal was told he was progressing steadily. It was not sufficient of a spur for Olazábal to do better than rounds of 67, 72, 67 and 67, 15 under par. And this in turn did not earn him enough money to dislodge Miguel Angel Martin from the tenth position he held for months. Broadhurst calculated he needed a 63 in the last round and though he birdied his last three holes he could do no better than a 66 for a share of sixth place. 'Good but not good enough,' he said. 'I left myself too much to do in the last two weeks.'

Harrington started brilliantly, his 64 in his second round being described by Colin Montgomerie, no less, as 'a helluva round'. On his birthday he fought to the 72nd hole before he admitting that rounds of 66, 64, 71, 68 were a couple of strokes too many for him to finish sufficiently far ahead of Olazábal to overtake him. Harrington, a relatively modest hitter with a razor-sharp short game, started with three successive birdies but three-putted from five feet on the ninth and though he birdied three more holes coming home it was not enough.

Ballesteros had phoned him the night before. 'It gave me a boost but it didn't put any more pressure on me,' Harrington said. 'He wished me good luck, told me to relax, play my own game and not to look

T H E   C O U R S E

One of the flattest courses in Europe with few trees that came into play. The course has four par fours of less than 380 yards, and places a high premium on a good short game.

Robert Karlsson (left) comes out of the shadows during the play-off. José Maria Olazábal (right) in overdrive.

Fabrice Tarnaud (left) and Carl Watts (right) celebrate success while Padraig Harrington (centre) reflects on what might have been.
Bernhard Langer (below) with his golden club award marking his 50 tournament victories.

at the scoreboards and so I didn't.'

So after 72 holes and thousands of strokes the Ryder Cup table remained as it had been at the start of the week with Martin retaining tenth place. Because of Martin's wrist injury Ballesteros was unable to announce his Ryder Cup team on the Sunday evening.

Two players felt truly fulfilled by the week's events. The first was Robert Karlsson, the tall Swede, whose form had been so poor he had had to resort to going to a counsellor to rediscover how to win. And he did this successfully, with rounds that totalled 24 under par. First he birdied the 71st and 72nd holes to force a play-off and then he defeated Carl Watts on the third extra hole where Watts drove into a pond and dropped one stroke.

The other was Watts who, far from being disappointed probably felt he had won the Ryder Cup. On the Wednesday he had been 149th on the Volvo Ranking and had missed the cut at 12 events this season. If the Ryder Cup contenders had been under pressure, then so was he. He had just got married, just taken out a mortgage on a house and was desperate to retain his card for a second season. Second place, a cheque for £83,000 did just that. No wonder he was serving champagne to his friends on the flight back to London that night.

John Hopkins.

GOLFCLUB MÜNCHEN NORD-EICHENRIED, AUGUST 28-31, 1997 · YARDAGE 6923 · PAR 72

Pos	Name	Country	Rnd 1	Rnd 2	Rnd 3	Rnd 4	Total	Prize Money £
1	Robert KARLSSON	(Swe)	67	67	64	66	264	125000
2	Carl WATTS	(Eng)	64	68	67	65	264	83320
3	Colin MONTGOMERIE	(Scot)	65	67	67	66	265	46940
4	Fabrice TARNAUD	(Fr)	63	68	68	67	266	37500
5	Thomas BJORN	(Den)	68	65	68	66	267	31770
6	Phillip PRICE	(Wal)	65	69	68	66	268	22500
	Paul BROADHURST	(Eng)	68	67	67	66	268	22500
	José COCERES	(Arg)	69	66	66	67	268	22500
9	Miguel Angel JIMÉNEZ	(Sp)	67	70	69	63	269	15180
	Padraig HARRINGTON	(Ire)	66	64	71	68	269	15180
	Eduardo ROMERO	(Arg)	67	70	64	68	269	15180
12	Stephen SCAHILL	(NZ)	66	71	69	64	270	10490
	Niclas FASTH	(Swe)	66	71	63	70	270	10490
	Mark MOULAND	(Wal)	67	68	71	64	270	10490
	Bernhard LANGER	(Ger)	68	69	68	65	270	10490
	Jarmo SANDELIN	(Swe)	67	69	68	66	270	10490
	Marc FARRY	(Fr)	68	69	66	67	270	10490
	Wayne WESTNER	(SA)	64	70	68	68	270	10490
	Paul LAWRIE	(Scot)	66	69	67	68	270	10490
	Ronan RAFFERTY	(N.Ire)	69	70	64	67	270	10490
	Greg TURNER	(NZ)	68	68	72	62	270	10490
22	Jay TOWNSEND	(USA)	66	70	66	69	271	8212
	Gary ORR	(Scot)	69	69	64	69	271	8212
	Domingo HOSPITAL	(Sp)	71	65	64	71	271	8212
	Paul CURRY	(Eng)	65	69	72	65	271	8212
26	Mark ROE	(Eng)	70	68	66	68	272	7200
	Mathias GRÖNBERG	(Swe)	65	69	66	72	272	7200
	Costantino ROCCA	(It)	69	70	65	68	272	7200
	Stephen AMES	(T&T)	69	63	72	68	272	7200
	Ernie ELS	(SA)	67	70	70	65	272	7200
31	Daniel CHOPRA	(Swe)	67	71	69	66	273	5934
	Patrik SJÖLAND	(Swe)	64	71	69	69	273	5934
	Peter MITCHELL	(Eng)	69	68	67	69	273	5934
	José Maria OLAZABAL	(Sp)	67	72	67	67	273	5934
	Angel CABRERA	(Arg)	67	71	68	67	273	5934
	Per HAUGSRUD	(Nor)	68	71	66	68	273	5934
	Christy O'CONNOR JNR	(Ire)	69	69	69	66	273	5934
	Jon ROBSON	(Eng)	69	68	66	70	273	5934
39	Paolo QUIRICI	(Swi)	68	66	69	71	274	4875
	Scott HENDERSON	(Scot)	69	70	69	66	274	4875
	Roger CHAPMAN	(Eng)	66	70	68	70	274	4875
	Mark JAMES	(Eng)	70	64	69	71	274	4875
	Ross MCFARLANE	(Eng)	71	68	65	70	274	4875
	Steve WEBSTER	(Eng)	68	71	67	68	274	4875
45	Iain PYMAN	(Eng)	69	70	68	68	275	3975
	Michael LONG	(NZ)	65	72	68	70	275	3975
	Carl SUNESON	(Sp)	65	70	69	71	275	3975
	Peter O'MALLEY	(Aus)	69	69	70	67	275	3975
	Russell CLAYDON	(Eng)	68	69	68	70	275	3975
	Adam HUNTER	(Scot)	70	69	69	67	275	3975
51	Dennis EDLUND	(Swe)	66	70	69	71	276	3075
	Stephen FIELD	(Eng)	68	68	70	70	276	3075
	Per-Ulrik JOHANSSON	(Swe)	68	70	69	69	276	3075
	Thomas GÖGELE	(Ger)	69	70	68	69	276	3075
	Gary CLARK	(Eng)	68	70	65	73	276	3075
	Derrick COOPER	(Eng)	69	68	72	67	276	3075
57	Fredrik JACOBSON	(Swe)	66	67	73	71	277	2300
	Gordon BRAND JNR.	(Scot)	69	69	71	68	277	2300
	Paul MCGINLEY	(Ire)	70	69	67	71	277	2300
	Raymond RUSSELL	(Scot)	65	69	70	73	277	2300
	Jim PAYNE	(Eng)	72	67	67	71	277	2300
	Diego BORREGO	(Sp)	71	67	68	71	277	2300
63	Rodger DAVIS	(Aus)	70	69	70	69	278	1743
	Peter BAKER	(Eng)	64	68	70	76	278	1743
	Andrew COLTART	(Scot)	67	72	72	67	278	1743
	Daren LEE	(Eng)	69	69	74	66	278	1743
67	Peter HEDBLOM	(Swe)	64	72	74	69	279	1121
	Steven RICHARDSON	(Eng)	73	66	71	69	279	1121
	Martin GATES	(Eng)	71	68	75	65	279	1121
70	Clinton WHITELAW	(SA)	70	69	71	70	280	1115
	Darren COLE	(Aus)	71	66	74	69	280	1115
	Katsuyoshi TOMORI	(Jap)	68	69	69	74	280	1115
73	Mårten OLANDER	(Swe)	69	70	74	69	282	1111
74	Jonathan LOMAS	(Eng)	66	70	74	73	283	1109

Seve Ballesteros and Ken Schofield in Ryder Cup press conference.

Rocca on a Swiss roll

A final round of 62

put Costantino Rocca

on a high in the Alps

*F*or Costantino Rocca, the 40-year-old Italian from Bergamo, the season had been a poor one. The former polystyrene box-maker, who only decided to make golf his career at the age of 23 when offered a post at his local club back in 1979, had finished fourth in the Volvo Ranking the previous two years but, coming in to the Canon European Masters, he was a lowly 45th and not even sure to retain his place in Europe's Johnnie Walker Ryder Cup side. He had made £30,000 less in prize-money from his 21 appearances during the year as the Swiss first prize of £133,330.

His fitness – or his lack of it – had been the main problem. First a shoulder injury incurred at the Deutsche Bank Tournament Players' Championship of Europe in Hamburg and then bruised ribs preventing him swinging through with his normal fluidity. Yet there had been signs that he was getting back his form and that certainly pleased Severiano Ballesteros, the Ryder Cup captain. He wanted Rocca on his side for Valderrama and did not want to have to pick him as a wild card choice.

What happened that week high above the Rhone Valley at Crans-Montana made them both happy. Helped by a career low final round of 62, lower than any score he had ever made while playing with his chums at Bergamo and better by one than his three previous low rounds on Tour,

THE COURSE

There is no more spectacular venue on Tour than Crans-sur-Sierre. As you wind your way up the narrow road from Sion it is difficult to imagine you will come to a level piece of ground for even a nine-hole-short course but suddenly you are at Crans, best known as a winter ski-resort but with a golf course useable five months a year. Built on a plateau 5,000 feet above the Rhone Valley and 5,000 feet below the Pleine Mort glacier, the tricky course offers the players not just staggeringly beautiful panoramic views, but the inspired opportunity to produce some of the lowest scores of the season. It is a magical combination.

Rocca scored a marvellous victory.

The win was not achieved without some nail-biting drama. Rocca finished well ahead of most of his rivals on the final day but as he, his wife Antonella and children Chiara and Francesco, waited in the players' lounge, the threat to his 72-hole 22 under par total of 266 receded only when Aberdeen's Scott Henderson's putt to tie finished tantalisingly for him, but happily for the Italian on the lip of the hole at the last.

Rocca, the Tour's most dramatic performer who wears his heart on his sleeve, had survived the tense last hour. He had won the title with a total most had thought might have been a shot or even two shots short of being good enough for victory, but he had done it.

Nick Faldo, the victim of an ice-cold putter, defending champion Colin Montgomerie and young Henderson, Robert Karlsson, who had brought his BMW International winning form of the previous week up the mountain, firing nine birdies in a closing 64, and Patrik Sjöland, talented Peter Lonard, Lian-Wei

Zhang, Ronan Rafferty and Darren Clarke just failed to make enough birdies on the final day to head him.

Rocca, the first Italian to win the title since Roberto Bernardini won in 1968 and 1969, took a massive leap into the top 12 in the Volvo Ranking and breathed a sigh of relief about his Cup place. The smile was broader than ever on the face of the man who once earned £50 a week making boxes and now makes considerably more making birdies.

If the winner had any regrets it was that he did not become the first man to break 60 on the European Tour. After he had birdied the 15th hole he knew he needed three birdies to do it and with the adrenalin pumping through his veins he genuinely felt he could.

The last two holes are eminently birdieable short par fours but the worry was the par three 16th, redesigned by Severiano Ballesteros. When he threaded his tee shot down the avenue of trees to under six feet from the hole it looked good for a two but he missed the putt and the chance was gone. Not making a birdie

at the last two either ensured the Crans fans had what they have now come to expect – a close finish.

His victory in Crans, where low scoring in the rarefied air has long been a tradition, was achieved by Rocca playing his best golf since scoring his first triumph on Tour at Lyon in 1993, although he is probably better remembered for forcing that play-off with John Daly for the 1995 Open Championship title at St Andrews by holing from 60 feet through the Valley of Sin, or for his 1996 Volvo PGA Championship success at Wentworth when he held off the determined challenge of Faldo.

Ironically, Rocca's last round heroics did not produce the best round of the week on greens which, because of a combination of unfortunate factors, not least the Alpine weather, were not at their best. Concerns about the putting surfaces were put in perspective on the first day when Gary Orr, still chasing his first overdue win on Tour, fired a 61 – just a shot outside the course record and Henderson a 62. While Henderson, whose joint-second finish with Karlsson, was his best on

Tour, moved up 50 spots in the Ranking to 22nd. Orr could not maintain that first day form and finished joint 25th.

Ballesteros, whose anxiety about the Ryder Cup had been affecting his form all year, missed the halfway cut and Scott Hoch, set to make his Ryder Cup debut at the age of 41, nearly did after opening with a jet-lagged 73 to be 12 strokes off Orr's hot pace. Hoch showed his class, however, with succeeding rounds of 66, 67 and 65 to finish tenth and make his trip across the Atlantic for a week of a fondues and racclettes, all washed down with a bottle of the local Dole, very worthwhile.

On hand at the end, as always, was the local band adding a touch of local

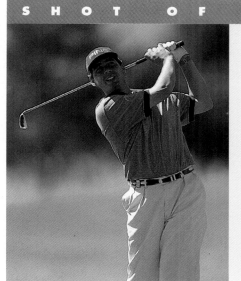

SHOT OF THE WEEK

Tricky pin positions on the short holes did not make holes-in-one easy to come by on the final day of the Canon European Masters but Scott Henderson, who finished joint second with Robert Karlsson, behind winner Constantino Rocca, came desperately close to his first Tour ace at the 202-yard 13th. Although Henderson, who had learned much from playing the previous day with Nick Faldo, admitted that on his first visit to the mountains he had sometimes felt breathless at 5,000 feet, he left the fans breathless with his five iron tee shot which finished just three inches away from the jackpot bonus of a car; and as it would turn out, three inches away from an eventual play-off for the title.

Scott Hoch in Alpine setting.

drama to the occasion as its music echoed round the snow-clad Alps looking even more impressive in the late afternoon sunshine, so welcome after the initial three-hour delay in starting because of low cloud. Certainly Rocca was glad it cleared. If the event had had to be reduced to 54 holes Nick Faldo, the leader with a round to go, would have taken the title for the second time.

This, however, was destined to be Rocca's week and as the champagne and the chianti flowed at the end nobody shared his joy more than his fellow Italian, Aldo Casera who won the title back in 1950 and is still playing in the event. Now

78, Casera teed up for the 49th consecutive time and in the first round shot his age which was remarkable enough. On the second day he did even better shooting a 73, the same as Ballesteros. He missed the cut but his week, in its own way, had been just as significant as that of the winner.

Renton Laidlaw

CRANS-SUR-SIERRE, SEPTEMBER 4-7, 1997 · YARDAGE 6663 · PAR 71

Pos	Name	Country	Rnd 1	Rnd 2	Rnd 3	Rnd 4	Total	Prize Money £
1	Costantino ROCCA	(It)	72	64	68	62	266	133330
2	Robert KARLSSON	(Swe)	68	66	69	64	267	69475
	Scott HENDERSON	(Scot)	62	66	73	66	267	69475
4	Patrik SJÖLAND	(Swe)	71	66	65	66	268	36940
	Peter LONARD	(Aus)	66	67	67	68	268	36940
6	Lian-Wei ZHANG	(Chi)	67	67	67	68	269	22460
	Ronan RAFFERTY	(N.Ire)	65	66	69	69	269	22460
	Darren CLARKE	(N.Ire)	67	64	69	69	269	22460
	Nick FALDO	(Eng)	66	65	68	70	269	22460
10	Scott HOCH	(USA)	73	66	67	65	271	15360
	Colin MONTGOMERIE	(Scot)	65	72	64	70	271	15360
12	Mathias GRÖNBERG	(Swe)	68	71	69	64	272	11395
	Alex CEJKA	(Ger)	68	70	68	66	272	11395
	Domingo HOSPITAL	(Sp)	68	69	68	67	272	11395
	Jon ROBSON	(Eng)	68	69	68	67	272	11395
	Mathew GOGGIN	(Aus)	66	69	69	68	272	11395
	Stephen SCAHILL	(NZ)	71	67	66	68	272	11395
	Santiago LUNA	(Sp)	69	66	68	69	272	11395
	Gordon BRAND JNR.	(Scot)	69	67	67	69	272	11395
	Niclas FASTH	(Swe)	67	67	68	70	272	11395
21	Joakim HAEGGMAN	(Swe)	66	69	70	68	273	9000
	Jeff HAWKES	(SA)	69	70	65	69	273	9000
	Silvio GRAPPASONNI	(It)	67	65	71	70	273	9000
	Phil GOLDING	(Eng)	66	68	68	71	273	9000
25	Stephen ALLAN	(Aus)	71	68	70	65	274	7680
	Ignacio GARRIDO	(Sp)	71	66	72	65	274	7680
	Michael LONG	(NZ)	66	71	68	69	274	7680
	Gordon J BRAND	(Eng)	71	68	66	69	274	7680
	Retief GOOSEN	(SA)	66	68	69	71	274	7680
	Gary ORR	(Scot)	61	68	72	73	274	7680
	Thomas GÖGELE	(Ger)	66	65	70	73	274	7680
32	Max ANGLERT	(Swe)	67	66	73	69	275	6160
	Martin GATES	(Eng)	69	70	68	68	275	6160
	Steven BOTTOMLEY	(Eng)	71	68	68	68	275	6160
	Fredrik JACOBSON	(Swe)	66	69	72	68	275	6160
	Ian GARBUTT	(Eng)	70	68	70	67	275	6160
	Richard BOXALL	(Eng)	68	71	67	69	275	6160
	Phillip PRICE	(Wal)	67	68	70	70	275	6160
	Robert LEE	(Eng)	66	73	66	70	275	6160
40	Jarmo SANDELIN	(Swe)	69	68	70	69	276	5200
	Barry LANE	(Eng)	67	69	72	68	276	5200
	Wayne WESTNER	(SA)	71	66	68	71	276	5200
	Jean VAN DE VELDE	(Fr)	68	69	67	72	276	5200
44	Michael CAMPBELL	(NZ)	69	66	71	71	277	4240
	Roger CHAPMAN	(Eng)	67	71	70	69	277	4240
	Daniel CHOPRA	(Swe)	72	64	72	69	277	4240
	Anders HANSEN	(Den)	68	71	70	68	277	4240
	Paul AFFLECK	(Wal)	70	68	72	67	277	4240
	Klas ERIKSSON	(Swe)	72	65	73	67	277	4240
	Mark ROE	(Eng)	68	68	69	72	277	4240
	John BICKERTON	(Eng)	68	70	67	72	277	4240
52	Alberto BINAGHI	(It)	70	67	72	69	278	3520
53	Eduardo ROMERO	(Arg)	70	69	68	72	279	3280
	Francisco VALERA	(Sp)	69	67	70	73	279	3280
55	Peter O'MALLEY	(Aus)	68	69	70	73	280	2628
	Gary EMERSON	(Eng)	69	67	72	72	280	2628
	Miguel Angel JIMÉNEZ	(Sp)	67	72	70	71	280	2628
	David HIGGINS	(Ire)	70	68	71	71	280	2628
	Emanuele CANONICA	(It)	68	69	72	71	280	2628
	Daren LEE	(Eng)	68	70	73	69	280	2628
	Carl SUNESON	(Sp)	71	67	73	69	280	2628
62	Massimo FLORIOLI	(It)	71	68	71	71	281	2240
63	Gary EVANS	(Eng)	70	67	71	74	282	1727
	Ignacio FELIU	(Sp)	66	73	71	72	282	1727
	Mårten OLANDER	(Swe)	69	69	74	70	282	1727
	Padraig HARRINGTON	(Ire)	68	69	75	70	282	1727
	Fernando ROCA	(Sp)	65	74	74	69	282	1727
68	John MELLOR	(Eng)	66	72	72	74	284	1196
69	Per HAUGSRUD	(Nor)	70	69	74	72	285	1194
70	José Maria CAÑIZARES	(Sp)	69	69	75	74	287	1192
71	Marc FARRY	(Fr)	69	70	75	74	288	1190
72	Mark DAVIS	(Eng)	69	69	75	76	289	1188

Robert Karlsson shared second place.

Life on Mars? The abominable Golfman? Another double bogey?

WRITE YOUR
OWN STORY WITH THE
CANON EOS500N

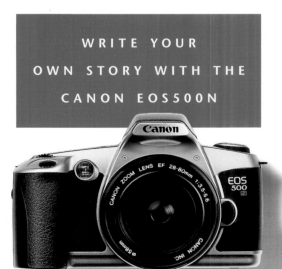

Canon EOS 500 N

http:\\sport.europe.canon.com

O'Meara edges home

Mark O'Meara saved par on
the final two holes to gain
a narrow victory in Paris

*I*t would ultimately prove to be American Mark O'Meara's week, but anybody visiting this picture-postcard setting on the outskirts of the French capital would remember it for the day Severiano Ballesteros rolled up his sleeves and rolled back the years while the game rolled out the red carpet for the master golfer.

The Sizzling Seve tabloid headlines had long since been replaced by Suffering

Seve messages as the Spaniard sought peace with his game and mind. But for five glorious hours on a crisp, early autumn morning, the three-time Open, double US Masters winner produced the kind of spectacular which used to be the norm.

Ballesteros knew there was something wrong when he arrived on the practice range. He felt good… and it had been many a topped drive, sliced iron and three-putt since that had happened.

But Ballesteros told his caddie to expect fireworks and what followed

rivalled the displays frequently illuminating the night air above the nearby Palace of Versailles.

He was at his flamboyant best – lashing the ball vast distances, showing the touch of a porcelain polisher around the greens and blowing the dust off a long-

time redundant bag of tricks.

Playing companion Darren Clarke could only shake his head in amazement at one piece of escapology. Trapped under a fir tree, Ballesteros weighed up the alternatives and opted for the high risk shot. Actually, it was more impossible than high risk, but he has always specialised in miracles.

The Spaniard went on his knees to hit the ball with the heel of a four wood through a gap scarcely big enough to squeeze a tennis ball through. Everybody else was praying he got out at all. Ballesteros looked somewhat disappointed that he had not

A strong contender for shot of the season was the one Severiano Ballesteros played from his knees during his first round 65. Trapped under a giant fir tree, anybody else would have chipped out sideways. Not him. He took out his four wood, went down in prayer position, flattened his swing and lashed the ball 180 yards through a tiny gap. A potential six was turned into a birdie four by a stroke of genius.

made the green some 230 yards away.

But Ballesteros did punch the air and his birdie four was one of seven in an opening 65 which took him to the top of the leaderboard alongside Australian Peter O'Malley.

Normal service was resumed as soon as it took Ballesteros to complete his second round. A 73, which he did not beat in his last two rounds, starting the quick descent to a tied-43rd finish. Not that he was too disappointed. At least he had made the cut and proved that whenever he really wants it, his game is

Bernhard Langer (left) demonstrates his ball-balancing skills from sand.
The unmistakeable silhouette of Greg Norman (above).

THE COURSE

One of the most beautiful settings on the Tour. Just five miles from Versailles and cut through an apple orchard, also featuring just about every species of tree imaginable, including Japanese maple. This year saw the introduction of a new hole – the 522-yard par five sixth, whose main feature is a three-tier green offering a variety of pin positions.

still there.

Others would show that they were more than one-round wonders. O'Malley would feature all the way, fellow Australian Greg Norman would similarly threaten, while O'Meara would make steady progress until he was in position for a last day show of dominance.

It was only on the last day that a previously unconsidered element entered the equation. Sweden's Jarmo Sandelin had started the final round four shots behind joint leaders O'Malley and Norman and three behind O'Meara.

Per-Ulrik Johansson stripes one from the rough.

A best-of-the-day 67 would be good enough to take Sandelin above all but the 40-year-old American. O'Meara, thanks to

single putts on the last three greens, held on to triumph by the slimmest of margins.

O'Meara collected £116,660 and many believed had struck a mighty blow for American morale with the Ryder Cup so close.

But Ballesteros had had the first say of an outstanding week and would have the last. 'What happens here has no bearing on what will happen in Spain,' said Europe's captain. Those who had seen his miracle shot knew better than to question his judgement.

Martin Hardy

Saint-Nom-La-Bretèche, Paris, September 11-14, 1997 · Par 71 · Yards 6903

Pos	Name	Country	Rnd 1	Rnd 2	Rnd 3	Rnd 4	Total	Prize Money £
1	Mark O'MEARA	(USA)	69	67	66	69	271	116660
2	Jarmo SANDELIN	(Swe)	70	70	65	67	272	77770
3	Peter O'MALLEY	(Aus)	65	68	68	72	273	39410
	Greg NORMAN	(Aus)	67	66	68	72	273	39410
5	Sven STRÜVER	(Ger)	71	65	68	72	276	25046
	Eduardo ROMERO	(Arg)	68	68	68	72	276	25046
	Patrik SJÖLAND	(Swe)	75	66	69	66	276	25046
8	David GILFORD	(Eng)	69	68	73	67	277	15703
	Paul LAWRIE	(Scot)	68	71	70	68	277	15703
	Lee WESTWOOD	(Eng)	68	68	74	67	277	15703
11	Silvio GRAPPASONNI	(It)	66	69	72	71	278	12460
	Rolf MUNTZ	(Hol)	72	70	69	67	278	12460
13	Bernhard LANGER	(Ger)	72	65	67	75	279	10318
	Retief GOOSEN	(SA)	70	67	73	69	279	10318
	José COCERES	(Arg)	67	74	70	68	279	10318
	Paul AFFLECK	(Wal)	67	72	71	69	279	10318
	Phillip PRICE	(Wal)	69	68	71	71	279	10318
18	Martin GATES	(Eng)	73	69	68	70	280	8575
	Per-Ulrik JOHANSSON	(Swe)	71	68	69	72	280	8575
	Fabrice TARNAUD	(Fr)	69	70	73	68	280	8575
	Stephen AMES	(T&T)	69	70	71	70	280	8575
22	Rodger DAVIS	(Aus)	71	71	68	71	281	7560
	Colin MONTGOMERIE	(Scot)	71	72	69	69	281	7560
	Ronan RAFFERTY	(N.Ire)	69	73	72	67	281	7560
	Jonathan LOMAS	(Eng)	69	70	74	68	281	7560
	Andrew OLDCORN	(Scot)	71	66	70	74	281	7560
27	Peter MITCHELL	(Eng)	69	69	74	70	282	6510
	Mathias GRÖNBERG	(Swe)	74	67	67	74	282	6510
	Tony JOHNSTONE	(Zim)	67	65	76	74	282	6510
	Miguel Angel JIMÉNEZ	(Sp)	70	71	70	71	282	6510
	Peter HEDBLOM	(Swe)	71	68	71	72	282	6510
32	Raymond RUSSELL	(Scot)	69	71	71	72	283	5670
	Iain PYMAN	(Eng)	72	68	70	73	283	5670
	Greg TURNER	(NZ)	69	71	72	71	283	5670
	Adam HUNTER	(Scot)	68	69	71	75	283	5670
36	Jim PAYNE	(Eng)	74	67	71	72	284	4900
	Dennis EDLUND	(Swe)	73	70	72	69	284	4900
	Jesper PARNEVIK	(Swe)	73	69	69	73	284	4900
	Ian WOOSNAM	(Wal)	68	73	70	73	284	4900
	Joakim HAEGGMAN	(Swe)	72	71	72	69	284	4900
	David HOWELL	(Eng)	66	72	72	74	284	4900
	Paolo QUIRICI	(Swi)	70	71	72	71	284	4900
43	Gary EVANS	(Eng)	69	71	74	71	285	4130
	Seve BALLESTEROS	(Sp)	65	73	74	73	285	4130
	Ian GARBUTT	(Eng)	74	68	70	73	285	4130
	Mark ROE	(Eng)	71	69	73	72	285	4130
47	Stephen FIELD	(Eng)	69	68	76	73	286	3360
	Diego BORREGO	(Sp)	72	71	71	72	286	3360
	Richard GREEN	(Aus)	72	71	68	75	286	3360
	Philip WALTON	(Ire)	70	71	75	70	286	3360
	Russell CLAYDON	(Eng)	69	70	74	73	286	3360
	Paul BROADHURST	(Eng)	71	71	72	72	286	3360
	Pedro LINHART	(Sp)	73	68	73	72	286	3360
54	Eamonn DARCY	(Ire)	76	66	70	75	287	2461
	David CARTER	(Eng)	73	70	74	70	287	2461
	Michael JONZON	(Swe)	67	71	75	74	287	2461
	Sam TORRANCE	(Scot)	71	70	73	73	287	2461
	Robert ALLENBY	(Aus)	74	69	74	70	287	2461
	Mark MOULAND	(Wal)	73	69	74	71	287	2461
60	Barry LANE	(Eng)	72	69	73	74	288	2030
	Ross DRUMMOND	(Scot)	73	68	73	74	288	2030
	Andrew SHERBORNE	(Eng)	71	72	78	67	288	2030
63	Robert COLES	(Eng)	73	69	73	74	289	1855
	Daniel CHOPRA	(Swe)	68	74	73	74	289	1855
65	Des SMYTH	(Ire)	69	67	78	76	290	1400
	Peter LONARD	(Aus)	72	71	71	76	290	1400
	Sergio GARCIA (AM)	(Sp)	71	72	73	74	290	1400
67	Jeff REMESY	(Fr)	73	69	79	70	291	1045
	Malcolm MACKENZIE	(Eng)	71	71	75	74	291	1045
	Steven BOTTOMLEY	(Eng)	70	71	76	74	291	1045
	Wayne RILEY	(Aus)	68	75	77	71	291	1045
71	Marc FARRY	(Fr)	76	67	73	76	292	1038
	Carl SUNESON	(Sp)	71	66	78	77	292	1038
	Emanuele CANONICA	(It)	71	70	75	76	292	1038
74	Miles TUNNICLIFF	(Eng)	72	71	72	78	293	1033
	Gary CLARK	(Eng)	71	69	77	76	293	1033
76	Mark DAVIS	(Eng)	73	70	73	78	294	1030
77	Paul EALES	(Eng)	70	69	79	77	295	1027
	Pierre FULKE	(Swe)	71	72	75	77	295	1027
79	Gordon BRAND JNR.	(Scot)	72	71	80	78	301	1024

Greg Norman pitched into joint third place.

Turner hangs on

Greg Turner staved off a strong challenge from Colin Montgomerie for the biggest win of his career

Colin Montgomerie once remarked that Nick Faldo was the last person that any player wanted to see in his rear view mirror. In more recent times that mantle has assuredly passed to Montgomerie himself.

Imagine, therefore, what was going through Greg Turner's mind as he stood on the 18th tee at the Forest of Arden, the leader by a stroke in the One 2 One British Masters. He had just dropped a shot at the previous hole after hitting his approach through the green.

Now, a glance at the scoreboard would have told him that Montgomerie was sitting in the locker room with a 12 under par total of 274 and that he had to confront a daunting par three without a single shot to spare. When Turner's tee shot finished in a greenside bunker, Montgomerie was not so much in the rear view mirror as pulling up alongside.

Turner's year to that point had not been a particularly good one, without a single top ten finish all season. His last victory had been in 1995 and he had never won an event in Europe boasting such a distinguished field.

'My putting has been the problem this season,' he explained. 'All year I have had to be patient, waiting for it to come right. I started to feel something happen at the BMW International in Germany.'

THE COURSE

In the weeks leading up to the event, it was feared that some unseasonally hot weather in August would mean the greens would not be up to the standard of previous years. As it turned out, the greenkeeping staff worked wonders, and the course was seen in a true light. It has plenty going for it, with wildlife roaming its acres, and with many millions now earmarked for improvements, it is only going to get better.

Two weeks later, it certainly did come right at the Forest of Arden, where rounds of 68, 71, and 66 took him into the lead after three rounds.

On day one it had been Raymond Russell and Mark Roe who had held the attention. Roe shot 65, which certainly made for a happier memory of the Forest of Arden than his appearance there in 1994, when he was hit on the head by an amateur's stray ball during the pro-am.

Russell, meanwhile, calmly began his round with eight straight birdies to equal a European Tour record. It says everything about the way the players cocoon themselves in concentration that Russell had to be reminded of his feat at the end of the round. 'I had how many birdies in a row did you say?' he remarked.

A second successive 69 gave Peter O'Malley a one-shot lead going into the third day, but Turner had made his move, and was among a group of five who shared second place.

For many of the crowd and nearly all of the media, attention was fixed on the Ryder Cup competitors who were in the field.

None were in contention at this stage but several players shone over the weekend. In the third round Thomas Bjorn shot 66 to be in second place, two shots behind Turner, who came in with the same score. Bjorn, who had taken a week off to work with his coach, had reaped immediate benefits.

But it was Montgomerie who was to challenge Turner on the last day. 'I figured it was a two-horse race

Thomas Bjorn contended strongly.

230

Michael Jonzon, Darren Clarke and the ever-present view in the rear mirror, Colin Montgomerie.

SHOT OF THE WEEK

Not the most spectacular but context is everything and Greg Turner's bunker shot at the 18th which set up his victory meant everything too. Think what was at stake: play the shot properly and he would win the biggest tournament of his career; play it badly and he would be in a play-off with Colin Montgomerie. In such circumstances, it was a fine effort to get it so close.

between me and Thomas but halfway through the final round the horse changed.' Turner said. Montgomerie was mounting one of his last round specials.

In two previous tournaments at the Forest of Arden, Montgomerie had finished third and second, but this time had scraped into the weekend play on the 36-hole cut limit.

Now he made rapid progress through the field. A 67 on Saturday was followed by a 63 in the final round, and now we awaited to see whether Turner would hold his nerve.

Jarmo Sandelin (top) and José Maria Olazábal (above).

What a long walk it must have been from the 18th tee, round the lake, before descending into the bunker. 'Certainly

there were a lot of things going through my mind.' Said Turner. 'It was hard not to look back with regret to the 17th where I had dropped a silly shot.'

By the 18th green, his heavily pregnant wife, Jane, kept her fingers crossed. In the locker-room, Montgomerie was wondering whether he would have to slip on his golf shoes.

Turner's bunker shot was a brave one, the ball coming to rest five feet from the hole.

The putt never looked like missing.

Derek Lawrenson

MARRIOTT FOREST OF ARDEN HOTEL & CC, SEPTEMBER 18-21, 1997 • PAR 72 • YARDAGE 7134

Pos	Name	Country	Rnd 1	Rnd 2	Rnd 3	Rnd 4	Total	Prize Money £
1	Greg TURNER	(NZ)	68	71	66	70	275	125000
2	Colin MONTGOMERIE	(Scot)	72	74	67	63	276	83320
3	Mark ROE	(Eng)	65	74	70	70	279	46940
4	Thomas BJORN	(Den)	69	72	66	73	280	34635
	Raymond RUSSELL	(Scot)	64	75	71	70	280	34635
6	Sam TORRANCE	(Scot)	69	75	66	71	281	24375
	Phillip PRICE	(Wal)	71	68	72	70	281	24375
8	Robert ALLENBY	(Aus)	71	73	69	69	282	16072
	Angel CABRERA	(Arg)	71	75	67	69	282	16072
	Alberto BINAGHI	(It)	72	74	70	66	282	16072
	Patrik SJÖLAND	(Swe)	68	74	71	69	282	16072
12	Darren CLARKE	(N.Ire)	71	72	70	70	283	12146
	Michael JONZON	(Swe)	70	72	67	74	283	12146
	Peter O'MALLEY	(Aus)	69	69	72	73	283	12146
15	Paolo QUIRICI	(Swi)	70	74	70	70	284	10138
	Klas ERIKSSON	(Swe)	70	73	73	68	284	10138
	Sven STRÜVER	(Ger)	69	73	71	71	284	10138
	Mark JAMES	(Eng)	71	71	67	75	284	10138
	Retief GOOSEN	(SA)	72	69	73	70	284	10138
20	Russell CLAYDON	(Eng)	68	76	69	72	285	8775
	Jean Louis GUEPY	(Fr)	74	70	69	72	285	8775
	Richard BOXALL	(Eng)	71	72	75	67	285	8775
23	Dennis EDLUND	(Swe)	69	75	70	72	286	7650
	Thomas GÖGELE	(Ger)	73	72	68	73	286	7650
	Stephen AMES	(T&T)	71	72	71	72	286	7650
	Peter HEDBLOM	(Swe)	67	75	75	69	286	7650
	Jay TOWNSEND	(USA)	71	71	72	72	286	7650
	Gary ORR	(Scot)	70	71	72	73	286	7650
	David GILFORD	(Eng)	71	70	69	76	286	7650
30	Santiago LUNA	(Sp)	72	72	70	73	287	6345
	José Maria OLAZABAL	(Sp)	72	73	70	72	287	6345
	Brian DAVIS	(Eng)	69	73	72	73	287	6345
	Stephen SCAHILL	(NZ)	70	72	73	72	287	6345
	Daniel CHOPRA	(Swe)	67	75	74	71	287	6345
35	Gordon BRAND JNR.	(Scot)	71	73	73	71	288	5325
	Gary EVANS	(Eng)	71	73	68	76	288	5325
	Ian GARBUTT	(Eng)	73	72	73	70	288	5325
	Peter BAKER	(Eng)	74	72	72	70	288	5325
	David J RUSSELL	(Eng)	72	71	70	75	288	5325
	Wayne WESTNER	(SA)	69	74	72	73	288	5325
	Ronan RAFFERTY	(N.Ire)	71	71	75	71	288	5325
	Mark DAVIS	(Eng)	71	69	75	73	288	5325
43	Paul LAWRIE	(Scot)	69	76	72	72	289	4275
	Ignacio GARRIDO	(Sp)	76	70	76	67	289	4275
	Carl MASON	(Eng)	70	76	70	73	289	4275
	Andrew SANDYWELL	(Eng)	71	75	74	69	289	4275
	Ross DRUMMOND	(Scot)	72	74	71	72	289	4275
	Emanuele CANONICA	(It)	71	70	76	72	289	4275
49	Jonathan LOMAS	(Eng)	68	77	71	74	290	3525
	Peter LONARD	(Aus)	75	70	73	72	290	3525
	Eamonn DARCY	(Ire)	70	76	72	72	290	3525
	Mårten OLANDER	(Swe)	68	71	78	73	290	3525
53	Jean VAN DE VELDE	(Fr)	73	71	72	75	291	2775
	Robert COLES	(Eng)	72	74	73	72	291	2775
	Costantino ROCCA	(It)	75	71	73	72	291	2775
	Roger CHAPMAN	(Eng)	75	68	74	74	291	2775
	Wayne RILEY	(Aus)	70	72	78	71	291	2775
	Jarmo SANDELIN	(Swe)	69	73	71	78	291	2775
59	Diego BORREGO	(Sp)	72	72	75	73	292	2175
	Andrew SHERBORNE	(Eng)	72	74	74	72	292	2175
	Ian WOOSNAM	(Wal)	73	73	75	71	292	2175
	Tony JOHNSTONE	(Zim)	70	73	74	75	292	2175
	Richard GREEN	(Aus)	72	71	76	73	292	2175
64	Andrew COLTART	(Scot)	71	73	75	74	293	1518
	Phil GOLDING	(Eng)	70	74	72	77	293	1518
	José RIVERO	(Sp)	71	72	75	75	293	1518
	Darren COLE	(Aus)	72	70	77	74	293	1518
68	Max ANGLERT	(Swe)	73	72	73	76	294	1121
69	Peter MITCHELL	(Eng)	75	71	74	75	295	1119
70	Ben TINNING	(Den)	70	75	80	73	298	1117

Sam Torrance has a happy one 2 one with the Press.

Supercharged Langer leaves his rivals standing

Bernhard Langer went from 0 to 60 in the third round and accelerated to his fourth victory of the season

Nine members of Europe's victorious Johnnie Walker Ryder Cub team teed up alongside captain Severiano Ballesteros in the Linde German Masters at Motzener See near Berlin feeling physically and mentally drained by the heroics of Valderrama four days earlier.

But, as Colin Montgomerie pointed out, they were all 'still on a high,' which explained why seven of them finished in the top 12, with Bernhard Langer, whose last afternoon victory over Brad Faxon ensured Europe kept the Cup, winning by six strokes from the Scot, whose last gasp half with Scott Hoch secured a cliffhanging one point victory over the Americans.

Astonishingly, iron man Langer, who recorded his fourth Tour triumph of the summer and his 38th in 21 years of European campaigning, powered a Tour record-equalling 12 below par 60 in round three.

Montgomerie, Thomas Bjorn, who finished third, and José Maria Olazábal, who shared fourth place with Costantino Rocca and Swede Patrik Sjöland, all fired fighting 66s that Saturday afternoon – and instead of gaining on leader Langer, one

ahead at the off, they all, incredibly, slipped six strokes further back.

It was a magical effort by the 40-year-old Bavarian, who 24 hours earlier had ended his second round on a low note by running up a double bogey six after his drive ended in a deep-sided, sand filled divot, from which he 'fatted' his second

shot into a pond fronting the green.

Montgomerie conceded: 'He was desperately unfortunate because he hit a perfect tee shot. I put mine in a bush but hacked out and hit my third to eight feet to save par, so instead of losing another stoke to go five behind him I picked up two. Bernhard's misfortune gave us all a

THE COURSE

Motzener See, home of the Berlin Country Club and sited in the former German Democratic Republic, is built on an old Soviet Army camp and was designed by Kurt Rossknecht. The rough was allowed to grow in to toughen the course after Darren Clarke's 24 under par 1996 triumph. Water abounds on the back nine and when the wind blows, as it usually does, it is a tough test. The 18th, demanding a courageous second shot to an island green across a lake twice saw Severiano Ballesteros come to a soggy end.

Seve Ballesteros (left) and Colin Montgomerie (right) in differing follow-through positions.
Tom Lehman (opposite) was out of sorts.

glimmer of hope.'

It was hope shortlived as Langer squeezed no fewer than 11 birdies and an eagle next day into his 60, the eighth to be recorded on Tour but the first since 1992, when, surprisingly, the feat was performed four times.

It could so easily have been 59. Had Langer not fractionally overhit, from three feet, a birdie putt at the 14th, the ball would not have spun right around the hole and tantalisingly skipped back out towards him.

It might even have been 58 for his only bogey, at the seventh, came when he three-putted from 20 feet.

They were uncharacteristic errors from the steely double US Masters Champion as he strode towards a truly impressive tenth Tour victory on German soil.

He said: 'To card 60 was a great thrill, especially in front of my own people.

'Perhaps my 62 on the links of El Saler near Valencia to win the 1984 Spanish Open was a better round of golf, and of course my 62 when I won the Volvo Masters at Valderrama in 1994 was also a great round. But it's the first time I ever shot 12 under par.'

Langer required only 23 putts and Sergio Gomez, who was caddieing for Bernhard's playing companion Olazábal, who himself shot 61 when winning the World Series in 1990, declared: 'We've just played with ET!'

Langer bettered his 20 under par winning score of 264 in the Chemapol Trophy Czech Open when he added a 70 for a 21 under par total of 267 to win £125,000 and step up his challenge to Montgomerie for a third European number one title.

Montgomerie picked up a prize of £83,320 to stay nearly £46,000 ahead of Langer at the top of the Volvo Ranking, thanks to three brave birdies in the last six holes – two threes from inside eight feet and a two from 12 feet at the 17th.

It edged him a stroke ahead of Bjorn and three clear of Sjöland, Olazábal and Rocca, who had tamed Tiger Woods on that memorable last day in Spain and followed a tired opening 75 with a best of the day closing 64.

The seven iron second Bernhard Langer hit to within four inches of the flag on the first green in round four for a birdie, which stretched his lead to nine strokes, was a killer blow but the key shot of a memorable week for the German was his 20 yards pitch-in for an eagle three at the 558-yards fifth after he powered a drive and three wood through the green on day three. It inspired him to birdie six out of seven holes from the seventh en route to a Tour record equalling round of 60.

Defending champion Darren Clarke, who fired a 65 in round three, kept alive his slender hopes of a first Vardon Trophy with gutsy birdies at the last two holes to share seventh place a stroke further back with Jamie Spence, Andrew Coltart and Gary Orr, and another Cup man, Per-Ulrik Johansson whose closing 68 tied him for 11th with Peter Baker.

Ignacio Garrido missed the cut by a

stroke and Lee Westwood was forced to retire in round two with a hip strain, but it was a hugely impressive performance by Europe's weary Cup warriors and a truly majestic one by Langer.

Amazingly, it was the third time he had bounced back to win on Tour the week after a Ryder Cup. In 1991, after that agonising last green missed putt to retain the Cup against Hale Irwin at Kiawah

BERLINER G & CC, MOTZENER SEE, BERLIN, OCTOBER 2-5, 1997, • YARDAGE 6848 • PAR 72

Pos	Name	Country	Rnd 1	Rnd 2	Rnd 3	Rnd 4	Total	Prize Money £
1	Bernhard LANGER	(Ger)	68	69	60	70	267	125000.
2	Colin MONTGOMERIE	(Scot)	71	68	66	68	273	83320
3	Thomas BJÖRN	(Den)	71	68	66	69	274	46940
4	Patrik SJÖLAND	(Swe)	71	68	67	70	276	31840
	José Maria OLAZÁBAL	(Sp)	69	69	66	72	276	31840
	Costantino ROCCA	(It)	75	71	66	64	276	31840
7	Jamie SPENCE	(Eng)	71	68	67	71	277	18247
	Gary ORR	(Scot)	69	71	69	68	277	18247
	Darren CLARKE	(N.Ire)	73	69	65	70	277	18247
	Andrew COLTART	(Scot)	71	68	70	68	277	18247
11	Per-Ulrik JOHANSSON	(Swe)	72	67	71	68	278	13350
	Peter BAKER	(Eng)	74	67	68	69	278	13350
13	David HOWELL	(Eng)	68	72	66	73	279	11520
	Martin GATES	(Eng)	68	75	67	69	279	11520
	Phillip PRICE	(Wal)	75	68	68	68	279	11520
16	Max ANGLERT	(Swe)	72	69	69	71	281	9734
	Eamonn DARCY	(Ire)	72	68	71	70	281	9734
	Thomas GÖGELE	(Ger)	73	65	72	71	281	9734
	Phil MICKELSON	(USA)	73	71	69	68	281	9734
	Alberto BINAGHI	(It)	70	71	71	69	281	9734
21	Richard BOXALL	(Eng)	75	70	68	69	282	8212
	Retief GOOSEN	(SA)	74	72	68	68	282	8212
	Des SMYTH	(Ire)	77	67	69	69	282	8212
	Sven STRÜVER	(Ger)	74	71	67	70	282	8212
	Seve BALLESTEROS	(Sp)	74	70	70	68	282	8212
	Steve JONES	(USA)	74	67	70	71	282	8212
27	Padraig HARRINGTON	(Ire)	72	70	70	71	283	7200
	Philip WALTON	(Ire)	72	68	73	70	283	7200
	Paul MCGINLEY	(Ire)	71	71	73	68	283	7200
30	Paul LAWRIE	(Scot)	76	71	66	71	284	6431
	Robert KARLSSON	(Swe)	77	69	69	69	284	6431
	Tom LEHMAN	(USA)	73	70	69	72	284	6431
	Fabrice TARNAUD	(Fr)	72	72	70	70	284	6431
34	Rolf MUNTZ	(Hol)	72	69	75	69	285	5550
	Gordon BRAND JNR.	(Scot)	75	73	68	69	285	5550
	Andrew SHERBORNE	(Eng)	75	70	70	70	285	5550
	David CARTER	(Eng)	73	69	70	73	285	5550
	Mark ROE	(Eng)	78	66	70	71	285	5550
	Paul CURRY	(Eng)	74	73	69	69	285	5550
	Russell CLAYDON	(Eng)	74	74	66	71	285	5550
41	Henrik BJORNSTADT	(Nor)	77	71	69	69	286	4575
	Gary EVANS	(Eng)	77	68	69	72	286	4575
	Mark MOULAND	(Wal)	75	71	69	71	286	4575
	Adam HUNTER	(Scot)	75	72	69	70	286	4575
	Steven RICHARDSON	(Eng)	72	73	70	71	286	4575
	Mathias GRÖNBERG	(Swe)	75	73	67	71	286	4575
47	Derrick COOPER	(Eng)	74	67	72	74	287	3900
	Santiago LUNA	(Sp)	74	72	72	69	287	3900
	Wayne RILEY	(Aus)	75	68	69	75	287	3900
50	Peter HEDBLOM	(Swe)	78	69	69	72	288	3600
51	Jim PAYNE	(Eng)	76	71	73	69	289	3075
	Andrew OLDCORN	(Scot)	76	72	69	72	289	3075
	Peter MITCHELL	(Eng)	77	70	68	74	289	3075
	Alex CEJKA	(Ger)	75	72	73	69	289	3075
	Mark DAVIS	(Eng)	76	69	72	72	289	3075
	Howard CLARK	(Eng)	77	71	73	68	289	3075
57	Jeff HAWKES	(SA)	78	70	73	69	290	2381
	Sam TORRANCE	(Scot)	71	69	73	77	290	2381
	Ricky WILLISON	(Eng)	76	72	72	70	290	2381
	Raymond RUSSELL	(Scot)	74	73	72	71	290	2381
61	Stuart CAGE	(Eng)	73	75	72	72	292	2025
	José RIVERO	(Sp)	77	71	69	75	292	2025
	Malcolm MACKENZIE	(Eng)	73	72	76	71	292	2025
	Tony JOHNSTONE	(Zim)	75	69	73	75	292	2025
	Michael JONZON	(Swe)	76	71	70	75	292	2025
66	Per HAUGSRUD	(Nor)	70	75	72	76	293	1124
	Paul BROADHURST	(Eng)	75	71	75	72	293	1124
68	Paul EALES	(Eng)	78	70	74	73	295	1120
	Pedro LINHART	(Sp)	75	71	74	75	295	1120
70	Wayne WESTNER	(SA)	76	72	76	80	304	1117

Island, he won the same German Masters event, which he co-promotes with brother Erwin, in Stuttgart after a play-off. And he won in extra time again in the Smurfit European Open at Dublin's K Club after Europe's epic Oak Hill success in 1995.

He explains: 'There is no secret. Like everyone else I'm tired for two or three days but by Thursday I'm able to concentrate on the next tournament. The past is past and you have to look forward. If I can do it at 40 the guys in their 20s and 30s should have no problem.'

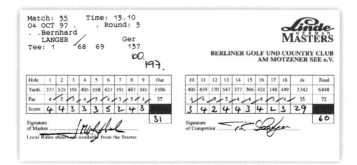

Bernhard Langer's course record 60 (above).

Mongomerie was full of admiration for the man he partnered to two key foursomes wins at Valderrama: 'He is the strongest golfer in the world mentally. When he is in this kind of mood he is unbeatable. After his 60 my sole objective

was to finish second and I got a result thanks to those three birdies in the last few holes.'

American Cup men Phil Mickelson (281) and Tom Lehman (284) were left trailing in the slipstream of Europe's Ryder Cup stars for the second week running. Even captain Ballesteros got in on the scoring act, following rounds of 74, 70, 70 with a 68 bristling with half a dozen birdies to end on 282 with former US Open champion Steve Jones, and underline his claims that a winning comeback was on the cards.

Gordon Richardson

Singh stops the run

In a repeat of last year's final,
Vijay Singh ended Ernie Els'
dominance at Wentworth

It had to end sooner or later of course. But it was not until the final green, of the final match, of the 34th Toyota World Match-Play Championship, that the record breaking Ernie Els era at Wentworth was ended by Vijay Singh. For Singh there was double delight in becoming the first player ever to beat Els and to gain revenge for his 3 and 2 defeat by the young South African star in the 1996 final.

When Singh was a young boy he used to watch the Championship (then The Piccadilly) on television and dream of one day emulating his heroes like Gary Player and Jack Nicklaus. That dream became a reality when the 34-year-old Fijian won a hard fought final by just one hole.

Ever since he had defeated Severiano Ballesteros in the first match of his debut in 1994, Els had been unbeatable over the Burma Road, setting a record of three successive titles. But for once he was unable to recapture the standard he had set in winning his previous 11 matches over 400 holes for which he was an extraordinary 77 under par.

'Today just was not my day at all,'

THE COURSE

Although prolonged rain made the West Course play its full length there was general approval among players and officials for making the 11th and 12th even longer. Twenty one yards were added to the par four 11th (making it 398 yards) by sharing the eighth tee. Shifting the 12th tee left 28 yards back (making it 510 yards) meant this par five was no longer an easy two-shotter, with many players taking woods off the fairway. 'We were delighted with the new tees and we shall almost certainly use the new 12th and probably the new 11th for 1998 Volvo PGA Championship,' said Tournament Director, Mike Stewart.

admitted a disappointed Els. 'I never managed to play like I played the last three years on this golf course. I was just hanging on trying to make something happen. I started off ok but I really got annoyed with myself. He won a lot of holes with pars and you just can't do that. I could have broken a couple of clubs out there.'

A Championship that experienced all four British seasons in one weekend began on a grey and blustery day with the first round clash of Ryder Cup team-mates Ian Woosnam and Jesper Parnevik. After Woosnam had complained about being left out of matches at Valderrama it was incumbent on him to prove his point on the course. He did so in style, jaw jutting

Ernie Els' (above) drive to a fourth win faltered.
Brad Faxon (right) exited in the semi-finals.

determinedly in the old Woosie fashion and swinging a new look driver to great effect as he finished six under in defeating Parnevik 4 and 3.

Meanwhile American Brad Faxon did a little to ease his Ryder Cup heartache by defeating Irishman Darren Clarke 2 and 1. Clarke won the first hole, Faxon was level by the tenth and from then on he was never headed.

His American team-mate Phil Mickelson was not so fortunate, staging a brave fight back against New Zealand's Frank Nobilo before finally succumbing at the 38th (second extra) hole.

Ever since 1986, Japanese interest in this Championship has ended at the first hurdle. Tsukasa Watanabe

proved just another failed wannabe as he was swept aside 4 and 3 by Singh.

On a gloriously sun-filled second day, Singh continued his largely untroubled and unheralded progress with an equally impressive 5 and 4 victory over Australian Steve Elkington, who had been seeded due to his US Tournament Players' title win.

Ian Woosnam was unable to maintain his newly rediscovered confidence or swing as he was comprehensively outgunned 7 and 6 by Els, who was playing his first competitive golf in five weeks. 'One day good, one day bad. You can't hope to do well if you play like that at this level,' admitted the little Welshman.

British interest in the Championship was ended when Colin Montgomerie, suffering badly from the onset of a heavy cold and weariness following a hectic five weeks of trying to seal the Volvo Ranking and help win the Ryder Cup went down 2 and 1 to Faxon. Montgomerie was two up after nine in the afternoon round, but after losing the next four holes in succession never looked like retrieving the match.

The semi-finals day provided the worst weather, yet almost certainly the best match of the Championship. Torrential and almost constant rain created miniature lakes all over Wentworth and only a magnificent effort by Course Superintendent Chris Kennedy and a mini-army of 24 greenkeepers allowed play to be completed. The umbrella, wellies and waterproof brigade of hardy fans were rewarded with some compelling golf. There was never more than two

SHOT OF THE WEEK

The shot that finally closed the door on Ernie Els's Wentworth reign came at the 36th hole of the final. Vijay Singh, having seen Els dump his approach in the greenside bunker, thought about hitting a hard six iron for his second shot but was persuaded by his caddie, Dave Renwick, to hit 'an easy five'. The resultant 185-yard blow finished perfectly on the front edge of the green, no more than 12 feet from the hole.

holes between Ernie Els and Nick Price all day, with both men shooting five under par 67s in the morning.

A fascinating see-saw afternoon, saw a two hole lead for Els turned into a one hole advantage for Price, only for Els to force extra holes with a birdie at the last and then claim a memorable victory with a long putt at the first extra hole. 'Walking down the last I thought my run was over and I would be playing for third and fourth place,' admitted Els.

In contrast, the Singh versus Faxon semi-final looked set for one of the biggest margins of victory in the Championship's history as Singh took an eight hole lead at one stage in the morning. Despite Faxon's brave comeback attempts, Singh was still seven up at the turn in the afternoon. Suddenly however, Faxon won three holes in succession to cut the deficit to four with six to play. But Singh held his nerve to eventually go through 4 and 3.

For the third year in succession there was no European in the final. Perhaps that added to the muted atmosphere, or maybe we had been so sated by the coruscating dramas of the Ryder Cup that anything else seemed tame by comparison.

In the final, Singh always did just enough to keep ahead of an opponent who seemed ill at ease from the start. Singh was four up after 14 in the morning and it seemed he might have his fourth comfortable win of the week. Els, who spent much of the lunch interval on the practice ground, managed to make some inroads in the afternoon.

For Singh it was the 21st win of a globe-trotting career and his fourth of 1997. 'It is a big achievement to win such a major international event and especially to beat Ernie on a course he seemed to have made his own, and it makes up for last year,' he declared. 'I was two under par in the morning, and one under in the afternoon. It was not as good as I can play, but in match-play you just have to play better than your opponent and I did that.'

John Whitbread

WENTWORTH CLUB (WEST COURSE), SURREY, OCTOBER 9-12, 1997 · YARDAGE 6957 · PAR 72

First Round

		Prize money
Ian Woosnam (Wal) beat Jesper Parnevik (Swe)	4 & 3	£30,000
Frank Nobilo (NZ) beat Phil Mickelson (USA)	at 38th	£30,000
Brad Faxon (USA) beat Darren Clarke (N Ire)	2 & 1	£30,000
Vijay Singh (Fij) beat Tsukasa Watanabe (Jap)	4 & 3	£30,000

Second Round

		Prize money
*Ernie Els (SA) beat Ian Woosnam	7 & 6	£40,000
*Nick Price (Zim) beat Frank Nobilo	6 & 5	£40,000
Brad Faxon beat *Colin Montgomerie (Scot)	2 & 1	£40,000
Vijay Singh beat *Steve Elkington (Aus)	5 & 4	£40,000

Semi-Finals

Ernie Els beat Nick Price	at 37th hole	—
Vijay Singh beat Brad Faxon	4 & 3	—

Play-Off for Third & Fourth Places

		Prize money
Brad Faxon beat	5 & 4	£60,000
Nick Price		£50,000

Final

		Prize money
Vijay Singh beat	1 hole	£170,000
Ernie Els		£90,000

*seeded into the second round

Semi-finalist Nick Price.

Swedish rhapsody

Anders Forsbrand and Michael Jonzon

struck the right notes in Bordeaux

Anders Forsbrand and Michael Jonzon, who did not team up until three days before the event began, came from four shots down with three holes to play to win the Open Novotel Perrier tournament at the Medoc Golf Club in Bordeaux.

The two Swedes won the £70,000 first prize when Jonzon sank a putt of 30 feet at the first extra hole in a play-off with Santiago Luna and Jose Rivero, but even Forsbrand admitted their victory was hardly believable.

Luna and Rivero had looked certain winners on the final day, when both men play singles, when they arrived on the 16th green, at 14 under par, four shots clear of the field but Luna then three-

THE COURSE

The Medoc golf course in Bordeaux is very challenging, despite wide fairways, with heather and gorse plus water, which comes into play at eight holes, particularly at the short fifth and eighth. A difficult par 71, especially when strong winds are blowing in from the nearby Atlantic.

putted to cut their lead to three. Rivero also three-putted the short 17th but the Spaniards were still two ahead of Forsbrand and Jonzon who, playing behind them, were only ten under as they played the penultimate hole.

Forsbrand then gave the Swedes hope by sinking a monster putt on the 17th green for a birdie two and Jonzon, with the Spanish pair watching on TV from the press room, holed out from 12 feet on the final green for another birdie to force a play-off.

Back to the 18th for the first extra hole, Forsbrand, Jonzon and Rivero all found the green in two but Luna, bunkered off the tee, took three to reach the putting surface and went 15 feet past the pin. Forsbrand then putted dead from 40 feet for his four, Jonzon holed from 30 feet for a birdie and the Spaniards had to sink both their putts to stay alive.

Rivero, however, missed his putt to end the contest. Later Forsbrand said that he and Jonzon were lucky on two counts. 'It's not often you make up four shots in the last three holes,' he said, 'and we weren't even supposed to be playing together. I was going to play with Per-Ulrik Johansson but he couldn't make it because, what with the Ryder Cup and then the Alfred Dunhill Cup coming up, he had too much on his plate. So I asked Michael and it worked out perfectly.'

Earlier in the day it looked as if the

José Maria Olazábal.

French pair, Jeff Remesy and Raphael Jacquelin, might gain a home victory, having set a hot pace for the first three days, which had been marred by almost persistent rain and blustery winds. The two Frenchmen, with Remesy at 159th on the Volvo Ranking and Jacquelin, three times a Challenge Tour winner earlier in the year, at 174th, had been joint leaders after

the first day four-ball with a seven under par 64.

Then they added a 69 on the second day foursomes to lead on nine under, two shots clear of Luna and Rivero, and with a 66 in the third day greensomes, went into the last day four shots ahead of Forsbrand and Jonzon.

Yet, despite preferred lies because the course was so wet and heavy, Remesy could shoot only 78 on the final day and, though Jacquelin had a creditable 72, the French pair fell back to sixth place, six shots behind the winners.

Before the start of this unique event, European Ryder Cup captain Severiano Ballesteros and José Maria Olazábal, playing together for the first time since winning this tournament in Paris in 1995, were strong favourites among the 30 competing pairs. But they had to be content with joint third place despite improving day by day. A four under par 67 in the four-ball left them in joint 18th place, a 73 in the difficult foursomes round in heavy rain took them to joint 13th, a 67 in the greensomes moved them up to joint seventh and Ballesteros shot a 70 and Olazábal 71 in the final day singles.

Ballesteros, with four birdies in his last six holes, was delighted with his form and believes there should be more events like this pairs tournament on the European Tour. 'These events are fun and break up the monotony of stroke-play

GOLF DU MÉDOC, BORDEAUX, OCTOBER 9-12, 1997 · YARDAGE 6909 · PAR 71

Pos	Names	Rnd 1	Rnd 2	Rnd 3	Rnd 4	Total	Prize Money £ each
1	A FORSBRAND / M JONZON	65	74	64	140	343	35000
2	S LUNA / J RIVERO	64	71	69	139	343	25000
3	M ROE / M FARRY	66	73	68	141	348	13000
	S BALLESTEROS / JM OLAZABAL	67	73	67	141	348	13000
	P HEDBLOM / P SJÖLAND	66	70	68	144	348	13000
6	J REMESY / R JACQUELIN	64	69	66	150	349	6500
7	J PAYNE / P PRICE	68	74	70	139	351	4916
	A CEJKA / F TARNAUD	69	73	69	140	351	4916
	D HOSPITAL / F ROCA	68	73	66	144	351	4916
10	P LAWRIE / R DRUMMOND	66	74	68	144	352	4250
11	W RILEY / C MASON	69	71	67	146	353	3875
	B LANE / JVAN DE VELDE	65	74	66	148	353	3875
13	T GÖGELE / M GRÖNBERG	68	75	68	143	354	3090
	I PYMAN / D CARTER	67	75	68	144	354	3090
	JL GUEPY / M BESANCENEY	64	75	70	145	354	3090
	J SPENCE / M MOULAND	66	78	65	145	354	3090.
	R MCFARLANE / D J RUSSELL	66	73	68	147	354	3090
18	M TUNNICLIFF / J ROBSON	65	77	67	146	355	2700
19	A HUNTER / G ORR	65	73	71	147	356	2550
	P CURRY / A SHERBORNE	65	72	69	150	356	2550
21	R LEE / M DAVIS	65	77	73	142	357	2300
	D HOWELL / S CAGE	66	72	75	144	357	2300
	P BAKER / P BROADHURST	67	76	70	144	357	2300
24	S RICHARDSON / R WILLISON	68	82	71	139	360	2050
	I GARRIDO / M CARRASCO	64	74	73	149	360	2050
26	W WESTNER / M MACKENZIE	68	75	70	148	361	1850
	R BOXALL / D COOPER	70	73	68	150	361	1850
28	M HARWOOD / S ALKER	68	78	67	151	364	1700
29	C SUNESON / P LINHART	64	80	72	150	366	1600
30	J LOMAS / S BOTTOMLEY	69	73	73	152	367	1500

Seve Ballesteros (above) and Peter Hedblom (below).

tournaments every week,' he said. 'More match-play tournaments would also help our younger players to get experience for the Ryder Cup. This is very important because, as you all know, I like to beat the Americans.'

John Oakley

SHOT OF THE WEEK

David Carter produced the shot of the week when he holed a three iron from a bunker 235 yards from the flag for an albatross two at the 514-yard tenth hole. 'I had an awkward downhill lie in the bunker but I hit it perfectly and it pitched just short of the green and then trickled into the hole,' said a delighted Carter.

The men for all seasons

South Africa coped best with
the changing conditions
at St Andrews

S outh Africa waited six years for this moment of retribution. Having lost 2-1 to Sweden in the 1991 final, Ernie Els, Retief Goosen and David Frost were bent on making amends. After a day which began in summer and ended in bleak mid-winter, it was the Springboks who proved to be men for all seasons.

Their reward for a 2-1 success over Jesper Parnevik, Per-Ulrik Johansson and Joakim Haeggman was a prize of £300,000 as well as a first opportunity to grasp the Alfred Dunhill Cup when dusk fell over St Andrews and the famous trophy glinted in the photographers' giddy flashlights. By then Els was wrapped up in a cashmere sweater and a woolly hat. He'd played in shirt sleeves during a glorious morning when South Africa dealt firmly with the challenge of New Zealand in a semi-final match illuminated by warm sunshine and a light, mild breeze.

In less time than it takes to pull a drive, however, the picture changed and the Old Course was transformed from a scene of blessed tranquility – Haeggman equalled the world record score for nine holes of 27 before lunch – to one of cold hostility. 'We don't get much weather like this in South Africa,' Els grinned later, 'and when we do we don't play golf in it.'

Long before they were preparing victory speeches, the South Africans were glad to get to dinner on Thursday night cheered by a tight 2-1 victory over the Irish. Having been drawn against Germany and Scotland as well as the Celts in Group Three. South Africa knew they had a scrap on their hands just to reach the semi-finals.

With the Scots inspired in front of their own folk by an unbeaten contribu-tion from Colin Montgomerie, it soon became apparent that the Group Of Death would be settled one way or another on Saturday morning when the local heroes jousted with the US Open champion and his chums.

Elsewhere, the USA took a grip on the outcome of Group One thanks to the

Colin Montgomerie against the backdrop of the 'Auld Grey Toun' (left). The Chinese Taipei team in alien surroundings (right).

Leonard, 26, first visited St Andrews 12 years previously with his father Larry and shot a highly respectable 82. His life changed quite a bit during the intervening years and no more so than in the preceding three months. 'My postman back home in Dallas has been a bit busier,' he revealed. 'Most of the letters have come from Scotland and have simply been addresssed 'Justin Leonard, Open Champion, Dallas, Texas.' They find me.'

With Mark O'Meara in assertive form – he won all three of his matches in Group One – it was no surprise that the defending champions saw off the challenge of England, Japan and Argentina. The 1996 finalists, New Zealand, also made solid progress in Group Four at the expense of Spain, Zimbabwe and Korea thanks to the leadership of Frank Nobilo. And in Group Two, Sweden signalled they were going to be a force to be reckoned with from the moment Parnevik matched Leonard's record 65 on Thursday afternoon.

The tournament didn't truly catch fire, though, until the Scots and the South Africans went head to head. Even the

example of Justin Leonard, who is a man transformed every time he gulps a lungful of Scottish air. The last time Leonard was in Scotland was in July when he won the Open Championship at Troon. He celebrated his return north of the border by setting a new Old Course record of 65.

Auld Grey Toun got caught up in the drama of this splendid contest. On a calm morning, Frost went to the turn in 30 and annihilated Raymond Russell. This left Gordon Brand Junior with plenty to do against Goosen. To his credit, the Scot made birdie to the South African's bogey

THE COURSE

There's no more historic golf course in the world than the ancient links at St Andrews. Not surprisingly, any changes are greeted with intense scrutiny. For this year's Alfred Dunhill Cup there was a first opportunity to assess the new tees which have added just over 160 yards to the Old Course and brought some of the traditional hazards back into play. Opinions among the players were divided. Ernie Els welcomed the alterations while Mark James described them as 'unimaginative, unnecessary and irrelevant.'

Frank Nobilo (above). Jesper Parnevik in the Road Hole bunker (below).

Joakim Haeggman was a modest one under par for the opening holes when he strode down the third fairway on Sunday morning in his match against the Open champion, Justin Leonard. Having dispatched his drive the best part of 270 yards, the Swede was left with just 133 yards to the cup. He picked out his wedge, executed a smooth swing and sent the ball scurrying into the hole for an eagle two. The shot set up Haeggman for a world record-equalling outward half of 27.

at the last and the match went down the 19th. By now Els and Montgomerie were locked in another instalment of their ongoing rivalry. When the South African rolled a birdie putt from 15 feet into the cup at the 18th for 68 it looked as if Montgomerie was about to be foiled again. However, the Scot holed from 12 feet himself to level the contest. As news filtered back to the first tee that Goosen had beaten Brand to take South Africa through, Els and Montgomerie relied on common sense, rather than the rules of the competition, and agreed a half.

By the time a shimmering Sunday morning rolled around it was the Swedes who made the headlines with their 2-1 win over the Americans. Haeggman, for one, will never forget his part in the triumph as he covered the outward half in just 27 blows, recording two fours, five threes and two twos before losing the plot on the way home and running up 41 for a lopsided round of 68. 'On the front nine everything went in,' the Swede recalled, 'even the bad shots.'

As South Africa eliminated New Zealand 2-1, the scene was set for a repeat of the 1991 final. Only this time the outstanding form of Goosen, who won all

JOAKIM HAEGGMAN'S RECORD-EQUALLING 27

Hole	Yards	Par	Score	
1	370	4	3	3 wood, wedge, 1 putt
2	411	4	4	Driver, 8 iron, 2 putts
3	400	4	2	Driver, wedge (133 yards)
4	463	4	3	Driver, 6 iron, 1 putt
5	564	5	4	Driver, 4 wood, 2 putts
6	416	4	3	Driver, 9 iron, 1 putt
7	372	4	3	Driver, sand wedge, 1 putt
8	178	3	2	8 iron, 1 putt
9	359	4	3	4 wood, wdge, 1 putt

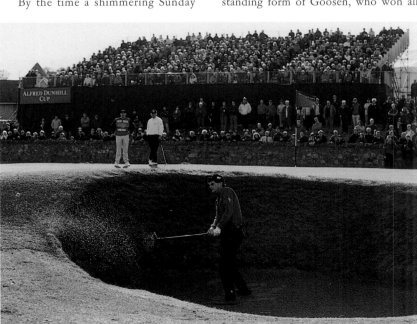

five of his matches, and the inevitable brilliance from Els won the day. The South Africans have needed to be patient in the Alfred Dunhill Cup. This year the wait was worthwhile.

Mike Aitken   253

Old Course, St. Andrews, 16th - 19th October 1997 • Yardage 7,094 • Par 72

Final

SOUTH AFRICA	2	1	SWEDEN
Retief Goosen	70	74	Jesper Parnevik
David Frost	74	71	Per-Ulrik Johansson
Ernie Els	69	72	Joakim Haeggman

Semi-Final

SWEDEN	2	1	USA
Jesper Parnevik	69	68	Mark O'Meara
Joakim Haeggman	68	72	Justin Leonard
Per-Ulrik Johansson	71	74	Brad Faxon

Semi-Final

SOUTH AFRICA	2	1	NEW ZEALAND
Retief Goosen	67	72	Michael Long
David Frost	72	76	Steve Alker
Ernie Els	70	66	Frank Nobilo

Group One

DAY 1

ENGLAND beat JAPAN 3-0
Russell Claydon (70) beat Tsukasa Watanabe (71)
Lee Westwood (70) beat Nobuhito Sato (73)
Mark James (73) beat Shigemasa Higaki (74)

USA beat ARGENTINA 2-1
Mark O'Meara (67) beat Eduardo Romero (67)
* 1st extra hole
Brad Faxon (72) lost to Angel Cabrera (68)
Justin Leonard (65) beat Jose Coceres (72)

DAY 2

USA beat JAPAN 3-0
Mark O'Meara (70) beat Tsukasa Watanabe (72)
Justin Leonard (74) beat Nobuhito Sato (82)
Brad Faxon (73) beat Shigemasa Higaki (79)

ENGLAND lost to ARGENTINA 1-2
Russell Claydon (74) lost to Jose Coceres (71)
Mark James (71) beat Eduardo Romero (72)
Lee Westwood (72) lost to Angel Cabrera (71)

DAY 3

USA beat ENGLAND 3-0
Mark O'Meara (67) beat Lee Westwood (69)
Brad Faxon (70) beat Russell Claydon (73)
Justin Leonard (69) beat Mark James (72)

ARGENTINA beat JAPAN 2-0
Eduardo Romero (72) beat Shigemasa Higaki (73)
Angel Cabrera (69) beat Tsukasa Watanabe (73)
Jose Coceres (70) halved with Nobuhito Sato (70)

Group Two

DAY 1

SWEDEN beat CHINESE TAIPEI 3-0
Joakim Haeggman (72) beat Hsieh Yu-Shu (72)
* 1st extra hole
Jesper Parnevik (65) beat Lu Hsi-Chuen (75)
Per-Ulrik Johansson (71) beat Chen Liang-Hsi (74)

AUSTRALIA lost to FRANCE 1-2
Robert Allenby (71) lost to Fabrice Tarnaud (70)
Steve Elkington (71) lost to Jean Van de Velde (71)
* 1st extra hole
Stuart Appleby (68) beat Marc Farry (71)

DAY 2

SWEDEN beat FRANCE 3-0
Joakim Haeggman (70) beat Fabrice Tarnaud (78)
Jesper Parnevik (73) beat Marc Farry (74)
Per-Ulrik Johansson (72) beat J Van de Velde (73)

AUSTRALIA beat CHINESE TAIPEI 2-1
Robert Allenby (74) lost to Hsieh Yu-Shu (71)
Steve Elkington (76) beat Chen Liang-Hsi (76)
*2nd extra hole
Stuart Appleby (77) beat Lu Hsi-Chuen (80)

DAY 3

AUSTRALIA lost to SWEDEN 1-2
Steve Elkington (72) lost to Per-Ulrik Johansson (72)
*2nd extra hole
Stuart Appleby (69) lost to Joakim Haeggman (66)
Robert Allenby (68) beat Jesper Parnevik (70)

FRANCE beat CHINESE TAIPEI 3-0
Marc Farry (70) beat Chen Liang-Hsi (73)
Fabrice Tarnaud (71) beat Lu Hsi-Chuen (75)
Jean Van de Velde (67) beat Hsieh Yu-Shu (76)

Group Three

DAY 1

SOUTH AFRICA beat IRELAND 2-1
Retief Goosen (70) beat Paul McGinley (71)
David Frost (69) lost to Padraig Harrington (67)
Ernie Els (66) beat Darren Clarke (71)

SCOTLAND beat GERMANY 2-1
Raymond Russell (68) beat Thomas Gogele (74)
Gordon Brand Jnr (69) lost to Alex Cejka (66)
Colin Montgomerie (67) beat Sven Strüver (73)

DAY 2

SCOTLAND beat IRELAND 2-1
Raymond Russell (74) lost to Paul McGinley (69)
Gordon Brand Jnr (73) beat Darren Clarke (77)
Colin Montgomerie (72) beat Padraig Harrington (76)

SOUTH AFRICA beat GERMANY 3-0
Retief Goosen (73) beat Thomas Gogele (73)
*2nd extra hole
David Frost (74) beat Alex Cejka (79)
Ernie Els (71) beat Sven Strüver (72)

DAY 3

IRELAND beat GERMANY 2-1
Darren Clarke (68) beat Alex Cejka (74)
Padraig Harrington (66) beat Sven Strüver (69)
Paul McGinley (71) lost to Thomas Gogele (67)

SOUTH AFRICA beat SCOTLAND 2-0
David Frost (68) beat Raymond Russell (71)
Retief Goosen (67) beat Gordon Brand Jnr (67)
*1st extra hole
Ernie Els (68) halved with Colin Montgomerie (68)

Group Four

DAY 1

ZIMBABWE beat KOREA 2-1
Nick Price (72) beat Kim Jong-Duck (74)
Mark McNulty (69) beat Mo Joong-Kyung (76)
Tony Johnstone (73) lost to Kang Wook-Soon (73)
* 1st extra hole

NEW ZEALAND beat SPAIN 2-1
Steve Alker (70) beat Miguel Angel Martin (73)
Frank Nobilo (70) beat Ignacio Garrido (75)
Michael Long (72) lost to Miguel Angel Jimenez (71)

DAY 2

NEW ZEALAND beat KOREA 3-0
Steve Alker (76) beat Mo Joong-Kyung (83)
Michael Long (75) beat Kim Jong-Duck (76)
Frank Nobilo (68) beat Kang Wook-Soon (70)

ZIMBABWE beat SPAIN 2-1
Tony Johnstone (76) beat Miguel Angel Martin (74)
Mark McNulty (70) beat Ignacio Garrido (74)
Nick Price (Rtd) lost to Miguel Angel Jimenez

DAY 3

KOREA lost to SPAIN 1-2
Kim Jong-Duck (70) beat Miguel Angel Martin (78)
Kang Wook-Soon (74) lost to MI Angel Jimenez (74)
*2nd extra hole
Mo Joong-Kyung (76) lost to Ignacio Garrido (70)

ZIMBABWE lost to NEW ZEALAND 0-3
Nick Price (Rtd) lost to Frank Nobilo
Tony Johnstone (75) lost to Steve Alker (70)
Mark McNulty (68) lost to Michael Long (67)

Prize Money

Winners

Country	Team £	Player £	Total £
S AFRICA (3)	300,000	100,000	300,000

Runners-Up

Country	Team £	Player £	Total £
SWEDEN (5)	150,000	50,000	150,000

Losing Semi-Finalists

Country	Team £	Player £	Total £
USA (1)	95,000	31,666	
N ZEALAND (7)	95,000	31,666	190,000

Group One

Country	Team £	Player £	Total £
USA (1)			
ARGENTINA	45,000	15,000	
ENGLAND (8)	25,500	8,500	
JAPAN	19,500	6,500	90,000

Group Two

Country	Team £	Player £	Total £
SWEDEN (5)			
FRANCE	45,000	15,000	
AUSTRALIA (4)	25,500	8,500	
CHINESE TAIPEI	19,500	6,500	90,000

Group Three

Country	Team £	Player £	Total £
SOUTH AFRICA (3)			
SCOTLAND (6)	45,000	15,000	
IRELAND	25,500	8,500	
GERMANY	19,500	6,500	90,000

Group Four

Country	Team £	Player £	Total £
NEW ZEALAND (7)			
ZIMBABWE (2)	45,000	15,000	
SPAIN	25,500	8,500	
KOREA	19,500	6,500	90,000

* Number in parentheses indicates seeds

McGinley is masterful in Madrid

Paul McGinley produced a stellar performance to capture the second title of his career

Self-belief is a priceless asset to a tournament professional and Paul McGinley displayed it in abundance to dominate the second OKI Pro-Am in Madrid. He had acquired a good measure two weeks prior to the Japanese company's promotion at La Moraleja when he won the Irish PGA title in Cork without either playing or putting to his usual high standard. Then his confidence rose several more notches when he bettered par on all three days in which Ireland were involved in the Alfred Dunhill Cup at St Andrews.

When, four days later, he opened his account in Spain with a 66 on La Moraleja's number one course, McGinley knew he was on the point of turning a moderate season into a year of significance.

By the end of a warm, sunny week in the Spanish capital, the 30-year-old Dubliner had become the eighth Irishman to gain membership of the European Tour's elite Millionaires' Club after producing the best golf in his six-year profes-

sional career.

McGinley counted an eagle and 22 birdies in a 22 under par winning total of 266 that gave him a four-stroke margin over the fast-finishing Iain Pyman. The 24-year-old former Amateur champion from Leeds closed with a 64 to more than dou-

ble his earnings in 26 previous events, and banish fears that he would be forced to forfeit his Tour card. It was a valiant effort as Pyman edged New Zealander Greg Turner, the newly-crowned One 2 One British Masters champion, into third place.

But he was unable to disturb the serenity of McGinley who had long since had a second European Tour title firmly in his grasp.

His first victory had arrived courtesy of a thunderous last round 62 in the 1996 Hohe Brücke Austrian Open. That maiden success had been gained after a succession of near misses that included losing to José Maria Olazábal and Costantino Rocca in play-offs. It proved that McGinley had the game and the determination to be a champion.

This latest showed he is now ready to step up to the higher level of consistent winner and become a contender for greater honours. Most importantly, that is what McGinley now believes. 'My game went to a new level in Madrid,' he said. 'As a 72 holes performance it was much

SHOT OF THE WEEK

Paul McGinley's putt from 95 feet at the 13th in the third round for a most unlikely birdie two. 'I had blocked my eight iron tee shot just on the green and was only trying to lag my ball to the flag,' he said. But the putt was struck with perfect pace and direction, and gave him the confidence to maintain an attack that brought three more birdies in the last four holes.

Raymond Russell (left) and Greg Turner (right) had good finishes.

more satisfying than my first win, particularly in the way I managed my game. I hit 67 out of 72 greens, and that was a very significant statistic. It has given me a new perspective on the game.'

There were two principal factors in the Irishman's emergence from a three-month period in which his game was becalmed. McGinley was making and missing cuts by one or two shots, but had only twice finished in the top 20 in 13 previous events.

The first was being re-united with coach Bob Torrance after the Scot's mid-summer illness, and the second was a suggestion from his father, Mick, that he should change the putter he had been using for the last three years. 'Dad felt that my putting was suffering because I was crouching too much over the ball by using a club with only a 31-inch shaft, three inches shorter than normal,' McGinley

said. Accordingly, when he tried an orthodox Scotty Cameron putter, owned by Irish team-mate Darren Clarke, during practice on the Old Course and found that by standing taller to the ball there was instant improvement, he decided to purloin it.

The work he did at St Andrews with Torrance, in particular, correcting overactive hands, meant McGinley's game was at its peak when he took on the more fancied Mark James, winner of the Peugeot Open de España on the course in May, home favourite Severiano Ballesteros, Ryder Cup men Costantino Rocca and Ignacio Garrido, course record holder Angel Cabrera, and all those, like Pyman, eager to take their last chance in the Volvo Ranking.

This last group included Kiwi Michael Campbell, who had endured 18 months of frustration since stamping himself as a

player of extraordinary ability by taking fifth place on the Volvo Ranking in 1995. Campbell's opening rounds of 67 and 66 gave him parity with McGinley at the halfway stage, two ahead of Scot, Raymond Russell and the Spanish trio of Miguel Angel Jimenez, Pedro Linhart, and Fernando Roca. But he faded with two 75s to finish 43rd.

After 54 holes all of them knew they were playing for second place as McGinley, an eagle and 11 birdies already to his credit, spreadeagled the field with a majestic 64. Five birdies in an inward 31, one of them from an enormous putt at the short 13th, took him to a 19 under par total of 197, equalling the season's best set by Ignacio Garrido in the Chemapol Trophy Czech Open, and Bernhard Langer in the Linde German Masters. McGinley had not incurred a single bogey in establishing a six-stroke lead. A closing

Runner-up Iain Pyman

66 would give him a record low 72 hole aggregate for 1997, and if he continued to play exemplary golf, McGinley would become the first since David J. Russell (1992 Lyon Open) to score a bogey-free victory.

Neither goal was attained as the new OKI title-holder had to settle for a 69 dur-ing which he dropped his first shot at the 66th hole, and another at the 68th, but nobody was complaining, least of all McGinley, who had beaten off the imme-diate challenge of Turner and Russell, and had far too much in hand to be disturbed by Pyman's birdie-sprinkled charge.

'I felt I was in control of the Tourn-ament after the first three or four holes of the last round, and I never let it out of my grasp,' he said. 'Now I want to use this second win as a springboard. I don't want to rest on my laurels.'

Mike Britten

THE COURSE

La Moraleja II, on which three of the four rounds were decided, is a prod-uct of the Jack Nicklaus design group. It first came to prominence as the venue for the 1992 World Cup when Fred Couples and Davis Love gained the first of four successive wins. Feature hole is the par five 16th, where the second shot with a long iron, or three wood if into wind, is over water to an island green.

GOLF LA MORALEJA I & II, MADRID, OCTOBER 23-26, 1997 · YARDAGE 7054 · PAR 72

Pos	Name	Country	Rnd 1	Rnd 2	Rnd 3	Rnd 4	Total	Prize Money £
1	Paul MCGINLEY	(Ire)	66	67	64	69	266	75000
2	Iain PYMAN	(Eng)	68	69	69	64	270	50000
3	Greg TURNER	(NZ)	69	68	67	69	273	28170
4	Raymond RUSSELL	(Scot)	66	69	68	71	274	22500
5	Howard CLARK	(Eng)	70	67	72	66	275	16103
	José RIVERO	(Sp)	65	73	68	69	275	16103
	Jonathan LOMAS	(Eng)	67	69	69	70	275	16103
8	Malcolm MACKENZIE	(Eng)	70	69	68	69	276	11250
9	Peter BAKER	(Eng)	69	72	68	68	277	9110
	Miguel Angel JIMÉNEZ	(Sp)	67	68	72	70	277	9110
	Stephen AMES	(T&T)	71	67	69	70	277	9110
12	Jarmo SANDELIN	(Swe)	74	67	70	67	278	6812
	Paul EALES	(Eng)	71	69	70	68	278	6812
	Angel CABRERA	(Arg)	70	70	69	69	278	6812
	Gary EVANS	(Eng)	70	67	71	70	278	6812
	Jamie SPENCE	(Eng)	66	72	70	70	278	6812
	Juan Carlos PIÑERO	(Sp)	67	70	68	73	278	6812
18	Andrew COLTART	(Scot)	74	69	70	66	279	5220
	Pedro LINHART	(Sp)	67	68	74	70	279	5220
	Anders FORSBRAND	(Swe)	71	69	69	70	279	5220
	Wayne RILEY	(Aus)	71	66	71	71	279	5220
	Padraig HARRINGTON	(Ire)	72	66	69	72	279	5220
	Patrik SJÖLAND	(Swe)	69	69	69	72	279	5220
	Fernando ROCA	(Sp)	65	70	71	73	279	5220
	Richard BOXALL	(Eng)	64	72	70	73	279	5220
26	Mark MOULAND	(Wal)	65	73	74	68	280	4387
	Paul CURRY	(Eng)	71	69	69	71	280	4387
	Gary CLARK	(Eng)	67	73	69	71	280	4387
	Santiago LUNA	(Sp)	70	69	68	73	280	4387
30	Seve BALLESTEROS	(Sp)	72	70	68	71	281	3757
	José SOTA	(Sp)	69	70	71	71	281	3757
	Paul AFFLECK	(Wal)	69	72	72	68	281	3757
	Ignacio GARRIDO	(Sp)	71	67	70	73	281	3757
	Sven STRÜVER	(Ger)	66	73	68	74	281	3757
	David HOWELL	(Eng)	71	71	65	74	281	3757
36	Dean ROBERTSON	(Scot)	69	70	72	71	282	3150
	Miles TUNNICLIFF	(Eng)	73	67	72	70	282	3150
	Stuart CAGE	(Eng)	70	68	74	70	282	3150
	Alberto BINAGHI	(It)	67	74	72	69	282	3150
	Peter MITCHELL	(Eng)	72	68	70	72	282	3150
	Jim PAYNE	(Eng)	72	68	70	72	282	3150
	Paul LAWRIE	(Scot)	71	66	69	76	282	3150
43	Des SMYTH	(Ire)	69	67	74	73	283	2475
	Domingo HOSPITAL	(Sp)	67	73	71	72	283	2475
	Massimo FLORIOLI	(It)	68	74	70	71	283	2475
	Manuel PIÑERO	(Sp)	68	72	73	70	283	2475
	Jon ROBSON	(Eng)	71	72	71	69	283	2475
	Fabrice TARNAUD	(Fr)	69	71	75	68	283	2475
	Miguel Angel MARTIN	(Sp)	72	69	68	74	283	2475
	Michael CAMPBELL	(NZ)	67	66	75	75	283	2475
51	Carl SUNESON	(Sp)	68	71	73	72	284	2025
	Gary ORR	(Scot)	72	67	69	76	284	2025
53	José COCERES	(Arg)	69	70	71	75	285	1755
	David CARTER	(Eng)	66	76	70	73	285	1755
	Mark JAMES	(Eng)	71	71	71	72	285	1755
	Ross DRUMMOND	(Scot)	71	68	75	71	285	1755
57	Gary EMERSON	(Eng)	69	71	71	75	286	1356
	Robert KARLSSON	(Swe)	70	73	69	74	286	1356
	Eduardo ROMERO	(Arg)	74	68	70	74	286	1356
	Thomas GÖGELE	(Ger)	73	67	74	72	286	1356
	David GILFORD	(Eng)	69	71	75	71	286	1356
	Derrick COOPER	(Eng)	69	71	75	71	286	1356
	Diego BORREGO	(Sp)	71	71	73	71	286	1356
64	José Maria CAÑIZARES	(Sp)	71	69	71	76	287	1170
65	Mathias GRÖNBERG	(Swe)	70	73	76	69	288	1125
66	Adam HUNTER	(Scot)	70	70	76	73	289	675
67	Jose ROZADILLA	(Sp)	75	65	78	74	292	673
68	Pello IGUARAN	(Sp)	72	71	78	76	297	671

Jonathan Lomas finished joint fifth.

Cellnet is the official supplier of mobile communications to the PGA European Tour.

Call 0800 21 4000 for details of what Cellnet can do for you.

on the Cellnet it's in your hands.

Westwood caps a marvellous season

Having come close on several occasions,
Lee Westwood ended his European Tour
campaign on the highest of notes

After nine years at Valderrama the Volvo Masters moved home. The best players on the 1997 European Tour gathered instead at Montecastillo, near Jerez, a city famous the world over for its sherry production, but now, for two weeks at least, a centre for sporting excellence too.

First the Formula One Grand Prix circus pitched camp. Central characters, Jacques Villeneuve and Michael Schumacher. High drama – Villeneuve goes to overtake, Schumacher crashes into him, but only puts himself out of the race. Villeneuve becomes world champion.

Enter Colin Montgomerie and Bernhard Langer. The former trying to make it a record five Volvo Ranking titles in a row, the latter looking for a fifth victory in the season and one which would enable him to regain top spot. A clean

263

fight is promised. Darren Clarke had an outside chance to top the Volvo Ranking as well, while for the other 63 players in the field the lure of one of the most prestigious titles on the Tour – and a first prize £166,000 was incentive enough.

Among them was Clarke's stablemate and close friend Lee Westwood. For all that he had achieved during the year, most notably in the majors and at the Ryder

Cup by Johnnie Walker, the 24-year-old from Worksop was aware of one significant gap. He had not won in Europe and this was his last chance. Montgomerie is among his admirers. 'I've always rated Lee Westwood,' said the Scot. 'His attitude is brilliant and he is talented at the same time. He is a confident lad and he has a very bright future ahead of him. Three years ago when Nick Faldo left we were

looking for good young players and there weren't any. Now there are Westwood, Clarke, Bjorn, Garrido and Harrington – and Lee may be the top of the tree.'

Montgomerie was not thinking of the future, but the present, however, when the tournament began. It made him uptight. He was just over £45,000 ahead of Langer, but did not need telling that it could still turn out just as close as in 1995,

Robert Karlsson (above). Colin Montgomerie out-of-bounds on the 16th (below). Top five finish for Peter O'Malley (opposite).

ing day to join the leaders on 11 under.

Still there was no need for Montgomerie to panic. He was 11 under as well standing on the tee at the dog-leg par five 16th, a hole where birdie and eagle putts were dropped like confetti at a wedding. Off a rare wayward drive, though, his second flew into an adjoining field and after a long debate over whether it constituted out-of-bounds, he had to play a second ball and walked off with a triple-bogey eight. It was no time to ask for his autograph. Now he and Langer were eight under, Clarke 11 and Westwood, adding a 67, joint leader with Sweden's Patrik Sjöland on 12 under.

The wind that had started to blow late in the second round was back with a vengeance for the third. The course was suddenly a totally different proposition. Langer scored 74, Clarke 77, but Montgomerie, thanks to three birdies in

the last four holes, returned a 71 that had him declaring: 'The champagne's on ice.' Even if he had a bad last day the other two would have to go crazy. Five titles in a row, a quite phenomenal feat, was within touching distance.

The Volvo Masters title was not, however. Westwood had produced a superb 68 and on the 16 under par mark of 200 had moved three clear of Harrington, himself round in an even better 67. And the importance of those scores became apparent the next morning.

The wind was joined by violent thunderstorms. Twice play was interrupted before the leaders had even teed off and

267

THE COURSE

The Jack Nicklaus designed course lives up to the Golden Bear's creed. 'I like to see what I'm getting,' he says and at Montecastillo he has practised what he preaches, offering the golfer superb views of the challenge before him. Raised tees feature strongly with none more spectacular than the 18th where the tee is perched 200 feet above the sweeping prospect of Montecastillo's finishing hole.

SHOT OF THE WEEK

Seve Ballesteros showed signs of improvement at Montecastillo where he finished on three under par. At the par four tenth on the first day he produced the shot of the tournament after hooking his tee shot onto a hillside. Discovering his ball in a flooded rivulet in the ground produced by a recent

rainstorm, he called upon John Paramor for a ruling. The Tour's Chief Referee awarded a free drop away from ground under repair and from a steeply downhill lie on compacted sand, Seve gripped down on his seven iron to punch a perfect shot to the lakeside green 120 yards away.

as conditions deteriorated the decision was reluctantly taken to cancel the final round.

'It was more nerve-racking sitting around than it was playing,' said Westwood. 'But a win is a win and I felt confident of holding onto my lead.'

Also celebrating, of course, was Montgomerie. Eighth in the tournament underlined once again what a consistent performer he had been not just all season, but for the last five triumphant years. 'When you are number one in anything, whether it's golf or in an office, the competition is increasing all the time,' he said. 'For that reason, each time I've won the Volvo Ranking has been more satisfying than the last. If I had stood still I would have been overtaken. I've had to improve every year on all aspects of my game, but my greatest asset is that I have an incredible desire and ambition to succeed, it's kept me going throughout my ten years as a professional. That has never wilted at all.'

Mark Garrod 269

MONTECASTILLO, SPAIN, OCTOBER 30-NOVEMBER 2, 1997 · YARDAGE 7025 · PAR 71

Pos	Name	Country	Rnd 1	Rnd 2	Rnd 3	Rnd 4	Total	Prize Money £		Name	Country				Total	
										Peter BAKER	(Eng)	71	69	74	214	7350
										Daniel CHOPRA	(Swe)	71	73	70	214	7350
1	Lee WESTWOOD	(Eng)	65	67	68		200	166000		ZHANG LIAN-WEI	(Chi)	69	69	76	214	7350
2	Padraig HARRINGTON	(Ire)	66	70	67		203	110000		Peter MITCHELL	(Eng)	70	66	78	214	7350
3	José Maria OLAZÁBAL	(Sp)	66	67	71		204	63000		Joakim HAEGGMAN	(Swe)	72	68	74	214	7350
4	Robert KARLSSON	(Swe)	68	67	70		205	50600		Niclas FASTH	(Swe)	71	68	75	214	7350
5	Peter O'MALLEY	(Aus)	68	69	69		206	35966		Mark JAMES	(Eng)	68	69	77	214	7350
	Patrik SJÖLAND	(Swe)	64	68	74		206	35966		Sven STRÜVER	(Ger)	72	75	67	214	7350
	Mark MCNULTY	(Zim)	64	69	73		206	35966		Anders FORSBRAND	(Swe)	70	69	75	214	7350
8	Colin MONTGOMERIE	(Scot)	65	71	71		207	25000	42	David GILFORD	(Eng)	68	73	74	215	5600
9	Eduardo ROMERO	(Arg)	71	69	68		208	19833		Retief GOOSEN	(SA)	75	66	74	215	5600
	Ian WOOSNAM	(Wal)	67	69	72		208	19833		Greg TURNER	(NZ)	72	69	74	215	5600
	Costantino ROCCA	(It)	69	65	74		208	19833	45	Sam TORRANCE	(Scot)	75	68	73	216	5200
12	Michael LONG	(NZ)	65	69	75		209	15866	46	Dennis EDLUND	(Swe)	75	68	74	217	4442
	Stephen AMES	(T&T)	67	69	73		209	15866		Carl WATTS	(Eng)	70	70	77	217	4442
	José COCERES	(Arg)	68	69	72		209	15866		Ronan RAFFERTY	(N.Ire)	68	71	78	217	4442
15	Paul BROADHURST	(Eng)	70	66	74		210	13700		Richard GREEN	(Aus)	69	73	75	217	4442
	Bernhard LANGER	(Ger)	66	70	74		210	13700		Thomas GÖGELE	(Ger)	65	74	78	217	4442
	Thomas BJÖRN	(Den)	70	66	74		210	13700		Paul MCGINLEY	(Ire)	74	67	76	217	4442
	Darren CLARKE	(N.Ire)	69	64	77		210	13700		Miguel Angel MARTIN	(Sp)	72	72	73	217	4442
	Per-Ulrik JOHANSSON	(Swe)	63	71	76		210	13700	53	Roger CHAPMAN	(Eng)	68	76	74	218	3750
	David CARTER	(Eng)	69	68	73		210	13700		Tony JOHNSTONE	(Zim)	71	74	73	218	3750
21	David HOWELL	(Eng)	70	68	73		211	11900		Gordon BRAND JNR.	(Scot)	72	72	74	218	3750
	Ignacio GARRIDO	(Sp)	70	66	75		211	11900		Russell CLAYDON	(Eng)	74	73	71	218	3750
	Paul LAWRIE	(Scot)	70	65	76		211	11900	57	Scott HENDERSON	(Scot)	73	70	76	219	3400
24	Miguel Angel JIMÉNEZ	(Sp)	71	74	67		212	10500		Wayne WESTNER	(SA)	73	71	75	219	3400
	Phillip PRICE	(Wal)	69	71	72		212	10500		Peter LONARD	(Aus)	72	72	75	219	3400
	Robert ALLENBY	(Aus)	71	68	73		212	10500	60	Alex CEJKA	(Ger)	72	76	72	220	3200
	Brian DAVIS	(Eng)	70	71	71		212	10500	61	Clinton WHITELAW	(SA)	76	72	74	222	3050
	Andrew COLTART	(Scot)	68	70	74		212	10500		Raymond RUSSELL	(Scot)	71	75	76	222	3050
29	Angel CABRERA	(Arg)	72	72	69		213	9300	63	Ross MCFARLANE	(Eng)	72	73	78	223	2900
	Jarmo SANDELIN	(Swe)	71	70	72		213	9300	64	CHENG JUN	(Chi)	72	77	77	226	2800
	Seve BALLESTEROS	(Sp)	72	71	70		213	9300	65	Michael JONZON	(Swe)	74	77	76	227	2650
32	Mark ROE	(Eng)	70	73	71		214	7350		Mike HARWOOD	(Aus)	76	73	78	227	2650

José Maria Olazábal completed a great comeback season.

VOLVO SUPPORTS GOLF

Golf and Volvo have been together since 1988, when the PGA European Tour became the Volvo Tour. Today, Volvo is the principal sponsor of the Volvo Scandinavian Masters, Volvo PGA, Volvo German Open and Volvo Masters. In the Far East, we have been the title sponsor of the Volvo China Tour and the Volvo China Open since 1995.

Easy to handle. Sophisticated, submissive, yet powerful. Safe, yet exciting. The Volvo C70 has the most powerful and advanced engine of any Volvo car to date, with five cylinders, 240 bhp and the capability to accelerate from 0-100 km/h in 7 seconds.

The Volvo C70 has been designed around the same safety features as the Volvo S70, by designers who were given free rein to create the car of their dreams. And, as you can see, that is exactly what they did.

Calcavecchia holds off Westwood

Mark Calcavecchia was victorious
in Georgia but Lee Westwood
chased him home

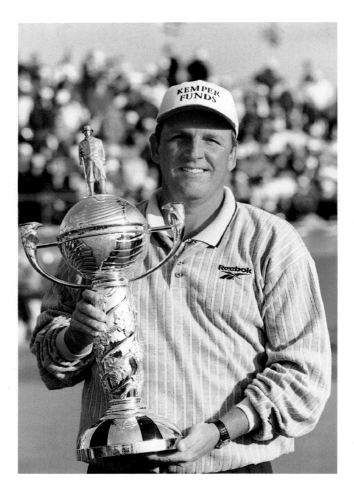

Lee Westwood and David Duval, fresh from their European and American Tour end-of-season triumphs, were significantly paired in the first two rounds of the $2 million Subaru Sarazen World Open on the Legends Course at Chateau Elan in Braseltor, Georgia.

But as Duval, a winner on his last three PGA Tour outings, marred his 26th birthday by slipping to joint sixth, 11 strokes behind, it was another American, Mark Calcavecchia, who emerged to challenge and ultimately beat by three strokes 24-year-old Volvo Masters winner Westwood, who ended five clear of joint third-placed Mark McNulty and Vijay Singh.

The 37-year-old from Nebraska, third, fourth and sixth in earlier Sarazens and fourth on his previous two outings in Las Vegas and the Tour Championship, built on a course record opening 62 to record a 17 under par 271 aggregate – one stroke inside New Zealander Frank Nobilo's 1996 tally in the event, a gathering of 108 champions from 67 countries to honour 95-year-old former Open, US Open, US Masters and USPGA champion, Gene Sarazen.

Calcavecchia who initially gained entry to the event with victory in the Argentine Open, earned $360,000, Westwood, after rounds of 71, 65, 70, 68, $218,000, which nudged his winnings in eight days to a princely £379,000.

Those are the nuts and bolts, but it was never that simple as young Westwood, looking every inch Europe's answer to Tiger Woods, battled from ten strokes behind after six holes of the final round to only two adrift with one to play.

It was drama all the way from day one with 44-year-old Sam Torrance threatening a happy ending to a miserable year with a pace-setting 68, despite a three-hour rain suspension.

Torrance who had slipped to the second lowest Volvo Ranking placing of his career – 56th – and missed out on a ninth successive Ryder Cup outing, collected seven birdies and would have had 67 but for a fluffed 12-inch putt on the tenth. He declared: 'I'm determined to start winning again. I've missed being in contention – it's my life and I'll be back.'

Sam could scarcely believe his eyes when he switched on his hotel room TV at lunchtime next day. 'I thought it said

Calcavecchia was four under after 14 holes but in fact he was 14 under after four holes on his second round,' explained the aimiable Scot, whose victory hopes were dashed by a second round 77, which plunged him 16 strokes behind the man who had beaten Greg Norman and Wayne Grady in the Open Champ-ionship's first four-hole play-off at Royal Troon in Torrance's native Ayrshire eight years earlier.

Calcavecchia led at halfway by seven strokes from Peter O'Malley and Westwood, who battled to an opening 71 after slipping two over par after eight, then added a magnificent 65.

The Worksop man, who earned his Sarazen place with victory in the Benson and Hedges Malaysian Open, was nine behind with six to play when bad light halted play on day two but he resumed in explosive style with a seven iron to five inches for a birdie three and picked up two more shots on the home straight. After covering 28 holes in ten under par, he launched his third round by downing birdie putts of 15 feet, then hit a three iron to four feet for a spectacular eagle three at the 517-yard ninth.

After another birdie at the 11th he

Lee Westwood (left) Vijay Singh (above).

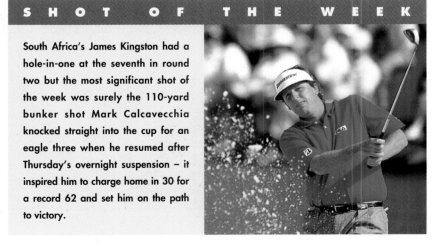

South Africa's James Kingston had a hole-in-one at the seventh in round two but the most significant shot of the week was surely the 110-yard bunker shot Mark Calcavecchia knocked straight into the cup for an eagle three when he resumed after Thursday's overnight suspension – it inspired him to charge home in 30 for a record 62 and set him on the path to victory.

was only three behind but a sad six at the long 14th, where he misshit the second and third shots and three-putted and Calcavecchia birdied, another birdie by the American at the 16th left him trailing by six.

Calcavecchia, who sank a succession of huge birdie putts, plus a bunker shot for an eagle, in his 62, looked home and dry when birdies at the first, third, fifth

THE COURSE

The Legends was designed by American Denis Griffiths, aided by Gene Sarazen, Sam Snead and Kathy Whitworth, featuring their favourite holes on great courses like Augusta National (the Legends' short 15th is a lookalike of the 12th and its long fifth inspired by the 13th at Amen Corner). Riviera, Merion, Winged Foot, Medinah, Pinehurst, St Andrews and Royal Troon have also been incorporated.

and sixth, where he chipped in, swept him 20 under par and ten strokes clear of Westwood, but the drama was just beginning.

After the youngster again eagled the ninth, Calcavecchia, forced to don a back brace at the turn after suffering painful muscle spasms, started to wobble, bogeying ten, 11 and 13 and failing to match Westwood's bold birdies at 14 and 16.

His ten-stroke advantage had shrunk to two after another nervous bogey at the 17th. It could have been one, for he bravely coaxed in a putt from ten feet there – indeed, Westwood would have been leading had he not narrowly missed birdie chances at the 11th and 15th.

It was his second stirring fightback of the week and the drama continued as Calcavecchia pushed his final drive into the rough and Westwood pulled his into a

Gentleman Gene Sarazen.

pine wood. He threaded an exquisite recovery between the tree trunks to within a few yards of the flag, only to have his hopes dashed as Calcavecchia got a fortuitous free drop away from a TV tower, found the green and audaciously knocked in a birdie putt from 40 feet.

Westwood, who sneaked a preview of the Legends Course prior to his Masters debut, refused to be downhearted: 'I'd never set foot in America until April but my worst finish in five starts – Masters, US Open, USPGA, World Series and here – was 29th and I've won more than $370,000. The Ryder Cup showed me I could play well under the most intense pressure and I believe I can win any tournament I tee it up in, including majors.' Fighting talk from the young man Calcavecchia called 'Golf's next superstar.'

Gordon Richardson

THE LEGENDS, CHATEAU ELAN, ATLANTA, GEORGIA, NOVEMBER 6-9, 1997 • YARDAGE 7025 • PAR 71

Pos	Name	Country	Rnd 1	Rnd 2	Rnd 3	Total	Prize Money $
1	Mark Calcavecchia		62	67	71	71	271	360,000
2	Lee Westwood		71	65	70	68	274	216,000
3	Mark McNulty		74	66	70	69	279	100,500
	Vijay Singh		69	69	70	71	279	100,500
5	Scott Hoch		69	69	69	74	281	70,000
6	Peter O'Malley		70	66	74	72	282	58,500
	David Duval		71	68	70	73	282	58,500
8	Steve Jones		69	68	74	73	284	49,500
	Frank Nobilo		71	69	69	75	284	49,500
10	Arden Knoll		72	70	71	72	285	45,000
11	Stewart Cink		70	77	71	68	286	40,500
	Per-Ulrik Johansson		69	70	72	75	286	40,500
13	Mathias Grönberg		70	72	75	70	287	35,000
	Retief Goosen		74	69	73	71	287	35,000
15	Ian Woosnam		73	72	74	69	288	27,250
	Craig Stadler		71	75	73	69	288	27,250
	Migel Angel Jiménez		72	73	71	72	288	27,250
	Sven Strüver		68	72	75	73	288	27,250
	Edward Fryatt		70	74	70	74	288	27,250
	Alex Cejka		70	71	72	75	288	27,250
21	Desvonde Botes		75	73	74	67	289	17,670
	P J Cowan		74	71	77	67	289	17,670
	Jaime Gomez		69	75	74	71	289	17,670
	Wayne Riley		70	74	73	72	289	17,670
	Steve Flesch		77	68	69	75	289	17,670
26	Elliott Boult		73	72	74	71	290	12,600
	Paul Broadhurst		75	73	70	72	290	12,600
	Christopher Williams		69	73	76	72	290	12,600
	Padraig Harrington		69	72	73	76	290	12,600
30	Paul McGinley		72	76	72	71	291	9,900
	Fuzzy Zoeller		76	70	73	72	291	9,900
32	Ricardo Gonzalez		71	75	76	70	292	7,164
	John Kernohan		71	76	75	70	292	7,164
	Jorge Berendt		74	73	74	71	292	7,164
	Tony Christie		74	73	73	72	292	7,164
	Sam Torrance		68	77	74	73	292	7,164
	Clinton Whitelaw		71	73	75	73	292	7,164
	Ignacio Feliu		71	76	72	73	292	7,164
39	Mike Miller		73	73	75	72	293	6,166
	Andrew Bonhomme		72	73	75	73	293	6,166
	Kevin Wentworth		73	73	73	74	293	6,166
42	Soren Kjeldsen		75	73	72	74	294	6,030
	Fabian Montovia		73	75	71	75	294	6,030
	Jyoung Ju Choi		78	70	71	75	294	6,030
	Michael Jonzon		73	72	73	76	294	6,030
46	Peter Hedblom		74	72	75	74	295	5,980
47	Kalle Brink		74	74	76	72	296	5,960
48	Marcello Santi		72	74	82	69	297	5,920
	Paul Fretes		72	73	78	74	297	5,920
	Gustavo Rojas		74	73	75	75	297	5,920
51	Peter Lonard		73	75	75	75	298	5,880
52	Phil Golding		73	71	75	80	299	5,860
53	Steve van Vuuren		71	75	78	76	300	5,830
	Mikael Lundberg		74	73	76	77	300	5,830
55	Payne Stewart		74	73	76	78	301	5,800
56	Mark Brooks		73	73	80	76	302	5,780
57	Anthony Musgrave		74	74	78	77	303	5,750
	James Kingston		74	71	80	78	303	5,750

Lee Westwood drives into second place.

New Zealand gets the call

The game's longest-running

world team event breaks

new ground in 1998

The World Cup of Golf took a huge step forward when, in 1995, it went to the People's Republic of China, so becoming the first major international golfing event to be held in mainland China, since when it has been played at Erinvale Golf Club in Cape Town, where South Africa was successful, and in 1997 at Kiawah Island in the United States where Ireland (Padraig Harrington and Paul McGinley) triumphed.

Now in November, 1998, the World Cup of Golf, first launched as the Canada Cup in 1953, will break new ground yet again by taking its 44th Championship to New Zealand, when it will be played at the Gulf Harbour course near Auckland, then to Malaysia in 1999 when the Mines Resort and Golf Club, near Kuala Lumpur, will be the venue.

Jonathan Linen, Chairman of the International Golf Association, the organiser of the World Cup, said: 'We are delighted to be taking our championship to New Zealand, a country that has produced such fine golfers as Bob Charles, Frank Nobilo, Greg Turner, Michael Campbell and Simon Owen. New Zealand has been a staunch supporter of the

Paul McGinley and Padraig Harrington, winners of the 1997 World Cup of Golf.

World Cup since 1954. Although it has never won our tournament, its team did come second to the United States in Mexico City in 1967. The New Zealand players have also had several top ten finishes in recent years so maybe 1998 will be their year at last. The World Cup is all about promoting goodwill between nations great and small and that's why it's become known as the Olympics of golf.'

David Ciclitira, Chairman and Chief

Executive of Parallel Media Group, the promoters of the World Cup, said: 'The World Cup has a proud tradition of taking its championship to all corners of the earth where the game is played. It has been staged in 21 different countries since its inception and we are confident that our visit to New Zealand will be an enormous success. New Zealand has great sporting traditions and I'm sure that golf lovers in the Auckland community will flock to the event, as enthusiasts did in Cape Town in 1996 and mainland China in 1995.'

The Gulf Harbour development, only a short drive out of Auckland, is one of the most spectacular in the South Pacific Region with marina, luxury hotel, conference centre and residential facilities. And the golf course, designed by Robert Trent Jones Junior, with all its exciting views, has been compared favourably to the famous American course, Pebble Beach, where the US Open Championship has been staged.

A group of international sponsors has been lined up for the event and the Government has pledged its full support.

The World Cup of Golf is a two-man team event featuring the top golfing

Ernie Els and Wayne Westner (above), winners of the 1996 World Cup. Fred Couples and Davis Love III, the undisputed kings of World Cup golf (below).

nations and in recent times a notable record was established when Fred Couples and David Love III became the first partnership in the history of the event to win four years in succession. This historic moment was sealed at Mission Hills, on the outskirts of Shenzhen, in 1995 when the United States won by 14 shots, as they had done in Puerto Rico in 1994.

Even so, in 1996 Ernie Els and Wayne Westner, representing South Africa, completed a record-breaking 18-stroke victory ahead of the United States and in front of a record-breaking 81,262 spectators at Erinvale. Els confessed: 'I guess we had a slight advantage with more than 30,000 people cheering us on during the last round.'

The popularity of the World Cup of Golf has most certainly grown since Argentina won the first edition in 1953 at Beaconsfield, Montreal, and the decision to play in 1997 at Kiawah Island, where the Ryder Cup unfolded in 1991, provided further evidence of its reputation as a truly prestigious event.

As Linen says: 'The IGA is the organising body for what is the game of golf's longest-running world team event and the principle under which it is organised – originally through the Canada Cup – is how we spread the understanding of the game of golf around the world and recognise its importance as manifested by people coming together to play this wonderful game.'

The IGA and the story of the World Cup began in 1953 when the first Canada Cup matches were held in Montreal. The event was the creation of noted Canadian

industrialist and educator, John Jay Hopkins, who dreamed of bringing the family of nations together for a truly global experience: 'Golf is a game for good neighbours', was one of his favourite sayings.

There were seven teams, but the next year the number of competing teams jumped to 25 and the event was poised to take its place in the history of championship golf. The venue then moved to Washington DC in 1955, and to Wentworth, England, in 1956, where Ben Hogan and Sam Snead formed one of the all-time great teams. The pattern had been set; this was a tournament that would be hosted all over the world.

As Burch Riber, Executive Director of the IGA, points out: 'It's important to know that we invite countries and not individuals. Each country selects its team based on what it feels are the proper qualifications for their particular set of circumstances and this applies to every country that participates.'

Mitchell Platts   279

Youth movement

The year's major championships
were dominated by the
youthful brigade

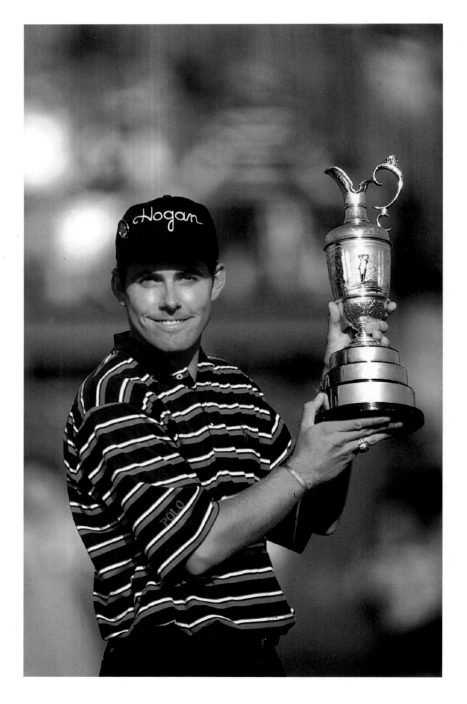

Something changed in 1997. Golf changed. Golf got younger, more with it, more hip. More right on. More popular. Tiger Woods started it, but Ernie Els and Justin Leonard continued the trend and Davis Love finally found his labours were not in vain.

Three of these men won majors for the first time, but more importantly three were under the age of 30. This was the first time, it was believed that the winners of the first three majors of the year were as youthful as Woods, Els and Leonard at 21, 27 and 25 respectively.

The 40-plus generation played some neat golf during the year, but not in the four championships that matter, Nick Faldo and Greg Norman setting the tone when, a year after their classic last day duel at Augusta, they both missed the cut at the US Masters. The 30-somethings, Colin Montgomerie, Tom Lehman, who both came close at the US Open, and Love, who succeeded at the USPGA, were around when it mattered most.

Suddenly this was a young man's game. A very young man's game in the case of Woods. The first Cablinasian – his own description of his mix of Caucasian, Black, Indian and Asian ancestry – to win

**Justin Leonard took the old claret jug
at Royal Troon (left).
Tiger Woods (right) dominated at Augusta.**

the Masters, Woods was also the youngest ever, at 21 years, three months and 15 days beating Severiano Ballesteros' previous mark. Only Young Tom Morris, in the last century, had won a major at a younger age.

His youth and his ethnic background – no Black player had been invited to the Masters until 1975 – made the victory into international front page news. But his golf had the back pages drooling, too. Despite his turning the 61st Masters into a one-man show, the final day drew record television audiences. The Augusta gallery, who have been lucky to witness the greatest the game has so far offered us, were at times stunned into silence. Jack Nicklaus saw no reason to change his estimate that Woods would surpass his and Arnold Palmer's combined total of ten Green Jackets.

Woods huge hitting overpowered the course. He needed only the short irons for his approach shots, usually only taking a wedge to reach the par five 15th green in two. But he also conquered Augusta's major defence, its slick and viciously undulating greens, with a touch and inspiration in his putting that was breathtaking.

He won by 12 strokes, a new record, just as his nine-shot advantage after 54 holes was. His putt at the last, inevitably holed, was not important for the victory but gave him a new record score at Augusta of 270, 18 under par. He tied the record for the lowest first 54 holes, broke the one for the last 54 and the middle 36 holes. Yet, he had gone to the turn in

Concern from Greg Norman and Colin Montgomerie (below). Joy from Ernie Els and caddie (bottom) at the US Open.

round one in 40. With the class of a champion, he returned in 30 and then added rounds of 66, 65 and 69.

There was talk of a Grand Slam, golf's first ever in the professional majors, but it was not to be. Woods went on to finish 19th, 24th and 29th in the remaining three majors, belying his inexperience in the first year as a professional on traditional tight, demanding, shot-making golf courses.

Els, however, was in his element at Congressional. His first US Open win came in 1994 when the South African was a member of the European Tour, and by coincidence he had rejoined in 1997.

As three years before, Montgomerie was one of his chief rivals. The Scot had set the course record in the first round with a 65, and managed to recover after a shaky 76 the next day. Lehman and Jeff Maggert added to a thrilling four-way tussle on the last afternoon, but eventually it was down to Els and Montgomerie. At the 17th, Els hit a brilliant five iron over the flag to 15 feet. It was a stunning blow. Montgomerie had bogeyed the hole all week and missed the green on the right. His chip was a good one, but just came up six feet short. His putt was a good one, just missing. 'I would not have either of those shots back,' he said.

In his moment of bitter disappointment at missing out so narrowly again, Montgomerie paid tribute to Els. 'He is so laid back it is

Justin Leonard (above) with significant background.
Davis Love III (below) conquered all in the USPGA.

frightening,' he said. After Leonard's victory at Royal Troon, where Darren Clarke and Jesper Parnevik finished joint runners-up, Montgomerie was again the leading European at the USPGA

Winged Foot played as a traditional US Open style course, but the Scot's putting was not at its best and twelve Americans finished in front of him. Love went into the final day tied with Leonard, but the young Texan's hopes of back-to-back majors faded early in the final round. Love produced his third 66 of the week to win by five strokes, as the 33-year-old son of a teaching professional got rid of the best-not-to-win-one-yet tag. His father, Davis Junior, had died in a plane crash nine years before and had never been at a tournament on a Sunday when his son won. 'My father always told me to 'follow my dreams and enjoy the trip',' Love said. 'Every day I play golf, I think about my dad. I know he would be extremely proud not only that I won a major, but that I won the PGA.'

But back to youth. In Europe, Lee Westwood, at the age of 24, emerged as a new rising star and never demonstrated that better than with his achievement in making the cut in all four majors, his worst finish being his 29th at the USPGA, his best the tenth place at Troon. It was a fine performance by a fine young man in a year of fine performances by fine young men.

Andy Farrell

Nick Faldo (left) and Colin Montgomerie (right) in dance of despair, while for Jesper Parnevik (centre) at Royal Troon, it's an Open and shut case. Synchronised mowing at Congressional during the US Open (below).

Charity is rewarded

The Canon Shoot-Out Series
proved popular for players
and charity alike

Canon Shoot-Out Grand Final
winners Alexander Cejka
and Sven Strüver.

The Canon Shoot-Out Series once again provided entertainment for players and spectators alike in Canon's seventh and final year of their sponsorship of the popular Shoot-Outs.

This year's Shoot-Out Series comprised ten events, beginning in South Africa in February, where local favourites Retief Goosen and Tony Johnstone triumphed at Houghton Golf Club, near Johannesburg, prior to the Alfred Dunhill SA PGA Championship.

Following South Africa, the Series next visited the Peugeot Open de España where the young pairing of Lee Westwood and Padraig Harrington pushed the partnership of Severiano Ballesteros and Costantino Rocca into second place. A chip-and-putt par at the final hole secured victory over the experienced Ryder Cup duo.

It was fitting that the Spanish Shoot-Out should feature pairings selected by this year's victorious Ryder Cup captain, Ballesteros. The European skipper was on hand to pick the partnerships at all of the remaining 1997 Shoot-Outs.

Charity was again a prominent feature in this year's Shoot-Outs and the most spectacular fund-raising of all was seen at the Canon Champions Challenge, which took place in damp conditions, prior to the Volvo PGA Championship, at Wentworth Club. An enthusiastic crowd, who turned up in their hundreds despite the poor weather, witnessed some magnificent golf by a truly world-class field which featured Ballesteros, Nick Faldo,

Colin Montgomerie, José Maria Olazábal, Bernhard Langer, Vijay Singh, Frank Nobilo, Ian Woosnam, Costantino Rocca and Jesper Parnevik.

The much-favoured British pairing of Montgomerie and Faldo emerged as victors over the strong pairing from the southern hemisphere of Singh and Nobilo. Although there could only be one victorious pair, charity was rewarded to the tune of over £40,000 from the efforts of the ten players involved.

The large crowd who turned up to watch the next leg of the Series prior to the Volvo German Open were rewarded with a real treat as local hero, Bernhard Langer, was able to confirm his participation only at the very last moment. The double US Masters champion's decision was shown to be extremely good as he and fellow German, Sven Strüver, triumphed.

Lightning threatened to halt proceedings after three holes, but Tournament Director Andy McFee's patience enabled the remaining ten players to resume after a short break to conclude matters. In a best-

Colin Montgomerie, and Nick Faldo (above) with Pat Guerin, Director of Communication Products, Canon, were victors in the Canon Champions Challenge. Lee Westwood and Padraig Harrington (right) were in Canon action throughout the season.

of-three Shoot-Out at the 18th hole, Langer's exquisite long bunker shot to three feet was enough to ward off the challenge of Eduardo Romero and Wayne Riley.

After four Shoot-Outs, Rocca had built up a six points lead in the Canon Shoot-Out Order of Merit. He led from Irishman Harrington, who shared second place with Strüver.

A crowd of well over 1,000 turned out for the next Shoot-Out, which was held at Druids Glen, prior to the popular Murphy's Irish Open. The Emerald Isle has been the scene of many great Shoot-Outs in recent years and 1997 was no exception. A splendid curling putt from 15 feet on the final green by Harrington meant that Italian maestro, Rocca had to hole from 12 feet to force a sudden-death shoot-out. The Italian's brave attempt slipped narrowly past, giving victory to Harrington and his fellow Celtic partner, Sam Torrance.

Hilversum Golf Club in Holland played host to the next Shoot-Out of the 1997 calendar. Rocca once again played bridesmaid as a tremendous display of chipping, pitching and putting from the Scottish pairing of Andrew Coltart and Raymond Russell ensured their first victory of the Series.

By the time of the Volvo Scandinavian Masters, Rocca must have been asking himself what he had to do to

287

Costantino Rocca (top), winner of the 1997 Shoot-Out Order of Merit, was in partnership with Seve Ballesteros in Spain. Bernhard Langer at St. Nom-la-Bretêche (centre). Nick Faldo (below) at Crans-sur-Sierre, Switzerland, venue for the Canon Shoot-Out final.

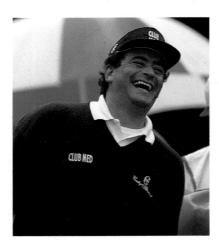

win his first 1997 Shoot-Out. Unfortunately for him, even being paired with the Welsh wizard, Woosnam, wasn't enough to secure his maiden 1997 victory.

A gallery of over 2,000 people were treated to a fine display of golf by a field which included local favourites Parnevik and Per-Ulrik Johansson. The Ryder Cup duo were unfortunately the first to be eliminated in a strong field which also included six other members of the year's triumphant Ryder Cup team. The year had seen the emergence of some fine young stars and Volvo German Open champion, Ignacio Garrido, together with Torrance, eventually triumphed at a windswept Barsebäck Golf Club.

The very first Shoot-Out in Eastern Europe took place prior to the Chemapol Trophy Czech Open. Local favourite, Alex Cejka, and Coltart were the winners, and it was no surprise to see that Rocca picked up, what, by now, had become a customary second place.

It was fitting that the Shoot-Out Final should once again take place at the Canon European Masters, held each year at the spectacular resort of Crans-sur-Sierre. Torrential rain threatened to put paid to the Shoot-Out Final, but sterling work by the green staff ensured that the golf course was playable. The patient crowd were treated to some excellent golf by many of the world's finest players, including Faldo, Montgomerie, Ballesteros and American, Scott Hoch. However, the much-coveted victory was secured by the lesser-fancied German pairing of Cejka and Strüver. Harrington and Hoch were the first to be eliminated at the third hole and a double-bogey by Montgomerie and Ballesteros at the short fourth sealed their departure.

Tournament Director John Paramor's decision to use the front bunker of the par

four seventh for a shoot-out heralded the exit of Faldo and Garrido, who were defeated by a near perfect bunker-shot by Strüver. As the two pairs headed up the last, it was evident that this was Rocca's big opportunity to avenge the numerous near misses of the 1997 Series.

After both pairings played excellent approaches in front of an appreciative crowd, Cejka holed bravely from eight feet to force Rocca to hole his slightly shorter, yet equally tricky effort. The Italian could only watch as his try slipped tantalisingly past, resulting in yet another second place.

The Italian nevertheless won the 1997 Shoot-Out Order of Merit by a considerable margin and took further consolation from the Final, winning the 'nearest the pin' competition at the seventh, for which he was rewarded with a pair of 15 x 45 Canon binoculars.

As in 1996, an extra Shoot-Out was staged after the Final in the delightful setting of St. Nom-la-Bretêche, prior to the Trophée Lancôme. A stunning final-hole birdie brought victory for Paul Lawrie and Jonathan Lomas over the unlucky Swedes Johansson and Parnevik, who, despite being four under par for the seven holes played, lost out to a magnificently struck four iron from Lawrie at the 18th.

As a mark of Canon's continued support for charity, each birdie made in this year's Shoot-Outs was rewarded with £50 and each eagle with £100. As in 1996, all funds raised from this initiative were donated to the PGA European Tour Benevolent Trust, a charity founded by the Tour to support members of the Tour and their families who fall upon hard times. All in all, the players managed to raise £2,750 for the Benevolent Trust.

Rocca matched his first place in the Shoot-Out Order of Merit with a similarly conclusive victory in the Birdie/Eagle Challenge Tables.

In addition to the popular Shoot-Outs, Canon's support of the 1997 PGA European Tour once again extended to their status as Official Copier/Fax. This important service ensures, that the latest news and results can be efficiently communicated to golf fans the world over.

Canon Shot of the Year

Colin Montgomerie,

18th hole, Valderrama,

Ryder Cup by Johnnie Walker

The 18th at Valderrama provided perhaps the most testing tee shot on the course during the Ryder Cup by Johnnie Walker. Certainly when matches were still in the balance, the trees which encroached onto the left-hand side of the left-hand dog-leg made the tee shot a daunting prospect.

When Colin Montgomerie came to the 18th in his singles with Scott Hoch the two were all square. Europe had already retained the Ryder Cup but Montgomerie knew that nothing less than outright victory for his team would do. To achieve this he had to gain at least a half with his opponent.

The design of the hole was not suited to Montgomerie's natural left-to-right shape of shot but showing great calmness under the most intense pressure, he fired his tee shot over the trees and landed the ball softly in the middle of the fairway.

'It was the best tee shot I have ever struck in my life,' said Montgomerie. 'I say tee shot because I didn't use the driver, it was a three wood. In fact, I always use a three wood at that hole. The idea is to hit the ball high over the the trees and land it softly. I managed that, and also got the length I was looking for as the ball travelled 280 yards.'

Former European Tour Director-General and world-renowned teacher, John Jacobs commented: 'Colin was faced with having to hit what was virtually a soft wedge shot only, on this occasion, it was with a wood. He pulled it off to perfection.'

Following that tee shot, Montgomerie was left with a nine iron second shot which he hit safely onto the green to ensure the half point which won the match for Europe.

The tee shot was a worthy winner of the 1997 Canon Shot of the Year and gave Montgomerie his second consecutive award in this category.

Canon

289

Ryder Cup trio sets standard

Former European Challenge Tour graduates
Costantino Rocca, Ignacio Garrido and Thomas Bjorn
provide the incentive for the future

**Italy's Michele Reale
was Challenge Tour number one in 1997.**

Europe's nail-biting Ryder Cup victory at Valderrama had most fans on the edge of their seats. Alain de Soultrait likewise, and as he watched the drama unfold he had a feeling of quiet satisfaction. After all, three of his 'old boys' were involved which made nine years of devotion to the European Challenge Tour all the more worthwhile.

Alain has been the man at the sharp end of that Tour since its formation in 1989. That year, Costantino Rocca was a graduate, Ignacio Garrido came through in 1993, and Thomas Bjorn in 1995. Now, this triumphant triumvirate are at the top of the golfing tree, proof, if any were needed, of the value of the Challenge Tour as a proving ground for future champions.

In 1989, only the top five players earned cards to the main Tour. Today it is 15 an there seems little doubt that with ever improving standards, more players will follow in Rocca, Garrido and Bjorn's footsteps.

That leaves Frenchman Alain to pon-

der, who of the 1997 graduates will influence the Ryder Cup come the millennium? It is easy to fly kites but two young men, Michele Reale and Raphaël Jacquelin, would seem to have all the credentials.

Reale, the 26-year-old Italian, who was a clear winner of the 1997 Rankings with a

record £51,679, is out of the Rocca mould. A year ago he finished 16th and missed his card by around £700. He was mortified. Fortunately, he shook off the disappointment to compete in 26 events, finishing in the top ten on eight occasions including two victories, and missing only five cuts.

His two triumphs, in the Canarias Challenge in Las Palmas, and the Sovereign Russian Open in Moscow, both came in play-offs which underlines how difficult he is to beat. 'It was hard for me to play again this year but now I think it turned out well because I won two tournaments,' said Michele. 'Maybe it was too early for me to go on the main Tour. It was important to be number one on the Challenge Tour because it shows to other players that you are special. I have enjoyed the Challenge Tour because the competition is so good and the standard so high. You play under pressure and this will help me next year.'

Jacquelin, 23, has clear objectives. 'I want to be world number one and to be the first Frenchman to play in the Ryder Cup,' he says. High ambitions, but he has proved to be the best of a large French contingent on the Challenge Tour.

He finished fourth on the Rankings, eclipsed Reale by recording three victories, in France, Switzerland and Holland, and amassed over £34,000 from 14 tournaments, again a better average than the Italian.

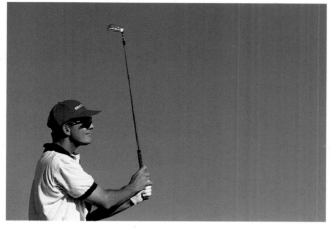

Leaney. They have the class to extend the long line of Aussie successes in Europe.

The other big influence on the Challenge Tour in 1997 was the weather. It was a bad year, torrential rain forcing the cancellation of two tournaments and the curtailment of three others including the Estoril Grand Final, the climax of the season, at Montado in Portugal.

Stephen Leaney (top). Greg Chalmers (left), Nicolas Joakimides (right) and Raphaël Jacquelin (below) all earned their cards to the main Tour for 1998.

Looking at the top 15 qualifiers, they represent 11 nations. Three come from Denmark (perhaps Bjorn's example was the catalyst), two each from Australia and France, and one each from Italy, Sweden, Finland, England, Germany, Belgium, Wales and the United States.

Watch also for the Australian duo, Greg Chalmers and Stephen

Three rounds were completed but a violent thunderstorm put paid to the fourth. It left Parisian Nicolas Joakimides the winner following a third round 62. The £11,662 first prize hoisted him from 26th to sixth, from obscurity to a Tour card. 'It was a gift from the sky,' he said. Such fairytales happen on the Challenge Tour, just ask Monsieur de Soultrait.

David Hamilton

Expansion and development herald the future

PGA European Tour Courses

is set to create outstanding golf facilities

throughout Europe

PGA European Tour Courses is looking forward to 1998. It is set to be an exciting year in its aim to develop golf facilities which will stage European Tour events. In 1998, the Volvo Scandinavian Masters will be held at ETC Stockholm, construction of a third course will begin at Woburn Golf and Country Club and PGA Golf de Catalunya near Barcelona is due to open in the autumn.

ETC Stockholm was developed as a 36-hole venue and opened in 1994. Tour Courses purchased the Club in 1995 and commissioned European Golf Design (EGD) to work with original designer, Anders Forsbrand, to upgrade the South Course for championship play. The extensive reconstruction work was completed last autumn and the course, carved through granite and pine forest, will be the scene for this prestigious tournament.

Soon after the Volvo Scandinavian Masters in August, Tour Courses' new venue, PGA Golf de Catalunya near Barcelona is scheduled to open. Designed by Neil Coles and Angel Gallardo, it is anticipated the course will become a jewel in the crown of the many delightful courses to be found in the Catalan region of Spain. The undulating land, dense with a variety of mature trees which now line the fairways and set against a backdrop of the Pyrenees in the temperate climate of the Costa Brava, has been sculptured

PGA European Tour Courses PLC

into a dramatic par 72, 7,200-yard course that will challenge the best players in the world. Angel Gallardo said: 'The opening of this facility has been a dream for nearly ten years. I am proud to have worked with Neil Coles and EGD to design a course that represents the best my country has to offer. There are many wonderful courses in the world and I believe PGA Golf de Catalunya will soon be ranked among them.' In time, a second course, hotel and other facilities will be developed to create a resort which will rival Tour Courses' 36-hole facility at Quinta do Lago on the Algarve, which has hosted seven Portuguese Opens.

Last year, Tour Courses joined forces with the Bedford Estate and acquired half of Woburn Golf and Country Club which has hosted 12 British Masters.

The 18th on the South Course at the ETC Stockholm (above). Angel Gallardo (below) surveys the work in progress at PGA Golf de Catalunya. Woburn Golf and Country Club (opposite).

Clearing has just begun to create a third course, designed by Peter Alliss and EGD, which will become the home of a European Tour event when it is ready for play. Alex Hay, Managing Director of Woburn, said, 'It is a pleasure to be working with Tour Courses to extend Woburn's already excellent facilities. It

takes considerable time, effort and money to go through the processes that are necessary to create a championship golf course. At Woburn we will have three such courses and with the support of the PGA European Tour, Woburn is set to play a leading role in European golf in the new millenium.'

Ken Schofield, Executive Director of the PGA European Tour and Director of Tour Courses summarises the future: 'PGA European Tour Courses now operates four facilities that have the potential to be among the best in Europe. The management is committed to developing and maintaining quality golf courses on which events will be played. The PGA European Tour is proud to be involved with Tour Courses which will play an integral part in the future of our game.'

293

Horton's dream continues

Six victories and a new record prize-money total put Tommy Horton on top for the second year running

*L*ike all top achievers in any walk of life, Tommy Horton has an acute sense of timing. So when he chose the final putt on the final green of the final tournament to roll in yet another birdie for his closing victory on the 1997 European Seniors Tour, it was more or less what had been anticipated.

Such is the level of performance and sense of theatre possessed by the 56-year-old Royal Jersey professional.

This crowning moment of yet another momentous campaign for Horton was adorned, appropriately enough, with the full colour of autumn at the lovely Buckinghamshire layout. Horton was capping not only a three-shot victory in the Seniors Tournament of Champions but a hat-trick of titles and a campaign that brought him six winning cheques, a new high of £158,427 in prize-money and, of course, the John Jacobs Order of Merit Trophy for the third time and second successive year.

For the record he opened the season with a two-stroke win over Maurice Bembridge in the Turkish Seniors Open over the vastly improved National course in Turkey and followed up with another

two-shot margin in the AIB Irish Seniors in Dublin.

Then followed his most cherished success, the Jersey Senior Open at La Moye. He took a rare rest from winning speeches during mid-season, but after an unsuccessful trip to the United States Senior Open where he missed the cut, Horton returned to close his season in dramatic style.

He took the Scottish Seniors Open at Newmachar by a record nine shots after an astonishing final round of 62 and a week later another record closing round of 64 at Benton Hall earned him a two-stroke margin over Ulster's David Jones in

the Clubhaus Senior Classic. Horton also collected three runners-up cheques and was four more times inside the top six.

If 1996 was described as Horton's year when he won four tournaments, what was 1997? Perhaps Tour Managing Director, Andy Stubbs summed it up best when he said: 'Tommy has taken us all to another level.' Certainly he inspired his contemporaries sufficiently to have them following him to the practice grounds in droves. They were all working harder to reach the next level.

And that neatly summed up the 1997 Tour. A campaign which offered £2 million prize money from 17 tournaments including the bonus of the £150,000 European Cup match against the WPGET Tour in Portugal. Indeed, Andy Stubbs now believes the Tour has grown sufficiently to offer a genuine career to which professionals can now commit fully and derive a main source of income.

Apart from Horton's phenomenal success, 1997 was memorable for producing five first-time winners. Two of them, Lincolnshire's Ian Richardson (Motor Senior Classic at Goodwood) and American T. R. Jones (De Vere Seniors Classic at Belton Woods) earned their places at the pre-Tour Qualifying School.

Atlantic to sample the Tour.

Another formidable challenger to finally realise his potential was Australian Noel Ratcliffe. After four second place finishes in his previous two years and yet another behind Horton in the AIB Irish

hole. And the small man in black underlined his enduring talent at the age of 61 by following up with a second victory in the Shell Senior Masters over Wentworth's Edinburgh course.

Another 'senior' senior, 62-year-old Neil Coles, demonstrated his liking for the Collingtree course at Northampton by winning there for the third time with an eight under par tournament record of 208.

Spain's Antonio Garrido, buoyant with his son Ignacio's rise to Ryder Cup status, enjoyed his best seniors year yet with a run to third in the Merit list, capped by victory in the Lawrence Batley at Hud-

Noel Ratcliffe (above), winner of the Swedish and German Senior Opens. Gary Player (left) victorious at Royal Portrush, and fellow countryman John Bland, runner-up to Player in the Senior British Open.

Seniors, the big Sydney professional took advantage of Horton's absence in America to win the Swedish Senior Open and followed up two events later with the German Senior Open title. They were to boost his season's earnings to £86,060 for second place in the Order of Merit.

Jim Rhodes demonstrated the opportunities for competitive-minded club professionals when he left his South Staffs shop in the hands of his assistants to earn £55,839 and fifth in the Merit list. His best form was reserved for a starring performance in the Senior British Open at Royal Portrush where he not only made the final round, but just missed a last green birdie that would have put him in a play-off for the title. He settled for a share of third and a cheque for £19,705.

It was, perhaps, appropriate that this Tour showpiece on one of the world's finest links courses should be won by South African legend Gary Player for the third time. He beat fellow countryman John Bland in the sudden-death play-off with a birdie putt on the second extra

dersfield. And Nottingham club professional Brian Waites also reminded us that he is not finished yet with a play-off success over the ever-consistent Malcolm Gregson in the Swiss Senior Open at the beautiful resort at Bad Ragaz.

Bryan Potter

Two other Americans, Deray Simon (Philips PFA Classic at St Pierre), and Walter Hall (PGA Championship at The Belfry) were among the new winners and the USA trio may well have signalled the start of a fresh surge on European titles by the increasing numbers crossing the

De Vere Hotels.
The king of the fairways.

When it comes to golfing resorts that are truly superb, just why do De Vere's rule all the rest?

Is it because our hotels offer some of the best golf resorts found in the United Kingdom?

Maybe it's because our challenging championship courses are matched by excellent off course facilities, making our golfing hospitality totally memorable.

Perhaps it's because our impeccable service and mouth-watering menus are as impressive as all our other golfing facilities on offer.

Whatever the reason, when it comes to golf holidays, we've clearly no handicaps.

Hotels of character, run with pride.

Golfer of the Month Awards 1997

The winners of the Johnnie Walker
Golfer of the Month Awards receive a trophy
designed by Tiffany & Co of London
and earn £1,000 for the PGA European Tour
Benevolent Trust and £1,000 for the Golf Foundation

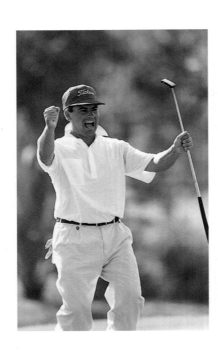

**Miguel Angel Martin (left), January; José Maria Olazábal (right), February and March; Colin Montgomerie (above), July.
There is also a Johnnie Walker Golfer of the Year Award. The winner in 1997 was Colin Montgomerie.**

Bernhard Langer (above left), May and October; Seve Ballesteros (above right), September.
Ernie Els (above), June.

Carl Watts (left), August; Mark James (right), April.

Volvo Ranking 1997

Colin Montgomerie

					£
	34	Richard GREEN	(Aus)	(20)	170116
	35	Jamie SPENCE	(Eng)	(24)	160986
#	36	Niclas FASTH	(Swe)	(24)	159370
	37	Miguel Angel JIMÉNEZ	(Sp)	(25)	158413
	38	Angel CABRERA	(Arg)	(23)	155429
	39	Phillip PRICE	(Wal)	(28)	151602
	40	Peter MITCHELL	(Eng)	(28)	148329
*	41	Dennis EDLUND	(Swe)	(25)	147234
#	42	Scott HENDERSON	(Scot)	(21)	147000
§	43	Michael LONG	(NZ)	(15)	144314
	44	Anders FORSBRAND	(Swe)	(24)	141727
	45	Michael JONZON	(Swe)	(25)	140078
	46	Andrew COLTART	(Scot)	(30)	140042
	47	David HOWELL	(Eng)	(31)	137703
§	48	Peter LONARD	(Aus)	(14)	134067
	49	Gordon BRAND JNR.	(Scot)	(25)	133541
	50	Wayne WESTNER	(SA)	(24)	129452
	51	Daniel CHOPRA	(Swe)	(30)	120241
	52	Paul LAWRIE	(Scot)	(27)	117919
#	53	Brian DAVIS	(Eng)	(23)	117575
#	54	Clinton WHITELAW	(SA)	(18)	116434
	55	Robert ALLENBY	(Aus)	(15)	116251
	56	Sam TORRANCE	(Scot)	(26)	115433
	57	Mark ROE	(Eng)	(27)	114542
	58	Thomas GÖGELE	(Ger)	(31)	113807
	59	Alex CEJKA	(Ger)	(21)	111263
	60	Ronan RAFFERTY	(N.Ire)	(26)	110314
*	61	Carl WATTS	(Eng)	(23)	109910
	62	Mark MOULAND	(Wal)	(29)	104767
#	63	Steve WEBSTER	(Eng)	(22)	104373
	64	Philip WALTON	(Ire)	(22)	102624
	65	Richard BOXALL	(Eng)	(29)	102007
	66	Iain PYMAN	(Eng)	(27)	98881
*	67	Van PHILLIPS	(Eng)	(26)	98109
	68	Carl SUNESON	(Sp)	(28)	97950
	69	Wayne RILEY	(Aus)	(26)	97913
	70	Jon ROBSON	(Eng)	(26)	97569
	71	Gary ORR	(Scot)	(27)	96667
	72	Peter HEDBLOM	(Swe)	(26)	94718
	73	Stuart CAGE	(Eng)	(27)	91482
	74	Mark MCNULTY	(Zim)	(13)	91318
	75	Santiago LUNA	(Sp)	(25)	90702
	76	Mats HALLBERG	(Swe)	(20)	88317
	77	Jean VAN DE VELDE	(Fr)	(25)	87829
	78	Fabrice TARNAUD	(Fr)	(27)	86639
	79	Jonathan LOMAS	(Eng)	(27)	84184
#	80	Katsuyoshi TOMORI	(Jap)	(23)	83460
	81	Marc FARRY	(Fr)	(27)	81545
#	82	Stephen ALLAN	(Aus)	(20)	80564
	83	Barry LANE	(Eng)	(24)	78046
*	84	Fredrik JACOBSON	(Swe)	(19)	77697
*	85	Ian GARBUTT	(Eng)	(27)	73421

					£						
1	Colin MONTGOMERIE	(Scot)	(22)	798947		17	Patrik SJÖLAND	(Swe)	(27)	245274
2	Bernhard LANGER	(Ger)	(20)	692398		18	Greg TURNER	(NZ)	(22)	239869
3	Lee WESTWOOD	(Eng)	(25)	588718		19	Joakim HAEGGMAN	(Swe)	(23)	228479
4	Darren CLARKE	(N.Ire)	(25)	537409		20	Russell CLAYDON	(Eng)	(23)	225005
5	Ian WOOSNAM	(Wal)	(19)	503562		21	Paul MCGINLEY	(Ire)	(27)	220278
6	Ignacio GARRIDO	(Sp)	(27)	411479		22	Peter O'MALLEY	(Aus)	(24)	208339
7	Retief GOOSEN	(SA)	(23)	394597		23	Sven STRÜVER	(Ger)	(28)	207006
8	Padraig HARRINGTON	(Ire)	(30)	388982		24	Peter BAKER	(Eng)	(30)	200819
9	José Maria OLAZABAL	(Sp)	(19)	385648		25	Paul BROADHURST	(Eng)	(30)	198426
10	Robert KARLSSON	(Swe)	(24)	364542		26	Ross MCFARLANE	(Eng)	(30)	187340
11	Per-Ulrik JOHANSSON	(Swe)	(18)	354580		27	Miguel Angel MARTIN	(Sp)	(20)	187289
12	Costantino ROCCA	(It)	(28)	315077		28	Jarmo SANDELIN	(Swe)	(26)	184981
13	Eduardo ROMERO	(Arg)	(20)	290469		29	José COCERES	(Arg)	(23)	184332
14	Mark JAMES	(Eng)	(26)	271510		30	Stephen AMES	(T&T)	(21)	183190
15	Thomas BJORN	(Den)	(24)	264938		31	David GILFORD	(Eng)	(24)	182619
16	Raymond RUSSELL	(Scot)	(28)	250633		32	Roger CHAPMAN	(Eng)	(26)	182354
						33	David CARTER	(Eng)	(27)	177820

Bernhard Langer

*	129	Kalle VAINOLA	(Fin)	(22)	42026
*	130	John MELLOR	(Eng)	(22)	41992
*	131	Robert LEE	(Eng)	(26)	40259
	132	Gary EMERSON	(Eng)	(25)	40076
	133	Michael CAMPBELL	(NZ)	(22)	38492
	134	Ross DRUMMOND	(Scot)	(27)	38026
*	135	Mårten OLANDER	(Swe)	(20)	37233
	136	Seve BALLESTEROS	(Sp)	(20)	36916
	137	Gary CLARK	(Eng)	(28)	36623
	138	Jean Louis GUEPY	(Fr)	(17)	36538
	139	Steven RICHARDSON	(Eng)	(27)	36119
	140	Pedro LINHART	(Sp)	(24)	35664
	141	Carl MASON	(Eng)	(18)	33187
#	142	John WADE	(Aus)	(20)	31463
	143	David A RUSSELL	(Eng)	(5)	31282
#	144	Mathew GOGGIN	(Aus)	(22)	31043
	145	Mark DAVIS	(Eng)	(28)	30444

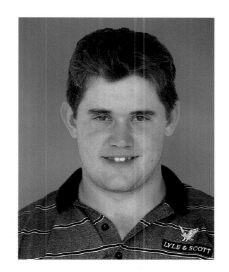

Lee Westwood

	86	Andrew OLDCORN	(Scot)	(23)	72041
	87	Klas ERIKSSON	(Swe)	(27)	70898
	88	Martin GATES	(Eng)	(24)	70535
	89	Jay TOWNSEND	(USA)	(23)	69123
	90	Domingo HOSPITAL	(Sp)	(24)	68242
	91	Silvio GRAPPASONNI	(It)	(22)	68185
	92	Dean ROBERTSON	(Scot)	(27)	67789
	93	Roger WESSELS	(SA)	(20)	66865
	94	Paul EALES	(Eng)	(25)	66577
	95	José RIVERO	(Sp)	(20)	65983
	96	Per HAUGSRUD	(Nor)	(27)	63405
	97	Raymond BURNS	(N.Ire)	(29)	62432
	98	Tony JOHNSTONE	(Zim)	(19)	61690
	99	Gary EVANS	(Eng)	(29)	61555
	100	Eamonn DARCY	(Ire)	(22)	61551
	101	Rodger DAVIS	(Aus)	(19)	61309
	102	Adam HUNTER	(Scot)	(28)	61109
	103	Derrick COOPER	(Eng)	(25)	58313
	104	Andrew SHERBORNE	(Eng)	(28)	57123
	105	Paul AFFLECK	(Wal)	(25)	57099
	106	Paolo QUIRICI	(Swi)	(21)	56688
	107	Malcolm MACKENZIE	(Eng)	(27)	56500
	108	Mathias GRÖNBERG	(Swe)	(22)	55236
#	109	Bob MAY	(USA)	(20)	55041
	110	Miles TUNNICLIFF	(Eng)	(29)	53950
	111	Pierre FULKE	(Swe)	(21)	52631
	112	Stephen FIELD	(Eng)	(22)	52238
	113	Robert COLES	(Eng)	(27)	51712
*	114	Massimo FLORIOLI	(It)	(26)	51282
#	115	David TAPPING	(Eng)	(22)	50914
	116	Rolf MUNTZ	(Hol)	(27)	50564
	117	Diego BORREGO	(Sp)	(21)	50436
	118	Paul CURRY	(Eng)	(22)	50057
	119	Howard CLARK	(Eng)	(18)	50003
#	120	Darren COLE	(Aus)	(21)	49437
	121	Emanuele CANONICA	(It)	(24)	48336
#	122	Max ANGLERT	(Swe)	(22)	48210
	123	Des SMYTH	(Ire)	(25)	47820
*	124	Stephen SCAHILL	(NZ)	(25)	47071
#	125	Alberto BINAGHI	(It)	(18)	46652
#	126	Daren LEE	(Eng)	(22)	46303
	127	Jim PAYNE	(Eng)	(25)	45473
*	128	Andrew SANDYWELL	(Eng)	(28)	42737

Darren Clarke

#	146	Ben TINNING	(Den)	(19)	30184
#	147	Gordon J BRAND	(Eng)	(15)	29057
*	148	Ignacio FELIU	(Sp)	(23)	27636
	149	Steven BOTTOMLEY	(Eng)	(28)	26631
	150	André BOSSERT	(Swi)	(14)	25952
§	151	Stephen LEANEY	(Aus)	(3)	25174
	152	Jeff HAWKES	(SA)	(26)	24878
#	153	Neal BRIGGS	(Eng)	(20)	23911
*	154	Joakim RASK	(Swe)	(18)	23084
	155	Stephen MCALLISTER	(Scot)	(8)	22179
#	156	Phil GOLDING	(Eng)	(15)	21797
	157	David HIGGINS	(Ire)	(29)	21252
	158	Christy O'CONNOR JNR	(Ire)	(14)	21184
	159	Juan Carlos PIÑERO	(Sp)	(21)	21156
#	160	Jeff REMESY	(Fr)	(16)	20573
	161	Fernando ROCA	(Sp)	(24)	19829
	162	Greg CHALMERS	(Aus)	(3)	18779
#	163	Anders HANSEN	(Den)	(16)	18543

§ Denotes Affiliate Member
* Denotes 1996 Challenge Tour Graduate
# Denotes 1996 Qualifying School Graduate
¶ Denotes Challenge Tour Member/Qualifying School Graduate
* Figures in parentheses indicate number of tournaments played

	164	Francisco VALERA	(Sp)	(12)	16908
#	165	John BICKERTON	(Eng)	(17)	16305
	166	Gordon SHERRY	(Scot)	(10)	16000
#	167	Stephen GALLACHER	(Scot)	(12)	14815
	168	Trevor DODDS	(Nam)	(3)	14550
	169	Ricky WILLISON	(Eng)	(27)	13582
	170	Manuel PIÑERO	(Sp)	(11)	12800
	171	Simon HURLEY	(Eng)	(12)	12510
	172	Michel BESANCENEY	(Fr)	(6)	12089
#	173	Anders GILLNER	(Swe)	(7)	11745
	174	Heinz P THÜL	(Ger)	(5)	11550
#	175	Raphaël JACQUELIN	(Fr)	(10)	11021
#	176	Ariel CAÑETE	(Arg)	(17)	10581
	177	Peter TERAVAINEN	(USA)	(7)	10575
*	178	Adam MEDNICK	(Swe)	(9)	9735
#	179	Johan SKOLD	(Swe)	(14)	9053
	180	Hugh BAIOCCHI	(SA)	(3)	8327
#	181	Fredrik ANDERSSON	(Swe)	(14)	8303
#	182	Daniel WESTERMARK	(Swe)	(13)	8035
	183	Gary NICKLAUS	(USA)	(7)	7890
§	184	Justin HOBDAY	(SA)	(5)	7304
	185	Francisco CEA	(Sp)	(2)	7206
	186	Mike HARWOOD	(Aus)	(12)	6430
#	187	Andrew BEAL	(Eng)	(13)	5727
	188	David J RUSSELL	(Eng)	(2)	5325
	189	Antoine LEBOUC	(Fr)	(4)	5159
	190	José Maria CAÑIZARES	(Sp)	(6)	5127
	191	Paul WAY	(Eng)	(6)	4760
	192	Mike MCLEAN	(Eng)	(8)	4560
#	193	Duncan MUSCROFT	(Eng)	(12)	3976
	194	Olle KARLSSON	(Swe)	(5)	3570
#	195	Christian CÉVAER	(Fr)	(13)	3478
	196	Mats LANNER	(Swe)	(7)	3075
	197	Brenden PAPPAS	(SA)	(4)	2764
	198	Carlos DURAN	(Swi)	(6)	2321
#	199	Alan TAIT	(Scot)	(12)	2108
	200	John MCHENRY	(Ire)	(6)	2010
#	201	Joe HIGGINS	(Eng)	(4)	1813
#	202	Massimo SCARPA	(It)	(7)	1675
	203	Bradley HUGHES	(Aus)	(4)	1630
#	204	Warren BENNETT	(Eng)	(9)	1381
#	205	Nicolas VANHOOTEGEM	(Bel)	(7)	1106
#	206	Joakim GRÖNHAGEN	(Swe)	(7)	948

The PGA European Tour

(A COMPANY LIMITED BY GUARANTEE)

BOARDS OF DIRECTORS
N C Coles MBE – Group Chairman
D Cooper (Tour)
A Gallardo (Tour, Properties)
B Gallacher OBE (Tour, Properties)
T A Horton (Tour, Properties)
M James (Tour)
D Jones (Tour)
M G King (Properties)
J E O'Leary (Tour, Properties)
R Rafferty (Tour)
D J Russell (Tour)
P M P Townsend (Properties)
P A T Davidson (Non Executive
        Tour Group Director)

EXECUTIVE DIRECTOR
K D Schofield CBE

DEPUTY EXECUTIVE DIRECTOR
G C O'Grady

ASSISTANT EXECUTIVE DIRECTOR
R G Hills

GENERAL COUNSEL
M D Friend

GROUP COMPANY SECRETARY
M Bray

**PGA EUROPEAN TOUR
TOURNAMENT COMMITTEE**
M James – Chairman
M Lanner – Vice Chairman
A Binaghi
R Chapman
R Claydon
D Cooper
B Langer
R Lee
C Montgomerie
R Rafferty
D J Russell
O Sellberg
J Spence
S Torrance MBE
J Van de Velde

PGA EUROPEAN SENIORS TOUR
A Stubbs – Managing Director
K Waters – Deputy Managing Director

CHIEF REFEREE
J N Paramor

**SENIOR REFEREE / DIRECTOR OF
TOUR QUALIFYING SCHOOL**
A N McFee

DIRECTOR OF TOUR OPERATIONS
D Garland

**ASSISTANT DIRECTOR OF TOUR
OPERATIONS**
D Probyn

**SENIOR TOURNAMENT
DIRECTOR**
M R Stewart

TOURNAMENT DIRECTORS
M Eriksson
M Vidaor

**PGA EUROPEAN CHALLENGE
TOUR**
A de Soultrait – Director

TOURNAMENT ADMINISTRATORS
M Haarer
J A Gray
G Hunt (Referee)
N Nesti
J M Zamora

TOURNAMENT OFFICIALS
P Talbot
D Williams

MARKETING DEPARTMENT
S Kelly – Marketing Director
G Oosterhuis – Corporate Sponsorship
        Director
I Barker – Account Director
A Crichton – Account Manager
M Haggstrom – Account Executive

STAGING DEPARTMENT
J Birkmyre – Director of Tournament
        Development
E Kitson – Director of Tournament Services

RYDER CUP LTD
R G Hills – Ryder Cup Director

PGA EUROPEAN TOUR (SOUTH)
A Gallardo – President

COMMUNICATIONS DIVISION
M Platts – Director of Communications
        and Public Relations
M Wilson – Consultant to
        Executive Director
R Dodd – Press Officer

GROUP FINANCIAL PLANNER
J Orr

GROUP FINANCE CONTROLLER
C Allamand

**CORPORATE RELATIONS
CONSULTANT**
H Wickham

Royal presence at Valderrama: King Juan Carlos of Spain with Seve Ballesteros and Bernhard Langer at the Ryder Cup opening ceremony.

The Contributors

Mike Aitken *(The Scotsman)*
Alfred Dunhill Cup
Mike Britten
Peugeot Open de España
Volvo German Open
OKI Pro-Am
Jeremy Chapman *(The Sporting Life)*
Ryder Cup by Johnnie Walker
Frank Clough
South African Open
Alamo English Open
Norman Dabell
Conte of Florence Italian Open
Sun Microsystems Dutch Open
Richard Dodd *(PGA European Tour)*
Moroccan Open
Madeira Island Open
Chemapol Trophy Czech Open
Bill Elliott
Volvo Ranking Winner
Andrew Farrell *(The Independent)*
Dubai Desert Classic
The Major Championships
Mark Garrod *(Press Association)*
Johnnie Walker Classic
Heineken Classic
Peugeot Open de France
Volvo Masters
Dermot Gilleece *(The Irish Times)*
Smurfit European Open

David Hamilton
European Challenge Tour
Martin Hardy *(The Daily Express)*
Trophée Lancôme
Alan Hedley *(The Journal)*
Compaq European Grand Prix
John Hopkins *(The Times)*
BMW International Open
Jock Howard *(Golf World)*
Benson and Hedges International Open
Jeff Kelly *(Andalucia Golf)*
Turespaña Masters – Open de Canarias
Renton Laidlaw *(The Evening Standard)*
Canon European Masters
Derek Lawrenson *(The Sunday Telegraph)*
One 2 One British Masters
Michael McDonnell *(The Daily Mail)*
The Year in Retrospect
John Oakley
Europe 1 Cannes Open
Open Novotel Perrier

Mitchell Platts *(PGA European Tour)*
Apollo Week
Andersen Consulting European
Championship
World Cup of Golf
Chris Plumridge *(The Sunday Telegraph)*
Volvo PGA Championship
126th Open Championship
Bryan Potter
European Seniors Tour
Gordon Richardson
Dimension Data Pro-Am
Linde German Masters
Subaru Sarazen World Open
Gordon Simpson *(The Daily Record)*
The Gulfstream Loch Lomond World
Invitational
Colm Smith *(Independent Newspapers)*
Murphy's Irish Open
Paul Trow
Alfred Dunhill South African PGA
Championship
Mel Webb *(The Times)*
Portuguese Open
Deutsche Bank Open – TPC of Europe
Volvo Scandinavian Masters
John Whitbread *(Surrey Herald Newspapers)*
Toyota World Match-Play Championship

The Photographers

David Cannon /Allsport
4, 6, 8, 9, 10, 19 top and centre, 23,
24 centre, 25 centre below, 29, 30, 31,
34-39, 40-45, 64, 66-69, 126, 130 top,
132, 135, 136, 148 below, 176-177,
178-179, 181 top, 217-219, 241,
245 top, 251, 254, 263, 264-266,
267 below, 269, 280-282, 284,
285 left and right, 286, 288-289,
291 top, 298 left and centre,
299 centre top and right,
299 below left, 302, 303

Phil Cole /Allsport
222-227

Mike Hewitt /Allsport
122-125

Rusty Jarrett /Allsport
7, 17 right

Craig Jones /Allsport
12 below, 13 both, 25 bottom,
283 below, 285 below

Ross Kinnaird /Allsport
19 below, 20, 172, 177 top, 178 below
left, 180 top, 205 centre

Alex Livesy /Allsport
65, 295

Andy Lyons /Allsport
294

Clive Mason /Allsport
279 top

Tim Matthews /Allsport
75-77, 80-85, 90-94, 110 centre,
119 top, 120, 156-160, 231 all, 233,
256-260, 291 left

Stephen Munday /Allsport
1, 3, 11 left, 12 top, 18-19, 22,
24 below, 25 above centre,
26 right and below, 96-101, 108, 109,
110 below, 114-118, 119 below, 127,
128, 130 centre and below, 134-135,
198 top right, 210-215, 240, 242-244,
275 below, 279 below, 287 below,
301 all

Andrew Redington /Allsport
11 right, 14-15, 17 centre, 24 right,
26 left, 27, 46-51, 52-56, 58-63, 102-105,
110 top, 111, 112, 144-147, 149,
150-155, 162-167, 168-171, 190-195,
202-205, 206 below, 208, 220,
245 below, 246-249, 250, 252 top,
253 right and below, 278, 285 centre,
287 top, 290, 291 right, 296 top,
298 right, 299 top left and below right

Paul Severn /Allsport
24 left, 28, 70-73, 74, 78, 86-88,
128-129, 133, 138-142, 184-189,
196-200, 228-230, 304, 232, 234-237,
252 below, 253 top, 262, 267 top,
268-269, 270, 291 below

Jamie Squire /Allsport
11 centre, 14-16, 17 left, 25 top,
182, 282 top, 296 left and right, 300

Matt Stockman /Allsport
272-277

Phil Inglis
32-33, 148 top, 206 top, 207 all

Alex Jackson
177 below, 216

Nick Walker
174, 175, 180 below, 181 below